HOUSTON
People ★ Opportunity ★ Success

A Special Publication of the

Greater Houston Partnership

Produced by MARCOA Publishing, Inc.

Ray Viator, Editor ★ Jim Olive, Photographer

People ★ Opportunity ★ Success

A Century of Progress	9
Shaping Houston in the 20th Century	20
Energy	26
Health Care	40
Space	50
Technology	60
Trade and Transportation	70
Business Climate	84
Quality of Life	108
Houston at the Beginning of the New Millennium	166
Houston Business Portraits	185

GREATER HOUSTON PARTNERSHIP

Chairman, Ned S. Holmes
Chairman & CEO, Parkway Investments/Texas Inc.
President & CEO, Jim C. Kollaer
Executive Vice President & COO, Charles R. Savino
President, Chamber of Commerce Division, George Beatty
President, Economic Development Division, Pamela House Lovett
President, World Trade Division, Miguel R. San Juan
Senior Vice President, Government Relations, Anne Culver
Vice President, Communications/Executive Editor, Marilou Schopper

MARCOA Publishing Houston, Inc.
Editor, Ray Viator
Photographer, Jim Olive
Publisher, Wallace Ryland
Associate Publisher, Scott Weaver
Account Executive, John Buck
Production Director, Jocelyn Boehm
Production Manager, Rudy Rey
Art Director, Patricia Cross
Contributing Writers, Anne Feltus & Joe Pratt

©1999 Greater Houston Partnership

With more than 25 million square feet of Class-A office space and 163,000 workers, downtown Houston (right) boasts a thriving Theater District and is home to many of Houston's largest companies, banks and law firms, as well as city, county and federal government offices. ★ The Uptown Houston area (pages 2-3), anchored by The Galleria and other high-end shopping centers as well as Class-A office buildings, upscale homes, condos and apartments, is one of several employment centers in the Houston region.

Downtown
With more than 25 million square feet of Class-A office space and 163,000 workers, downtown Houston boasts a thriving Theater District and is home to many of Houston's largest companies, banks and law firms as well as city, county and federal government offices.

Port of Houston
Houston's role as a major international trade center in the 20th century is a direct result of the foresight and vision of its early leaders in creating the Houston Ship Channel. The Port of Houston is the largest U.S. port for foreign cargo and the eighth largest port in the world.

Texas Medical Center
The world-renowned Texas Medical Center and its 42 non-profit institutions are dedicated to providing the very best in patient care, medical education and research. The Texas Medical Center includes two comprehensive medical schools, four schools of nursing, 13 renowned hospitals and two specialty institutions.

NASA/Johnson Space Center
NASA's Johnson Space Center, located 22 miles south of Houston, has been Mission Control for the U.S. space program since 1963. Using a full-scale mock-up of the Space Shuttle, astronauts are trained to conduct scientific, medical and engineering research projects.

The Galleria
The Galleria features more than 320 retail stores and restaurants and an indoor ice skating rink. As Houston's most popular shopping center, the Galleria also is one of the region's favorite destinations, drawing shoppers and visitors from throughout the Southwest, Mexico and Latin America.

Museum District
Houston's Museum District is home to a broad variety of collections and arts organizations ranging from the Museum of Fine Arts, Houston to the Contemporary Arts Museum, The Menil Collection, the Houston Museum of Natural Science, the Children's Museum of Houston, The Holocaust Museum, the Museum of Health & Medical Science and others.

Clear Lake Area
The Clear Lake region around Galveston Bay is the third largest boating center in the United States with over 7,700 boat slips and seven yacht clubs.

Bush Intercontinental Airport
More than 31 million passengers travel annually through George Bush Intercontinental Airport. The city's largest airport is served by 23 airlines offering direct or nonstop flights between Houston and more than 150 destinations worldwide.

Hobby Airport
Located nine miles from downtown Houston, Hobby Airport is used by 9 million passengers annually for direct and nonstop flights between Houston and 71 cities throughout the United States.

HOUSTON ★ People ★ Opportunity ★ Success

HOUSTON: A Century of Progress

Only the most creative artist, visionary businessman or most prescient futurist could have imagined all that has unfolded in Houston during the 20th century.

To say that Houston had humble beginnings at the start of the century would be a serious understatement. But one hallmark of Houston has been its dream and ambition to be a world-class city. And in the 20th century that dream became a reality as Houston grew to become the fourth largest city in America; the energy capital of the world; a leader in medical care, research and education; mission control for the U.S. space program; and the home of world-class cultural arts organizations.

At the beginning of the century, cattle and cotton dominated Houston's economy. Galveston was the boomtown of the Gulf Coast and Houston could only dream about becoming a major port and trade center. But it was a dream that had been growing since the city's founding in 1836. And it was a dream that Houstonians had been nurturing through repeated investments in deepening and widening Buffalo Bayou with the goal of creating a "Houston Ship Channel."

At the turn of the century, the "can-do" spirit of Houstonians – together with a combination of tragedy and geology – changed Houston's economy forever and catapulted the city onto the world stage.

The first was the Galveston hurricane of 1900 which devastated that city and laid the groundwork for Houston to assume a larger role in trade along the Gulf Coast. By 1914, Houston's perseverance and vision – together with its pioneering concept of matching local funds with federal funds – turned its dream of a deepwater port into a reality and ensured the city's future role as a world trade hub.

One year into the new century, the Spindletop gusher roared to life in nearby Beaumont, followed by the discovery of oil even closer to Houston in Humble and Goose Creek. The discoveries, combined with the arrival of thousands of wildcatters and new oil entrepreneurs, marked the beginning of Houston's emergence as the energy capital of the world.

Throughout the century, Houston and the energy industry have had a symbiotic relationship through good times and bad times. Houstonians provided not only the brawn but also the brains that have helped fuel the discovery of oil and gas in extreme conditions around the world, from the Arctic Circle to the deserts of the Mideast and from the depths of the Gulf of Mexico to the frigid waters of the North Sea.

The same drive, ambition and "can-do" spirit that made Houston the energy capital of the world also affected other defining areas of life in the 20th century.

Houstonians, for example, had the vision to create the Texas Medical Center, which today is the world's largest medical complex. In doing so, Houstonians have made significant contributions to the quality of life, not just locally, but for millions of other Americans and patients from around the globe who have come here for treatment by some of the best and brightest physicians in the world. And, though they will never visit a Houston hospital or research institution, millions more will benefit from the research and education that takes place every day in the Texas Medical Center.

There's an old saying among new residents of Texas that goes: "I may not have been born in Texas, but I had the good sense to get here as quickly as I could." It's doubly true for many Houstonians who have had the good sense not only to move to Texas, but also to call Houston their home. When the 20th century began, the Houston region had a population of about 182,000. Today the region is home to more than 4 million people who have come here from across the United States and all over the world.

Throughout the century, Houstonians have worked to improve their city and make it a better place to live and work. It's the people of Houston who make this city special. They are warm, friendly and caring. And Houstonians truly welcome newcomers. They've come here from from every state in the nation as well as Asia and Africa, Europe and the Mideast, Mexico and South America. You can come here from any city in the U.S. or around the world – as millions have during this century – and Houstonians will accept you and give you an opportunity to succeed.

Houstonians are the people who create new opportunities and contribute to the success of everyone they touch. ∎

The Port That Built a City. Houston's success in becoming a major international trade center in the 20th century is a direct result of the foresight and vision of its early leaders in creating the Houston Ship Channel. The Port of Houston is the largest U.S. port for foreign cargo and the eighth largest port in the world.

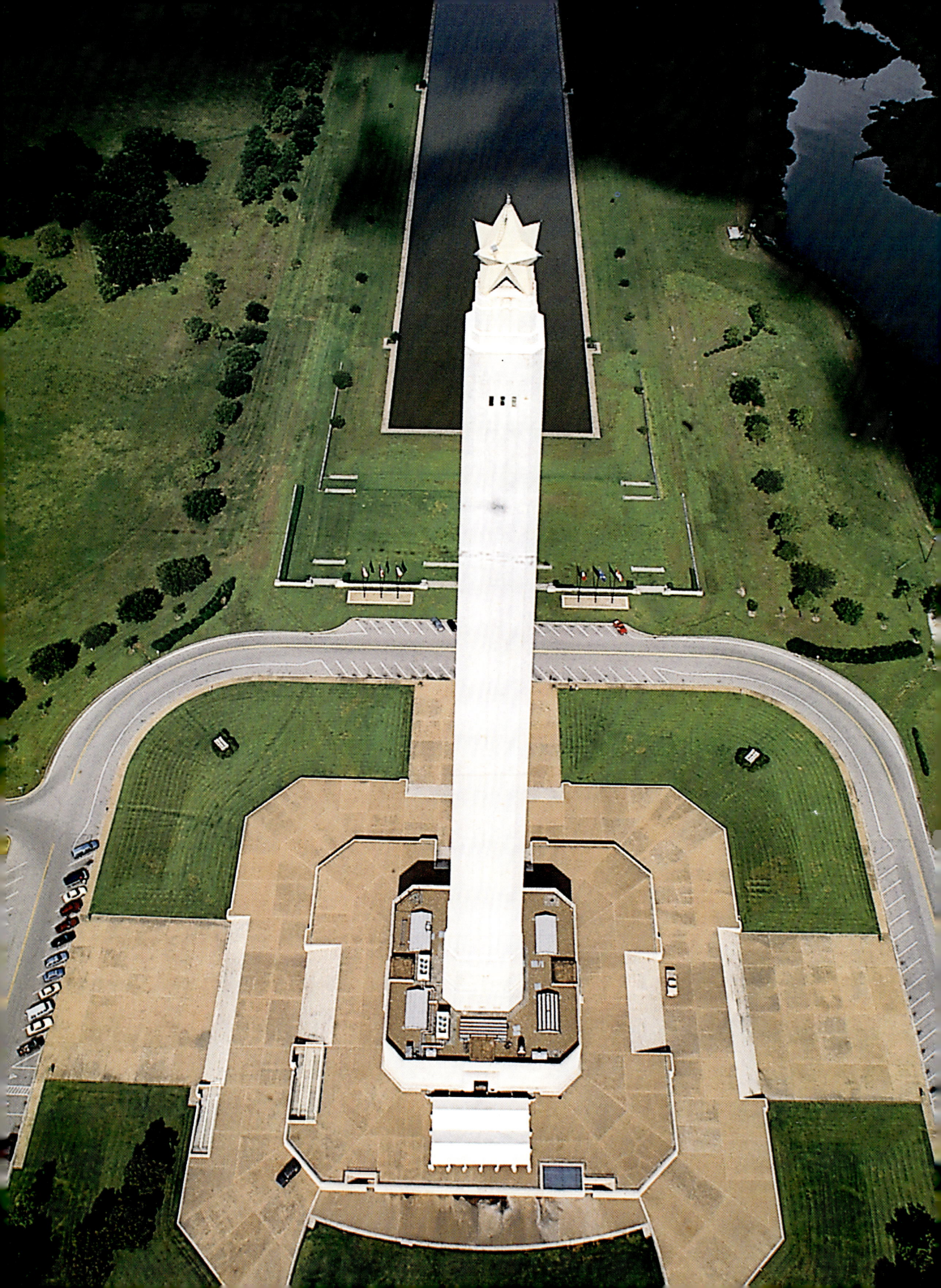

HOUSTON ★ People ★ Opportunity ★ Success

The Past and the Future. The statue of Gen. Sam Houston (above) in Hermann Park is positioned to point to the southeast and the San Jacinto battlefields where Texas won its independence in 1836. Ironically, NASA's Johnson Space Center, mission control for the Apollo moon missions as well as all U.S. space flights, is located just a few miles south of San Jacinto. ★ Built in 1936 to mark the centennial of the battle it honors, the 570-foot San Jacinto Monument (left) is the tallest monument column in the world.

HOUSTON ★ People ★ Opportunity ★ Success

***B**uilding a Heritage of Success. Representative of "modern" homes in 1905, the Staiti House (above) was originally owned by oil pioneer Henry T. Staiti. The 17-room house included the latest feature of its times: electricity. In 1986, the house was moved by the Heritage Society to Sam Houston Park in downtown Houston as part of a collection of eight homes, cottages and a church that date back to 1823. ★ With the Texaco Heritage Plaza as a backdrop, canoeists navigate the waters of Buffalo Bayou as it meanders through downtown Houston near where the Allen brothers founded the City of Houston in 1836.*

HOUSTON ★ People ★ Opportunity ★ Success

Houston's Agricultural Roots. When the 20th century began, agriculture was the primary economic engine for the Houston region. While no longer a dominant part of Houston's economy, cattle and horses can still be found on the hundreds of farms and small ranches scattered throughout the region. In 1998, for example, Harris County claimed 983 farms and ranches producing about $85 million worth of crops and livestock.

HOUSTON ★ People ★ Opportunity ★ Success

*C*ampfires *and Barbecue. Both native Houstonians and newcomers celebrate the region's western heritage at least once a year during the Houston Livestock Show & Rodeo, the largest rodeo in the country. One of the most popular events is the World's Championship Bar-B-Que Contest, which attracts more than 150,000 people hungry for a real taste of Texas. With more than 340 cooking spaces spread over 45 acres, the three-day event is the largest charitable barbecue contest in the world and raises more than $700,000 for the rodeo's scholarship programs.*

H O U S T O N ★ P e o p l e ★ O p p o r t u n i t y ★ S u c c e s s

King Cotton and Black Gold. *While the discovery of oil in 1901 at Spindletop near Beaumont ushered in the modern Texas oil era, it was the subsequent discoveries of nearby massive fields such as Humble in 1905 and Goose Creek (above) in 1906 that cemented Houston's position as a major center for the energy industry.* ★ *In 1900, cotton was king and Houston staked its claim on being a major center for growing and shipping cotton to markets around the world. Today, the Houston region exports 241,000 tons of cotton, including a large amount from some of the original fields (left) along the Brazos River bottomland in Fort Bend County.* ★ *The Port of Houston is the leading port for containerized cargo. The Port's Barbours Cut Terminal (pages 18-19) each year handles almost 1 million containers with more than 8 million tons of products from across the United States and around the world.*

Shaping Houston in the 20th Century

BY JOSEPH A. PRATT

Throughout its history, Houston has been a magnet for ambitious people. Some came to Houston by way of the small towns and farms of Texas and Louisiana; others ventured from more distant locales in search of a better future. Generations migrated to Houston, lured by opportunities to make something more of themselves in a fast-growing economy. Those who succeeded in business helped create the new jobs that drew still others to the region.

In comparison to older, more traditional cities, Houston embraced successful outsiders, quickly welcoming them into positions of civic leadership. Indeed, most of the business leaders of the city left smaller towns for the bright lights of Houston in search of a larger stage on which to play out their ambitions. Those who succeeded generally developed a lifelong love affair with Houston. Recognizing that their futures were tightly bound to the prosperity of their adopted hometown, they understood that what was good for Houston ultimately was good for their own business ventures. Several generations of business and civic leaders literally grew up with the city, helping it expand almost a hundredfold from a frontier town of about 45,000 people at the turn of the 20th century to a major metropolitan area of more than four million at the turn of the 21st century.

Pivotal Years for Houston

The years from the Civil War to World War I were pivotal for Houston's emergence as a major city. In this era, aggressive leaders firmly established Houston as a center of commerce, finance and law for a broad region of Texas and Louisiana. By attracting major national railroad systems to their city, this generation of leaders assured that Houston would become the transportation center of its region. Then, by pushing through the completion of a deep-water ship channel to the Gulf of Mexico, they strengthened the region's ties to the booming national economy.

Lawyers and bankers took the lead in Houston in these years. Their talents were vital in the emergence of the city as the capital of their region's trade and its key connection to the national economy. The symbol of Houston's influential civic leadership in this era was Captain James A. Baker, who came to Houston from Huntsville, Texas, in the 1870s to join his father's law firm, Baker & Botts. He practiced law in the city for the next 70 years, and his activities suggest the broad role played by a generation of lawyer/bankers in transforming a large town into a major city in the years before World War I.

Baker's clients included national railroads, local banks and utilities, and Rice University, where he served as the first chairman of the board of trustees from 1891 until his death in 1941. A prominent banker as well as lawyer, he spent portions of each year in New York City, where he maintained close contacts with a variety of nationally-active companies with interests in Houston. Along with other prominent lawyers such as Frank Andrews (Andrews & Kurth), Captain Baker and his generation helped create the legal and financial framework needed to assure Houston's future growth.

Around the turn of the century, waves of new business handily built upon this framework. Timber flowed from East Texas, financed in Houston by such entrepreneurs as John Henry Kirby (Kirby Lumber, Houston Oil). Cotton traveled from the Brazos River bottom down to Galveston and Houston, where M.D. Anderson and Will Clayton created one of the largest cotton trading companies in the world, Anderson Clayton. Thus even before the

Capt. James A. Baker

William Clayton

Joseph S. Cullinan

Howard Hughes Sr.

development of petroleum, Houston had created a sturdy economic base from which to expand.

A Coming of Age for Houston

But the discovery of oil in 1901 at Spindletop, some 100 miles east of the city near Beaumont, vaulted Houston to a new level of development. Much of the oil trade steadily moved to Houston, led by such emerging oil giants as Joseph S. Cullinan's Texas Company (now Texaco) and later the Humble Oil & Refining Company (now Exxon) of Will Farish and Ross Sterling. Houston also quickly became the center for the manufacture of the tools needed by the petroleum industry; here Howard Hughes Sr. and Walter Sharp led the way with the manufacture of drill bits for the world at Hughes Tool.

The potent combination of oil, cotton, and timber made Houston's economy the envy of its region, but the completion of the Houston Ship Channel secured its place in the world. Realizing that their city needed access to the sea to grow into an international center of trade, Houston's business and civic elite closed ranks to convince the U.S. government to become the city's partner in building a pathway to the Gulf. Led by U.S. Representative Tom Ball, the city's leaders gained acceptance for an innovative approach in which the city agreed to share the costs of deepening the ship channel with the U.S. Corps of Engineers. The celebration of the opening of the Houston Ship Channel in 1914 marked the coming of age of Houston as a major city.

The 1920s witnessed an extraordinary boom in Houston, as cotton and oil products flowed out of the ship channel and into the world economy. Giant petroleum refineries grew up along the Houston Ship Channel, providing thousands of new manufacturing jobs. Then, in the 1930s and 1940s, a new wave of refinery building and the coming of modern petrochemical plants made the region an industrial power. The expansion of this era attracted a new generation of migrants to the city, bringing both the work force and the business leadership needed to allow the city to escape the worst of the Great Depression and then to rebound strongly in the post-World War II era.

Jesse Jones: "Mr. Houston"

The symbol of the new Houston of the 1920s was Jesse Holman Jones, who made his way to Houston in 1898 from Tennessee via Dallas-Fort Worth. During the next 58 years, his leadership in all phases of the city's life earned him the nickname "Mr. Houston," although many of his younger colleagues called him simply "Uncle Jesse." Jones' primary business activities were banking, newspaper publishing and real estate development, which proved to be a lucrative calling as Houston grew by leaps and bounds. But, as he grew older, Jones devoted growing amounts of his time and energies to civic affairs. He almost single-handedly arranged for the Democratic Party's 1928 nominating convention to be held in Houston, putting it on the map as a city on the move. He then went to Washington in 1932 to run the Reconstruction Finance Corporation, which became one of the central agencies promoting economic recovery during the Great Depression. During World War II, he headed the effort to finance the industries needed by the war effort before becoming Secretary of Commerce.

Upon his return to Houston in 1945, Jones became a sort of elder statesman of the city. After his death in 1956, his philan-

Rep. Tom Ball

Jesse H. Jones

George R. Brown

Judge James Elkins

thropic foundation, the Houston Endowment, became the largest such foundation in Texas.

When Jones returned to the city to live after World War II, he found a new generation of business leaders poised to guide Houston through its extraordinary post-war boom. Natural gas, petrochemicals, oil, oil-related manufacturing, and construction fueled a surge of expansion from 1945 through the 1970s, pushing Houston rapidly up the ranks of the nation's largest cities.

The Influential 8F Crowd

During these years of economic boom, many regional businesses grew into national concerns. An array of forceful, colorful business leaders directed their energies toward building their enterprises and their city. Most visible among these were the "8F crowd," a loosely-knit group that became the symbol of the "can-do" attitude of Houston's leadership. Brothers Herman and George R. Brown rented Suite 8F in the downtown Lamar Hotel, and it gained notice in the 1950s as a regular meeting place for a group of movers and shakers who helped shape modern Houston.

The core group of 8F visitors included representatives of many of the booming regional businesses of the era: natural gas pipelines and construction (the Browns and W.A. "Bill" Smith); law and banking (Judge James Elkins); insurance (Gus Wortham); oil-related manufacturing (James Abercrombie); and communications (Governor William P. Hobby and Oveta Culp Hobby). Beyond this core group were many others in the city who often joined ranks with the Browns and their associates.

While contributing greatly to Houston's economic and cultural lives, the 8F crowd became best known for its political activities. It supported such important public officials as President and Senate Majority Leader Lyndon B. Johnson; U.S. Representative Albert Thomas; Senator Lloyd Bentsen; and numerous winning mayoral candidates, including – at one time or another – Oscar Holcombe and Louie Welch. These and other strong political leaders managed the extraordinary growth of Houston, whose rapid, sustained expansion placed great demands on government at all levels to provide the variety of public services needed by the emerging metropolis.

Leadership came from many others during the post-war boom. Contributing much to the city were independent oil men, best exemplified by Hugh Roy Cullen's long-term commitment to the University of Houston, Glenn McCarthy's building of the Shamrock Hotel, and John Mecom's success with the Warwick Hotel. A new cross-country natural gas pipeline industry emerged after World War II, and leading companies such as Tenneco and Texas Eastern made Houston the center of the natural gas trade. Gas executives such as Gardner Symonds of Tenneco became important civic leaders. Executives at major oil companies – Texaco, Gulf Oil, Humble Oil (Exxon), and later Shell – continued to contribute to the city's well-being. Oil-tool manufacturers such as Hughes Tool and Cameron Iron Works generated thousands of industrial jobs.

Creating a City of Medicine

By the 1950s, the regional economy began to diversify with the creation of the Texas Medical Center. Houston's emergence as the home of one of the world's largest medical centers was the result of the vision and generosity of M.D. Anderson, who had made his fortune in cotton earlier in the century in Houston. Anderson, who

Gus Wortham

Oveta Culp Hobby

Rep. Albert Thomas

Mayor Oscar Holcombe

believed in doing important things for society with the enormous fortune he amassed, asked his friends John H. Freeman and Col. William Bates (of the law firm Fulbright, Jaworski, Freeman and Bates) and Horace Wilkins of the Central Bank of Houston to think of good and beneficial ways to use the money in the foundation he had created.

Together with Dr. Ernst William Bertner, they conceived the idea of creating a city of medicine such as envisioned by Aesculapius in ancient Greece. They formed Texas Medical Center Inc. to carry out their goal of creating a medical center consisting of many different hospitals, academic institutions and various support organizations. When the state legislature decided in 1942 to create a state cancer hospital and to make it part of the University of Texas system, the M.D. Anderson Foundation and the Houston Chamber of Commerce pledged money to match the state funding of the hospital if it were to be located in Houston and named after M.D. Anderson. The project was blessed by the state three years after M.D. Anderson's death.

Expanding Opportunities for All Citizens

During the post-war boom, as in earlier years, Houston's growth was limited by its system of racial segregation. Since the late 19th century, Houston had been a "Jim Crow" city with a system of legal segregation that limited the opportunities of its growing African American population. By the mid-20th century, black Houston alone would have been the fifth largest city in Texas.

Excluded from equal participation in the larger society, blacks developed their own leadership to improve economic and educational opportunities while championing equal rights. The Reverend Jack Yates, born a slave, had helped build a community for freed slaves in Houston after the Civil War and the Reverend William Lawson and other religious leaders continued his tradition of leadership in the post-World War II era.

Black business leaders also emerged as forces for change. Carter Wesley, the son of a school teacher in the segregated Houston public schools, left the region to go to law school at Northwestern University before returning to Houston, where his ownership of a chain of newspapers made him one of the leading black businessmen in the South—and one of its loudest, most persistent voices for desegregation.

Finally, in the early 1960s, the national civil rights movement helped convince Houston's leadership that the time had come to dismantle segregation, and a quiet campaign to open public accommodations ended Jim Crow's reign in Houston.

Despite the fact that Houston tended to see race in terms of black and white, leaders in the city's growing Hispanic communities also emerged in these years. Such men as Felix Tijerina, a prominent restauranteur in Houston after World War II, led a movement to help Hispanic children get a head start in learning English. Tijerina also worked with the League of United Latin American Citizens (LULAC) on a variety of civil rights initiatives.

Entering the Space Age

As the city gradually embraced its diverse population in the 1960s, it also experienced an economic boom that elevated it to the status of one of the nation's largest, most prosperous cities. As the energy-related core of the city's economy grew, diversification continued. In the early 1960s, Humble's Morgan Davis joined

Hugh Roy Cullen

M.D. Anderson

Ernst W. Bertner

Carter Wesley

George Brown, U.S. Rep. Albert Thomas, then-Vice President Lyndon Johnson, and others to help convince NASA to choose the Clear Lake area south of the city as the site for its Manned Spacecraft Center. The space program quickly grew into an important economic force in the region.

Meanwhile, Judge Roy Hofheinz, R.E. "Bob" Smith and others helped bring major league sports to the city with the building of a new type of stadium, the air conditioned Astrodome, billed as "the Eighth Wonder of the World" when it opened in 1965.

A broad coalition of business leaders assisted the city in the 1960s in acquiring the site needed for a modern airport, and Intercontinental Airport (now Bush Intercontinental Airport) soon became an important transportation link between Houston and the world.

During the late 1970s, Houston experienced significant growth and Houston's skyline was dramatically transformed into an architectural showcase by architects and developers such as Gerald Hines, Kenneth Schnitzer, Walter Mischer and others.

Creating a Climate for the Arts

More than jobs and infrastructure are needed, however, to build a major city, and many different groups contributed to the development of world-class cultural institutions. The initial impetus for excellent cultural institutions came from several relatives of business leaders of the turn-of-the-century generation, Ima Hogg and Nina Cullinan. Their fathers—Governor James Hogg and Joseph Cullinan—had earned their fortunes in the early Texas oil industry, and the daughters used their wealth to create a better city. Through their own involvement and the activities of their philanthropic foundations, the leaders of the next generation – Jesse Jones, the 8F Crowd, and others such as Hugh Roy Cullen – contributed to the development of a first-class symphony and museums, performance halls and universities of the highest rank.

An outpouring of philanthropic contributions from Houston's civic leaders also encouraged the growth of world-class medical, educational and research facilities in the Texas Medical Center.

Such local traditions as the Houston Fatstock Show & Rodeo (now the Houston Livestock Show & Rodeo), preserved Houston's western heritage while providing financial support for area students. They also repositioned charity as social events that contributed greatly both to the life of the city and the social welfare of its citizens.

Building a Broader Community of Leaders

As Houston became both more prosperous and more diverse, the issues it faced became more difficult to resolve by such relatively small groups as the 8F crowd. The civil rights movement had cracked open doors of economic and educational opportunity for Houston's growing non-white population, which included increasing numbers of Hispanic-Americans and, beginning in the 1970s, a large number of Asians from Vietnam, China, Taiwan and other countries.

By the early 1980s, the boom and busts in petroleum made economic diversification an imperative. To address such issues, a new generation of leadership sought to build a broader-based coalition of leadership in the region. They set about to build a giant umbrella under which representatives of all Houstonians

Felix Tijerina

Judge Roy Hofheinz

Ima Hogg

Rev. William Lawson

could gain a voice in the city's civic affairs; the result was the creation of the Greater Houston Partnership.

Numerous business and civic leaders joined forces in this organization, led by Ben Love of Texas Commerce Bank, Charles Duncan of Duncan Interests, and Bob Onstead, founder of Randalls Food Markets. Among the emerging new generation of leadership in the city were representatives of some of the city's fastest-growing new industries, notably Kenneth Lay of Enron. The Partnership quickly became a focal point for cooperation on issues of importance to the Houston metropolitan area's future. Such leaders as George Mitchell—with a business headquartered in Houston, a founder's interest in the thriving suburban city of The Woodlands, and a longtime commitment to the redevelopment of Galveston—sought to span the broad geographical reach of modern Houston and develop a truly regional outlook.

Within the increasingly diverse region, leaders sought to build coalitions capable of defining a unified interest across the various ethnic and racial groups in the city. Mayors Kathy Whitmire, Bob Lanier and Lee P. Brown encouraged this quest to embrace the city's diversity, and the ranks of the city's civic leaders gradually expanded to include broader representation of all groups.

The 1980s also saw the emergence of several Houstonians as leaders at the national and international levels. The highest example was the election of Houstonian George Bush as President of the United States in 1988. Bush subsequently recruited several Houstonians to join his Cabinet in Washington, including James A. Baker III, who served as Secretary of both Treasury and State, and Robert A. Mosbacher Sr., who served as Secretary of Commerce. In the 1990s, Rep. Bill Archer took a leadership role in Congress as Chairman of the powerful House Ways & Means Committee while Rep. Tom Delay rose to become House Majority Whip.

Looking to the Future

The stewardship of Houston's prosperity will be in the hands of new generations of civic leaders in the next century. Many of their challenges will remain the same as those of generations past: shepherding a prosperous economy by creating more and better jobs, improving the region's educational systems, bettering the quality of life for all Houstonians and creating strength from diversity. In addition, Houston will face new challenges, especially as major strides in research and technology put our workforce to the test and push Houston onto the world stage in new areas.

The city has always had a "can-do" spirit. That spirit lifted Houston from a small frontier town in the late 19th century, to a regional industrial center before World War I, to the ranks of the nation and world's major cities at the end of the 20th century. It is that "can-do" spirit that will be called upon again and again if Houston is to continue its role as a world class city in the 21st century. ∎

Joseph A. Pratt is Cullen Professor of History and Business at the University of Houston.

Gerald Hines

Ken Lay

George Mitchell

President George Bush

HOUSTON ★ People ★ Opportunity ★ Success

Energy

If there is a single word that defines Houston in the 20th century – and is likely to define it well into the 21st century – it is energy.

First fueled by the Spindletop oil gusher in nearby Beaumont in 1901, and subsequent oil discoveries in the Humble area in 1905 and Goose Creek in 1906, Houston was propelled into the energy age. And Houston has staked a leadership position in the energy industry ever since.

Beginning with those early oil boom years, Houston earned one of its many sobriquets: "Energy Capital of the World." The title is fitting, as Houston throughout the century either developed, acquired or attracted a role in virtually every phase of the energy industry: from exploration and production to oilfield equipment manufacturing and services, from refining and gasoline marketing to pipelines and distribution, from petrochemicals to plastics manufacturing and from electricity marketing to the trading of crude, natural gas and other petroleum products.

Throughout the century, Houston and Houstonians have been involved in virtually any business or operation that involved finding, producing, transporting or marketing oil and gas around the world.

Today, for example, Houston accounts for almost 30 percent of all U.S. exploration and production jobs and more than 44 percent of all oilfield equipment manufacturing jobs. And the Houston region produces more than 20 percent of all U.S. gasoline and petroleum products and almost half of all U.S. base petrochemicals.

Houston also is home to many of the largest energy pipeline companies, controlling thousands of miles of pipelines that transport natural gas and other petroleum products across the United States.

The depth and breadth of Houston's role in the energy industry was sparked by home-grown energy entrepreneurs. Over the years, the city has been able to attract companies from energy-producing regions across the country and around the world. As the city reached critical mass in the energy industry, all roads – and most careers in the industry – led to Houston.

Today, more than 5,000 energy-related companies have operations in Houston and more than 1 million jobs – about half of Houston's total employment – are directly or indirectly tied to the energy industry.

In addition to its obvious economic impact on Houston, the energy industry has had a dramatic impact on the region's international stature. Reflecting the international nature of the energy industry, for example, Houston hosts 70 foreign consular offices, 27 foreign trade and commercial offices, 40 active foreign chambers of commerce and trade associations and 28 foreign banks from 13 countries.

The impact of the international energy industry on Houston is also reflected in: the area's population – nearly one in five Houstonians is foreign born; international air service – 11 airlines provide direct service to 40 foreign cities; shipping – the Port of Houston ranks first in the United State for foreign tonnage; and schools – more than 65 foreign languages are represented in Houston schools.

Throughout the century, Houston became known for industry icons such as Howard Hughes Sr., who pioneered new drill bits, his flamboyant billionaire son, Howard Hughes Jr., and legends like "hellfighter" Red Adair who capped hundreds of wild well fires around the world.

Houston also gained a reputation as the birthplace for many innovations in the energy business. While early Houston wildcatters may have hit gushers based on a combination of luck and gut instinct, modern explorationists in Houston now rely on sophisticated, computer-based 3-D seismic modeling to find giant oil and gas fields in deep waters offshore and in remote areas of the world. As a result of innovations first developed by engineers and researchers in Houston, records are set almost every year for new drilling or production depths in increasingly deeper waters offshore. ∎

Leading the Search. In addition to being the energy capital of the world, Houston continues to be a productive area for oil and gas exploration and production. Almost 800 wells are drilled in the Houston area each year, producing nearly 40 million barrels of oil and 920 mcf of natural gas. Houston also is the home of hundreds of companies that manufacture drilling rigs and all the pipes, valves, pumps and equipment needed to drill for and produce oil and gas. ★ The success rate for finding new oil and gas fields improved significantly during the 1990s with the development of new 3-D seismic interpretation software developed and used by companies in Houston such as Texaco. The company's 3-D Visualization Center (pages 28-29) is a large-scale theater for three-dimensional imaging and computerized maps that allow geoscientists to travel virtually through thousands of feet of rock and earth and evaluate a section of oil-bearing rock in seconds rather than days.   *Photo (pages 28-29) Courtesy of Texaco U.S.A.* ▶▶

HOUSTON ★ People ★ Opportunity ★ Success

***M**eeting Offshore Challenges.* In the ongoing search for oil and gas in ever-deeper waters offshore, Houston companies have played pivotal roles in the design, engineering and fabrication of offshore exploration and production platforms and vessels. In addition, Houston companies and their products, services and employees can be found in every major offshore oil-producing region in the world, from the Gulf of Mexico to the North Sea and off the coasts of Canada, Mexico, South America, Africa, Asia and Australia. ★ Conoco's Deepwater Pathfinder (above) is a state-of-the-art, ultra-deepwater vessel capable of drilling in 10,000 feet of water. The drillship features a dynamic positioning system that uses a combination of seabed and satellite systems that send signals to onboard computers to control six high-powered thrusters. The thrusters counter the forces of currents, wind and waves to keep the vessel exactly on target — usually averaging less than two meters off her mark — without an anchor, even in weather conditions as severe as a 10-year Gulf of Mexico storm.

HOUSTON ★ People ★ Opportunity ★ Success

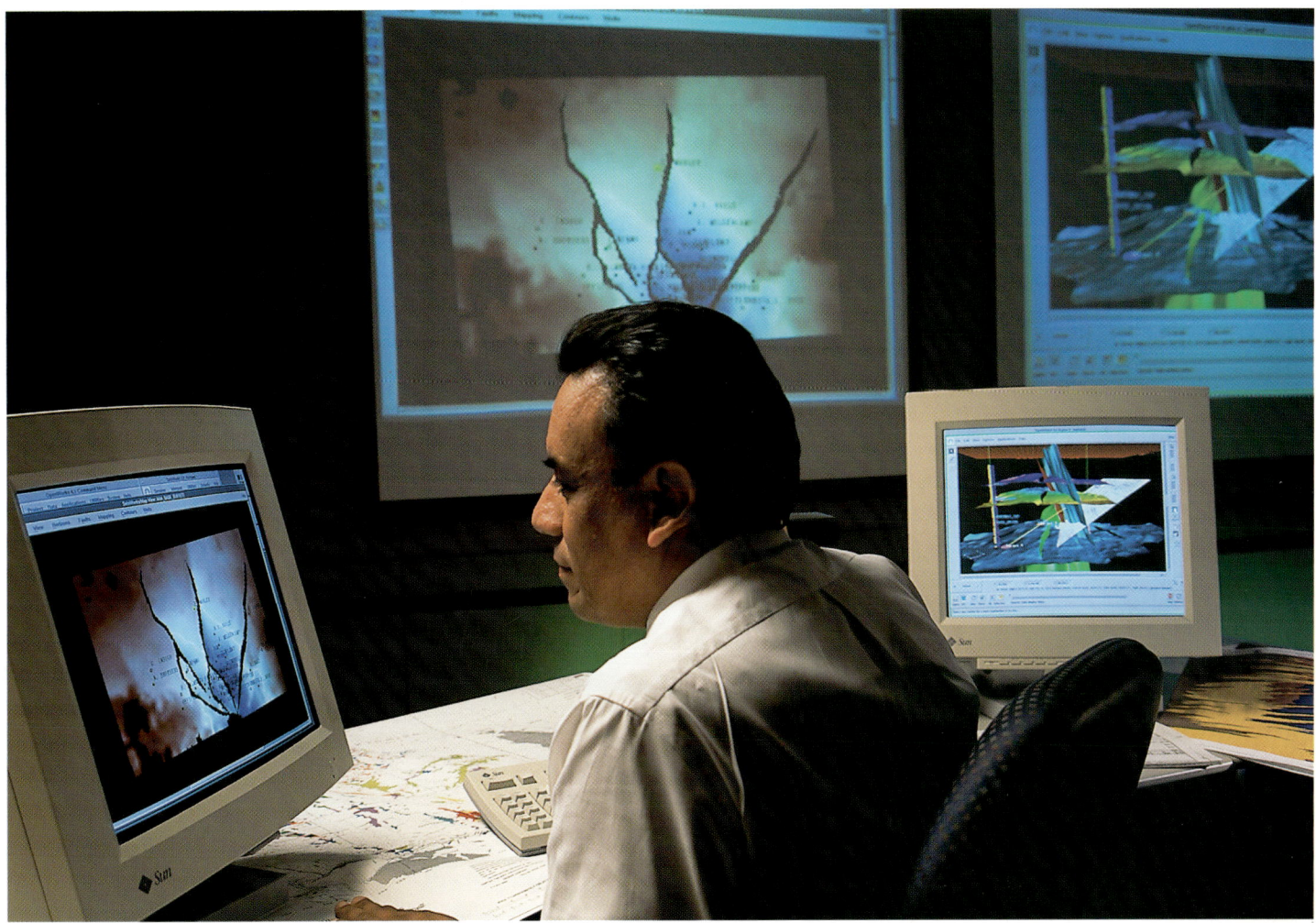

Harnessing New Technology Then and Now. *Using software that transforms vast quantities of seismic, well log and other data into detailed computer models of petroleum reservoirs, Landmark Graphics, a division of Halliburton Inc., (above) is able to help geologists and engineers analyze the earth's subsurface. Houston-based Landmark Graphics' systems are installed in more than 70 countries, and its customers include 90 percent of the world's largest oil and gas companies. ★ In the early 1900s, Houston's oil fields attracted not only wildcatters with a goal of finding gushers, but also men with new ideas on how to drill for oil. One of them, Howard Hughes Sr., developed, patented and manufactured a then-revolutionary approach to make rotary drill bits with two-cone cutters that significantly improved drilling performance. Through the years, Baker Hughes Inc. has further improved its drill bit designs and continues to manufacture drill bits (left) in a state-of-the-art plant in Houston.*

HOUSTON ★ People ★ Opportunity ★ Success

Fueling the World's Energy Needs. With a capacity to produce more than 3.5 million barrels of refined petroleum products every day of the year, Houston is the country's leading refining center, accounting for 22 percent of total U.S. production of gasoline and petroleum products. To store both crude and refined products, Houston area refineries are ringed by huge tank farms.

HOUSTON   ★   People   ★   Opportunity   ★   Success

Petrochemical Powerhouse. More than 45 percent of the country's base petrochemical manufacturing capacity is located in the 368 chemical plants in the Houston-Gulf Coast region. Base petrochemicals are the raw materials for producing plastics and resins used by a number of industries to make finished products.

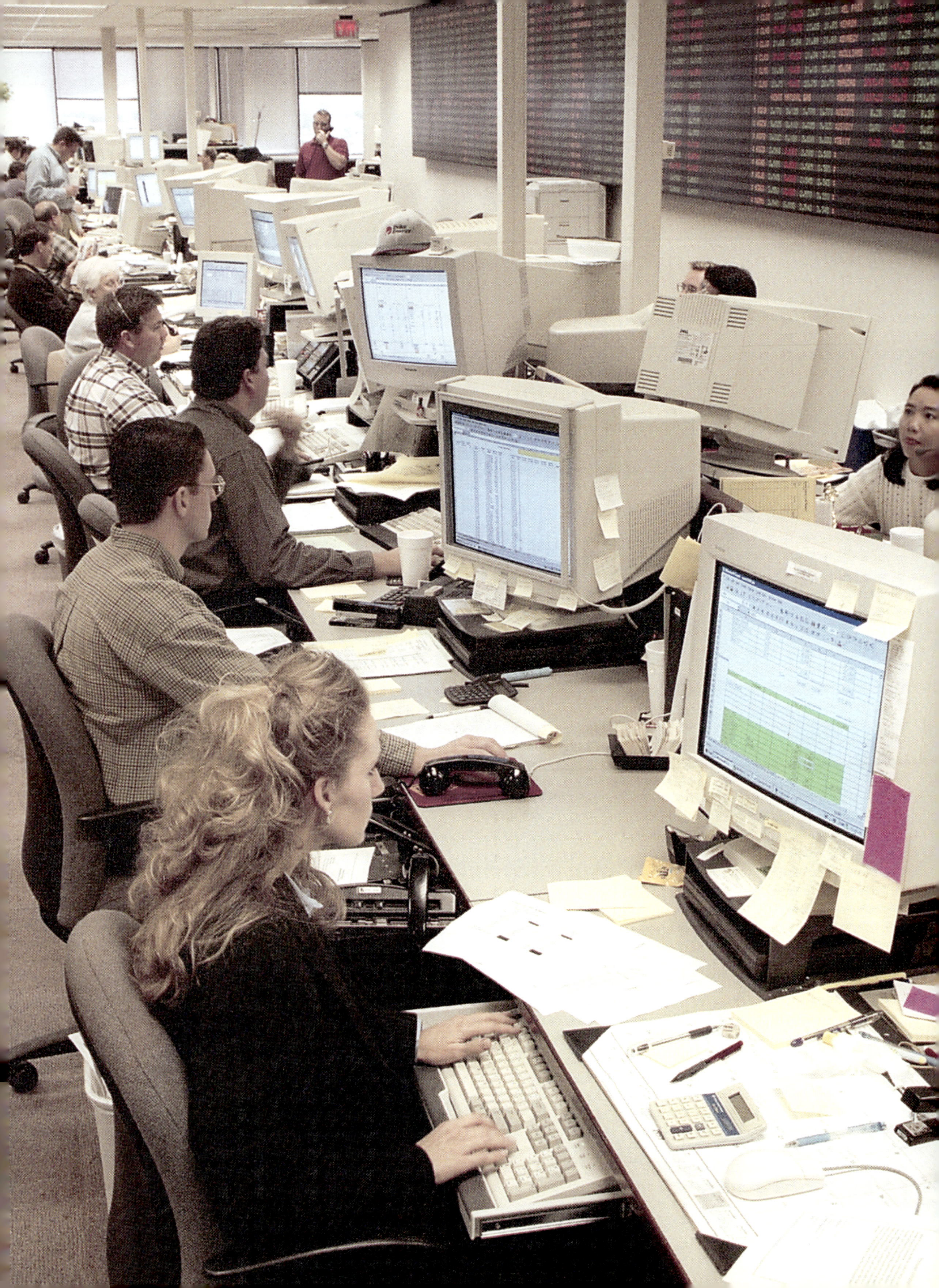

HOUSTON ★ People ★ Opportunity ★ Success

Mission Control for Pipeline Companies. *Thirteen of the nation's 20 largest natural gas pipeline companies have corporate or divisional headquarters in Houston. They account for 108,328 miles or more than 57 percent of the nation's total pipelines. El Paso Energy's control center (above) monitors and controls pumping along the company's network of pipelines that stretches from the Gulf of Mexico and along the Gulf Coast to the Northeast and Midwest.* ★ *Houston has become a 24-hour international center for dozens of companies engaged in trading energy-related products. On the trading floor of Duke Energy Trading and Marketing, (left), employees finalize transactions for trades involving natural gas, electricity and other energy products.* ★ *Attracting more than 45,000 attendees from 97 countries, the annual Offshore Technology Conference (pages 38-39) in Houston is the largest conference in the world dedicated to the offshore oil and gas industry.*

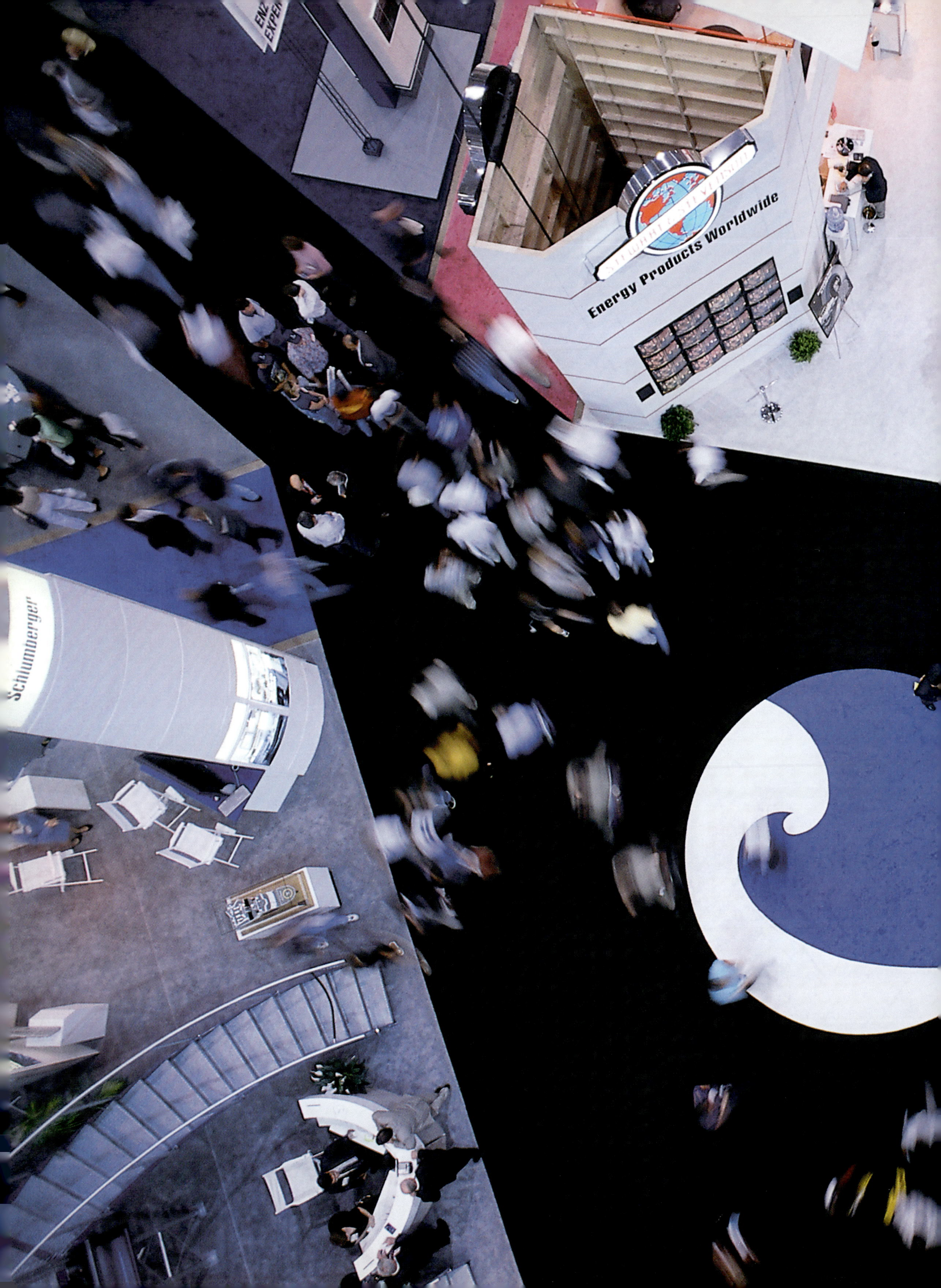
Energy Products Worldwide
Schlumberger

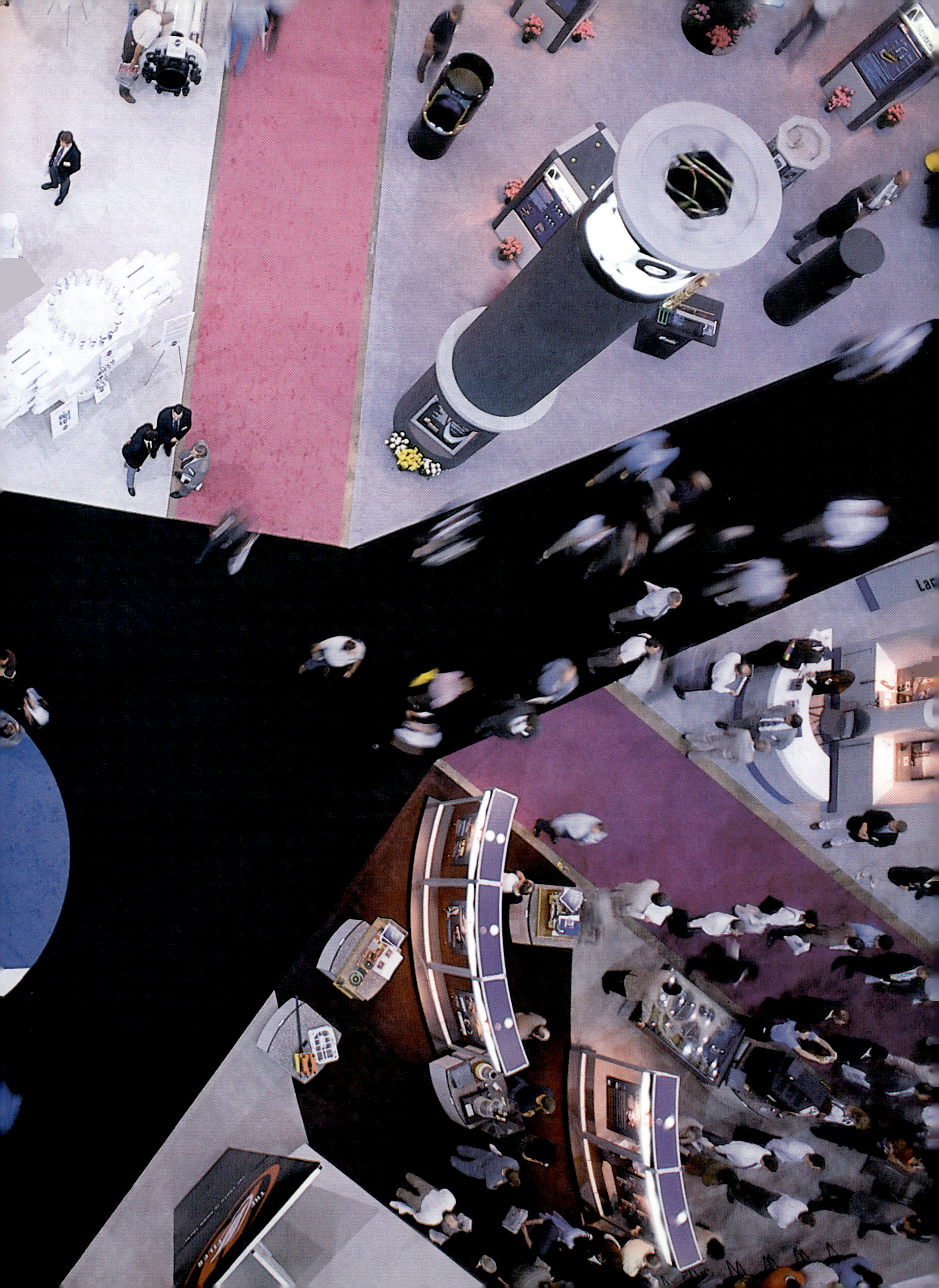

HOUSTON ★ People ★ Opportunity ★ Success

Health Care

If you are looking for a medical miracle, you may well find it in Houston. After all, major breakthroughs have become almost commonplace as a result of the tremendous research and resources invested in Houston's famed Texas Medical Center.

Houstonians, for example, founded the world's first trauma center, the nation's first critical wound unit, the first freestanding AIDS facility and the first germ-free environment for protecting immunosuppressed patients who are susceptible to life-threatening infections while undergoing cancer therapy.

The city's physicians performed the first successful heart transplant in the United States, the first successful implant of a partial artificial heart, the first operation to remove fatty plaques that clog the artery to the brain and one of the first surgeries on a blue baby, born with a congenital heart malformation that robs the blood of oxygen.

Houston introduced the first PET scanner for producing three-dimensional images of the heart and the first hospital-based cyclotron for treating certain types of radiotherapy-resistant cancers. Patients here were the first to receive Cobalt-60 radiotherapy for the treatment of cancer and streptokinase to open their blood vessels following a heart attack.

Health care in Houston had simple beginnings. More than a century ago, the Sisters of Charity, missionaries from France, founded the city's first general hospital, the 40-bed St. Joseph Infirmary. By the mid-1920s, Houston had more than a dozen public and private hospitals.

But it was the development of the Texas Medical Center in the 1940s that earned Houston its reputation as one of the greatest medical meccas on earth.

Starting out in an old army barracks that served as temporary headquarters for the M.D. Anderson Hospital and Tumor Institute, the Texas Medical Center quickly began setting global standards of excellence in health care. Today, it boasts, among other things, the world's largest cardiac catheterization facility, the nation's largest pediatric facility, one of the world's largest transplant centers and one of the country's largest air emergency services, shuttling critically ill or injured patients to the medical center from around the region and the globe. Houston is also home to two of the world's most renowned heart surgeons, Dr. Michael E. DeBakey and Dr. Denton A. Cooley.

Today, 4.8 million patients annually travel to the Texas Medical Center from other parts of Houston as well as Texas and around the world. One of the largest health-care complexes of its kind, the Texas Medical Center covers close to 21 million square feet – almost half the size of Houston's central business district – and it's expected to grow to 31 million square feet within the next 15 years. Truly a city within a city, it has more than 100 permanent structures linked by 12 miles of private and public streets and highways. As a whole, the Texas Medical Center employs nearly 55,000 full- or part-time personnel.

Most significantly, the Texas Medical Center boasts more than 40 not-for-profit institutions, including 13 hospitals and two specialty institutions, with a total of 7,000 licensed hospital beds and 400 bassinets. Six institutions in the Texas Medical Center are regularly among U.S. News and World Report's rankings of the top hospitals in the nation.

Complementing the Texas Medical Center's commitment to quality patient care is its dedication to ensuring a comprehensive education for the healthcare providers of tomorrow and to conducting leading-edge research into the cause, prevention and treatment of disease.

Each year, more than 20,000 students attend classes regularly and over 68,000 take short courses or professional training at the Texas Medical Center's two medical schools as well as its four schools of nursing and schools of dentistry, public health, pharmacy and other health-related fields.

Significant discoveries by researchers at the Texas Medical Center have led to major advances in medicine. The fact that its institutions have received more than $2 billion in research grants in the past five years testifies to the caliber and commitment of the researchers and scientists throughout the Texas Medical Center.

The standards of excellence established at the Texas Medical Center are echoed in the quality of care given patients at facilities throughout the Houston metropolitan area. The Houston region boasts more than 100 hospitals with almost 23,500 beds. Houston's stellar health-care system does more than ensure the highest quality in patient care, medical education and research. It also makes a major contribution to the area's economic vitality. ■

A Haven for Medical Care. For more than 50 years, the world-renowned Texas Medical Center and its 42 non-profit institutions have been dedicated to providing the very best in patient care, medical education and research. The Texas Medical Center includes two comprehensive medical schools, four schools of nursing, 13 renowned hospitals and two specialty institutions. ★ Located on 675 acres three miles south of downtown Houston, the Texas Medical Center (pages 42-43) annually receives more than 4.8 million patient visits, including 20,000 international patients. The institutions of the Texas Medical Center are also leaders in medical and biomedical research, receiving more than $2 billion in research grants during the past five years.

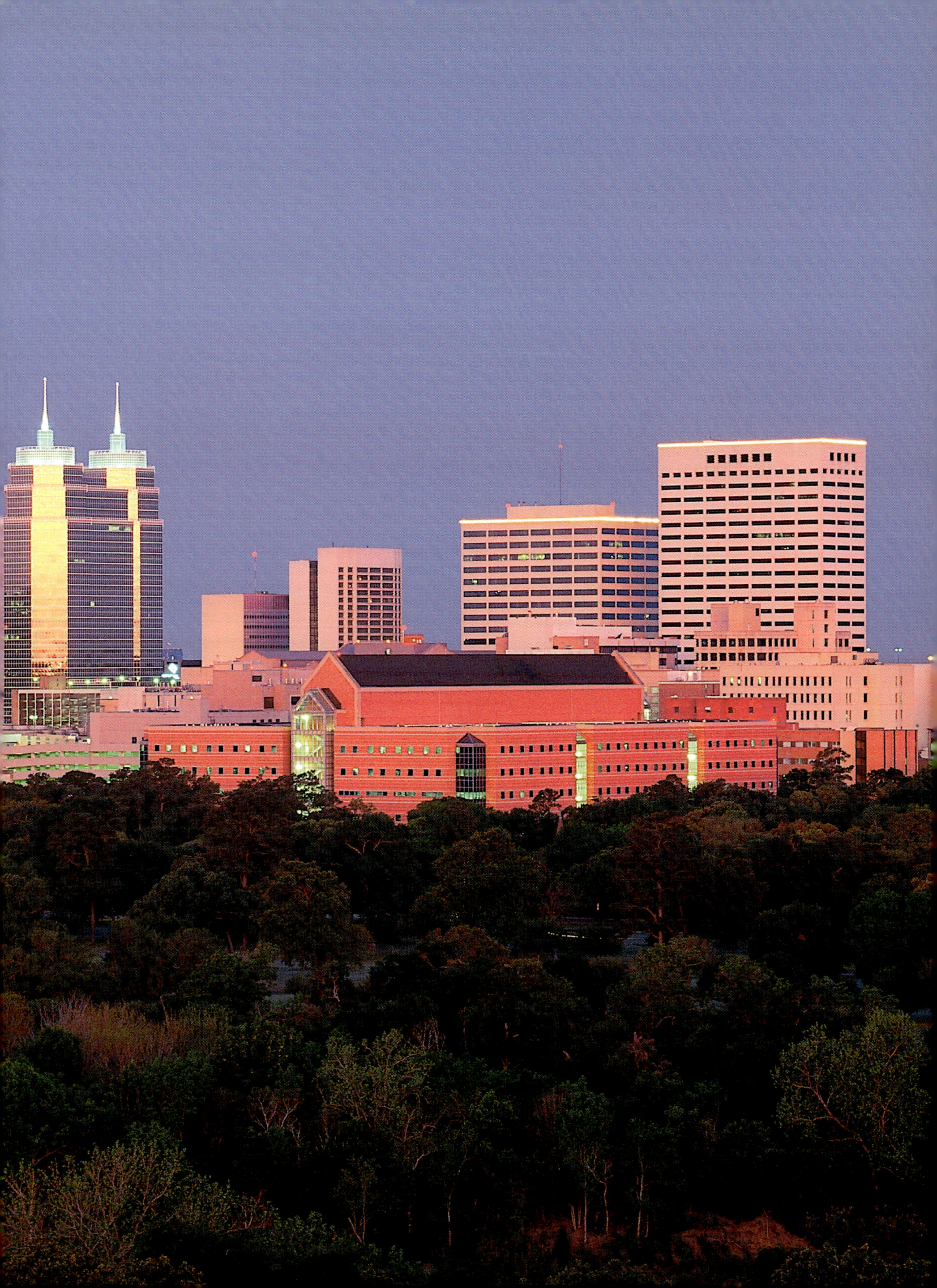

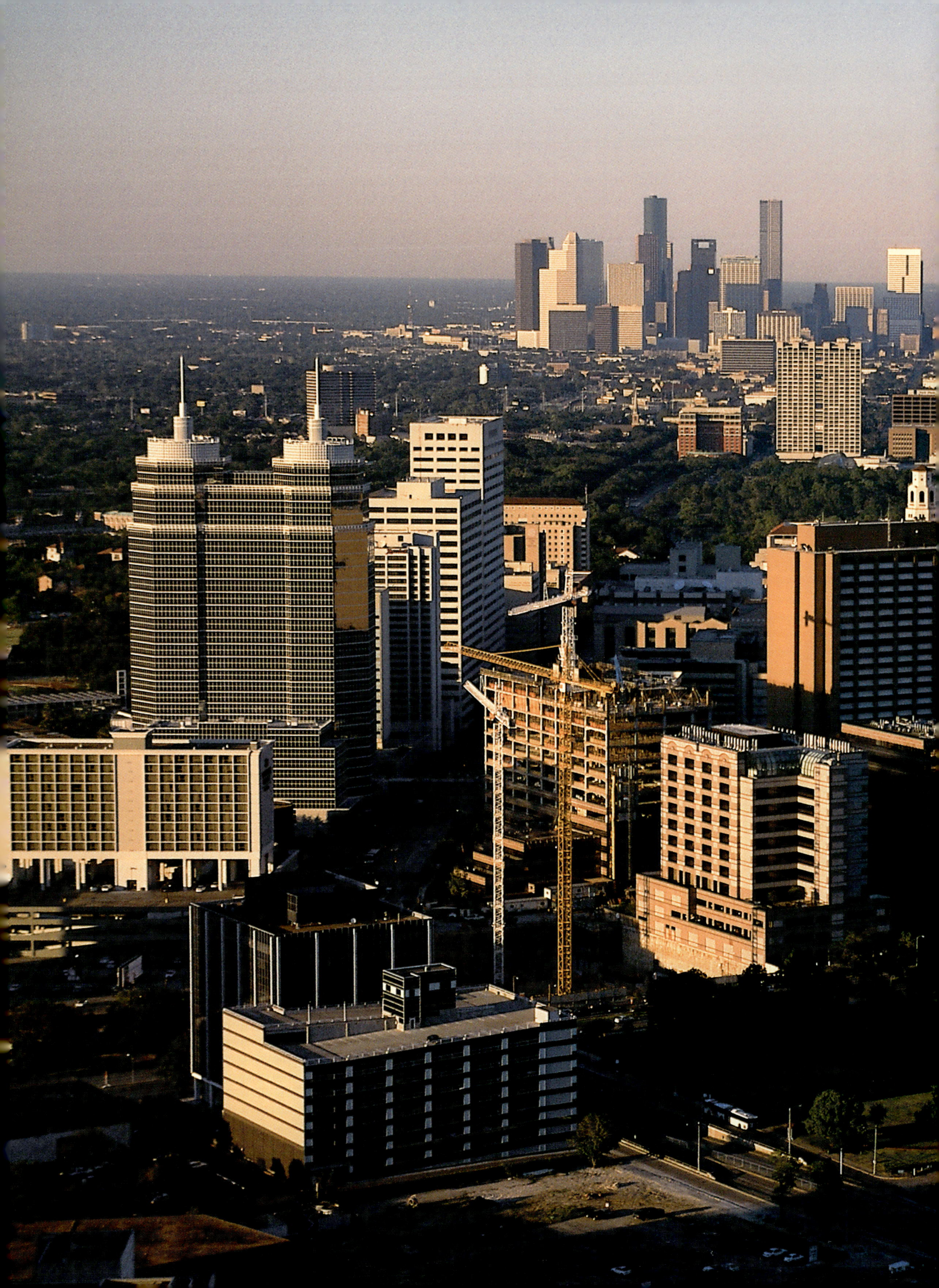

The University of Texas-Houston

HOUSTON ★ People ★ Opportunity ★ Success

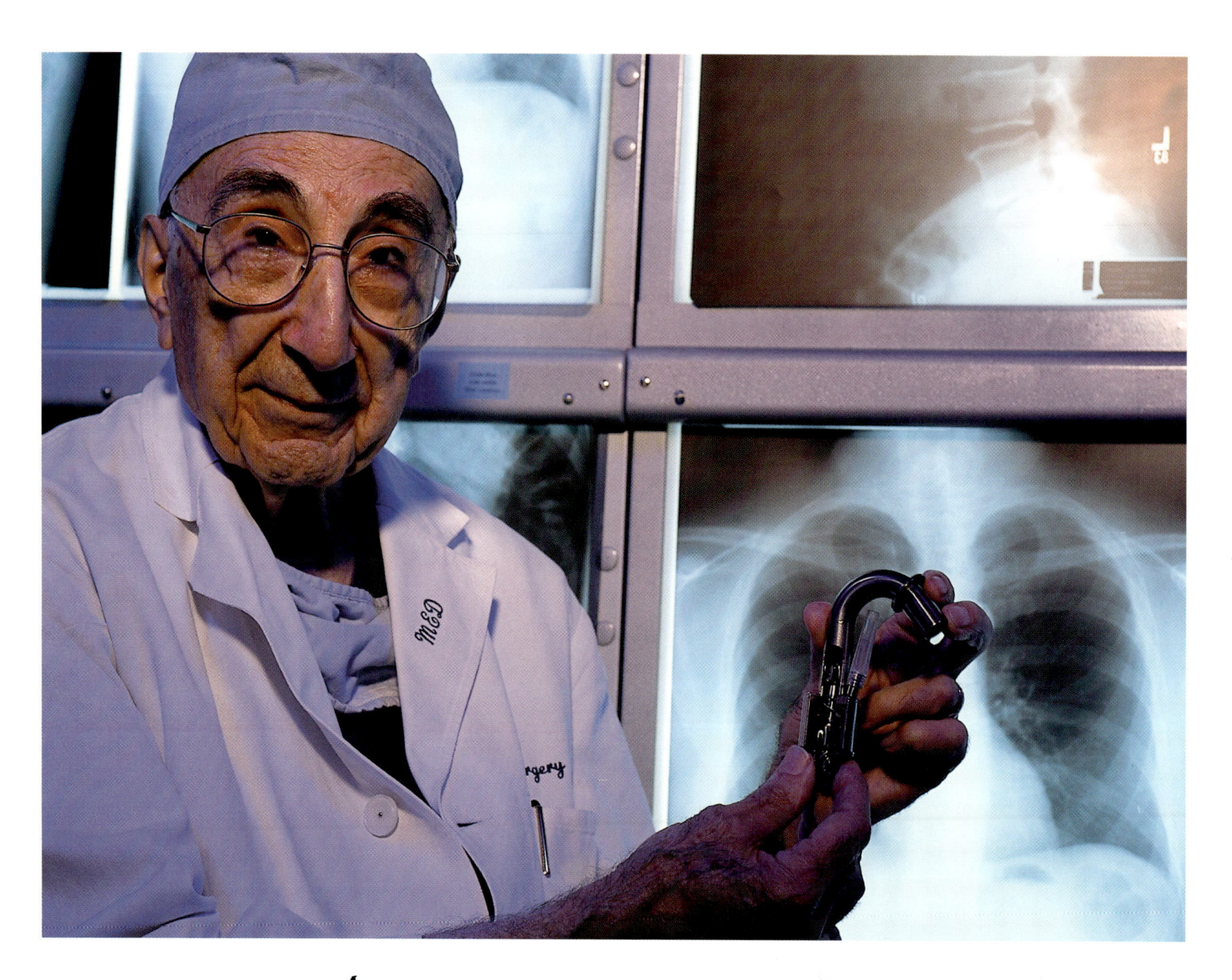

A **Medical Pioneer.** *Surgeon, innovator, medical educator and international medical statesman, Dr. Michael E. DeBakey is best known for his innovations in treating cardiovascular diseases. While still a medical student, he devised a pump that years later became one of the essential components of the heart-lung machine that made open-heart surgery possible. He has developed more than 50 surgical instruments, was a pioneer in the development of an artificial heart and was the first to use a heart pump successfully in a patient. His latest invention is a ventricular assist device, developed in part by applying engineering and technology from the U.S. space program. The DeBakey VAD™ is a miniaturized heart-assist device capable of pumping in excess of 10 liters per minute to provide increased blood flow to patients who suffer from heart disease.*

HOUSTON ★ People ★ Opportunity ★ Success

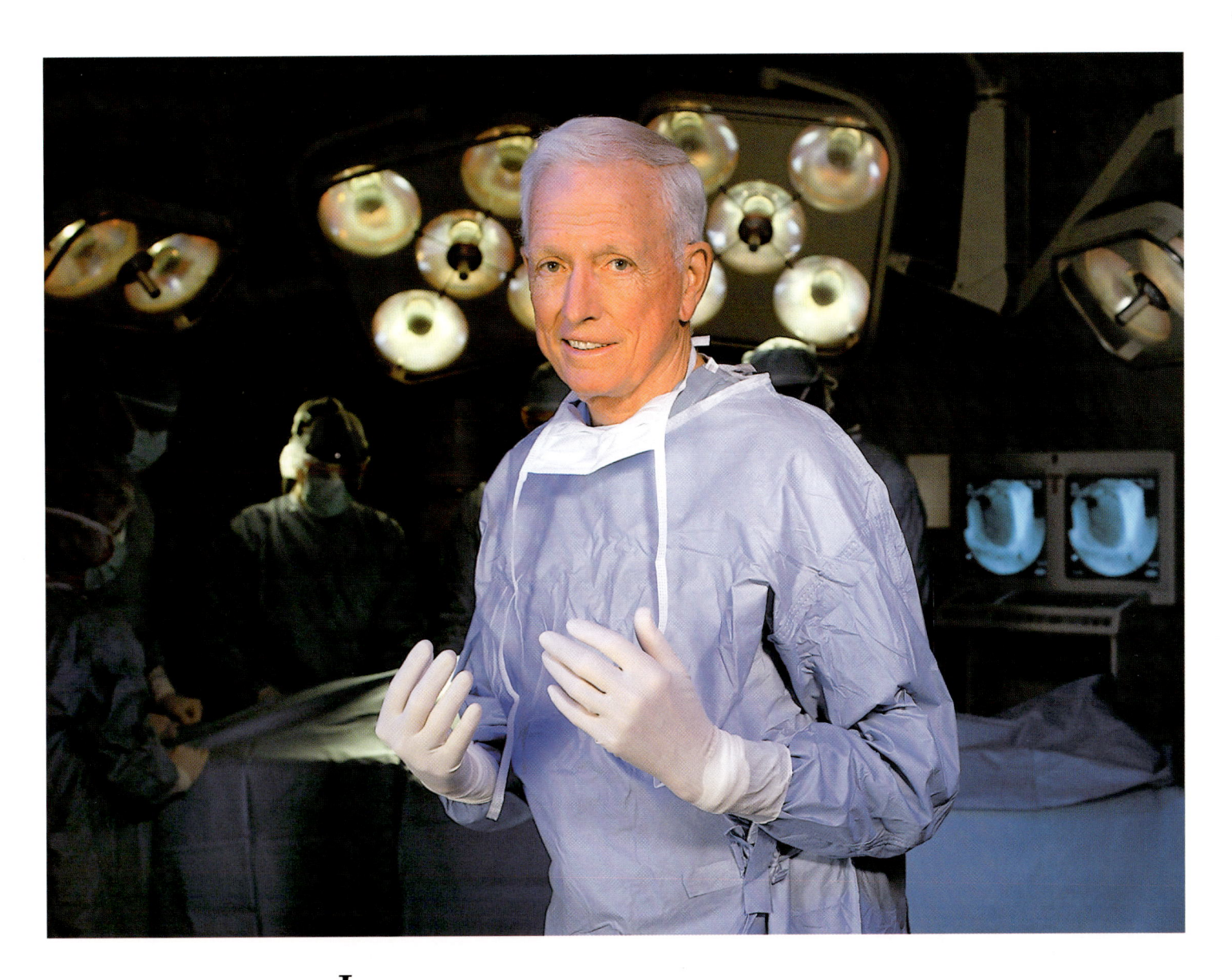

Leading with the Heart. Dr. Denton Cooley, president and surgeon-in-chief of the Texas Heart Institute in the Texas Medical Center, pioneered many techniques used in cardiovascular surgery. In 1968, he performed the first successful human heart transplant in the United States and in 1969 became the first heart surgeon to implant an artificial heart. Dr. Cooley and his associates have performed more than 98,000 open heart operations—more than any other group in the world

HOUSTON ★ People ★ Opportunity ★ Success

M*aking Medical History. Since its first mission in 1976 as one of the nation's first helicopter ambulance services, Hermann Life Flight has flown more than 50,000 missions to retrieve critically ill and injured patients within a 150-mile radius of Houston and transport them to trauma hospitals such as Memorial Hermann Hospital in the Texas Medical Center. On each mission, the helicopter is equipped with skilled medical personnel, advanced emergency equipment and necessary medications. Most locations in the Houston area are accessible in less than 15 minutes. ★ Ranked as one of the most respected and productive comprehensive cancer centers, the University of Texas M.D. Anderson Cancer Center is devoted exclusively to cancer patient care, research, education and prevention. One of the most promising new areas of treatment for the new century is gene therapy in which specially selected genes are manipulated and then inserted into a cancerous area to control growth or shrink a tumor.*

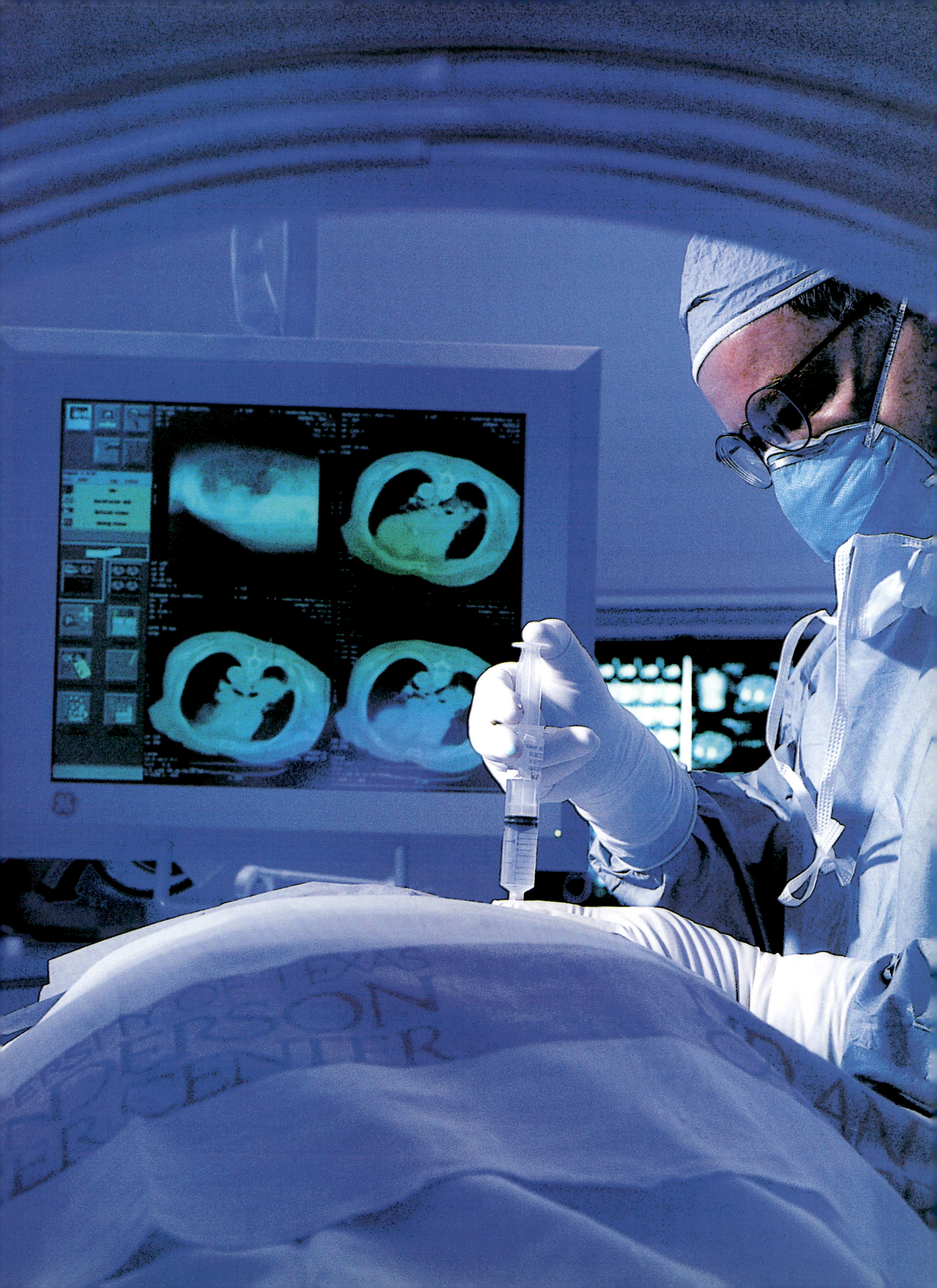

HOUSTON ★ People ★ Opportunity ★ Success

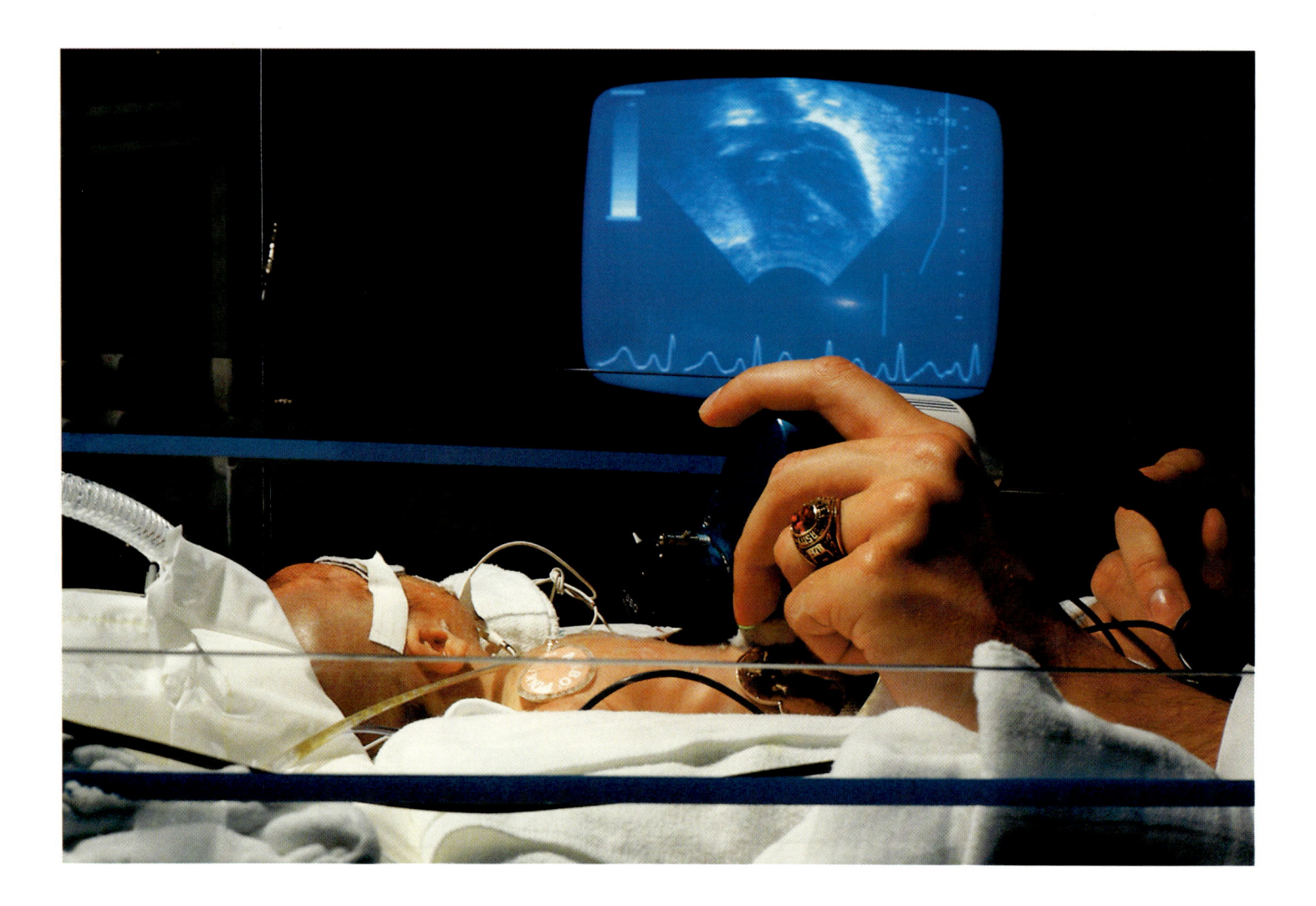

Miniature Medical Miracles. *Throughout the century, Houston has been a leader in pediatric medicine, with hospitals such as Texas Children's Hospital, Memorial Hermann Children's Hospital and others continuously setting new standards for the care and quality of life for even the tiniest of babies. Texas Children's Hospital, the largest pediatric facility in the United States, has garnered widespread recognition for its expertise and breakthrough developments in the treatment of cancer, diabetes, asthma, HIV, premature babies, and cardiogenic and attention-related disorders. Since 1954, Texas Children's Hospital has cared for more than one million children from every corner of the world. Memorial Hermann Children's Hospital's Turner Neonatal Intensive Care Center is a Level III nursery equipped to care for the most critically ill infants born as early as 23 weeks gestation and weighing as little as one pound.*

HOUSTON ★ People ★ Opportunity ★ Success

The Future of Medicine. In addition to their roles in patient care, one of the primary goals of the institutions of the Texas Medical Center involves educating, training and preparing future physicians, surgeons, nurses and other medical professionals. More than 20,000 students attend the two medical schools and four schools of nursing while more than 60,000 health professionals and others attend short courses or continuing education programs offered in the Texas Medical Center.

HOUSTON ★ People ★ Opportunity ★ Success

Space

"Houston, Tranquility Base here. The Eagle has landed."

Perhaps it was destiny that "Houston" was the first word spoken from the surface of the moon by Apollo 11 commander Neil Armstrong on July 20, 1969.

Afterall, the quest to put a man on the moon – one of the most ambitious goals and defining moments of the 20th century – was articulated by President John F. Kennedy during a speech at Rice University in Houston on September 12, 1962, when he said: "We choose to go to the moon and do the other things, not because they are easy, but because they are hard."

The hard challenges of humankind's dangerous venture into space captured the nation's imagination and determination. Nowhere was that more evident than in Houston during the 1960s as the city's leaders lobbied for Houston to be the site of Mission Control for the fledgling U.S. space program. Armed with donations of land from Rice University and other incentives from area companies, Houston won one of the biggest economic development plums of the century. In 1963, NASA's Manned Spacecraft Center – later renamed the Johnson Space Center – began operations with Gemini 4, the first flight to be controlled from Houston. Since then, every U.S. manned space flight has been controlled from Houston from the moment that each spacecraft broke its bonds with earth.

As the home for the manned space program, Houston became the home for every astronaut who ever flew aboard a U.S. spacecraft. From the original seven Mercury astronauts to the last astronaut class of the 20th century, more than 250 men and women astronauts have called Houston home before their journey into space.

The list of astronauts/Houstonians includes Alan Shepard, the first American in space; John Glenn, the first American to orbit the earth; Neil Armstrong, the first man to walk on the moon; Sally Ride, the first American woman in space; and Gene Cernan, the last man to walk on the moon. Some lived in Houston only while training and preparing for their missions. Others made Houston their permanent homes. Shepard, for example, later became a successful businessman in Houston and served as a commissioner on the Port of Houston Authority.

At its peak during the Apollo lunar missions, Johnson Space Center employed more than 5,000 Houstonians directly and thousands more through the variety of aerospace contractors and subcontractors that migrated to the NASA area to support the center.

As a result, Houston attracted engineers, computer programmers, researchers and scientists from across the nation and around the world to NASA's 1,620-acre campus.

Because such a large portion of space flight operations rely on computer controlled systems, Johnson Space Center also became a virtual software factory with programmers, computer analysts and engineers developing and maintaining systems to monitor and control every aspect of space flight activity.

Johnson Space Center also became a hub for research focusing on the life sciences. NASA's engineers were supported by researchers and scientists from the Texas Medical Center, Rice University, the University of Houston and other area institutions.

Collectively, Houstonians helped design and develop many of the key components of the U.S. space program, from the lunar lander, lunar rover and space suits to parts of the space shuttle and key elements of the international space station.

And it was Houstonians who went to work to devise and improvise solutions when disaster struck Apollo 13 and the crew radioed: "Houston, we have problem."

As the space program began to reflect the broader international interest in space exploration, so did Houston. Over the years, astronauts and researchers representing Canada, France, Germany, Italy, Japan, Russia and other countries have trained in Houston in preparation for their flights on U.S. spacecraft.

At the beginning of the new millennium, Houston's destiny in space is centered around the embryonic International Space Station, now being planned and built by 16 countries and assembled miles above the Earth. The Space Station will be the only laboratory free of the effects of gravity where long-term scientific research can be carried out. Scientists from around the world – including many based in Houston – will conduct medical research that could help to fight diseases such as influenza, diabetes, cancer, osteoporosis, and AIDS, and will conduct materials research that could lead to new manufacturing processes and products to benefit life on Earth.

Houston's continuing role in space will reflect each of the major areas of effort with which the city has been associated over the preceding years: mission control, astronaut training, life sciences research and applications. Wherever Houstonians are involved in the space program, they are sure to bring with them the spirit of dedication and adventure that have made dreams a reality. ■

Astronaut University. Every astronaut who has ever flown aboard a U.S. spacecraft has undergone rigorous and thorough training at NASA's Johnson Space Center in Houston. The Sonny Carter neutral buoyancy pool (right), allows Space Shuttle crews and trainers to test and validate techniques and procedures used by space-walking astronauts assembling the International Space Station. ★ Houston has been Mission Control (pages 52-53) for the U.S. space program since Gemini 4 was launched in 1963. ★ Full-scale mock-ups of the International Space Station (pages 54-55) are used for training astronauts at NASA's Johnson Space Center as part of the center's mission to design, develop and test spacecraft and associated systems for human space flight.

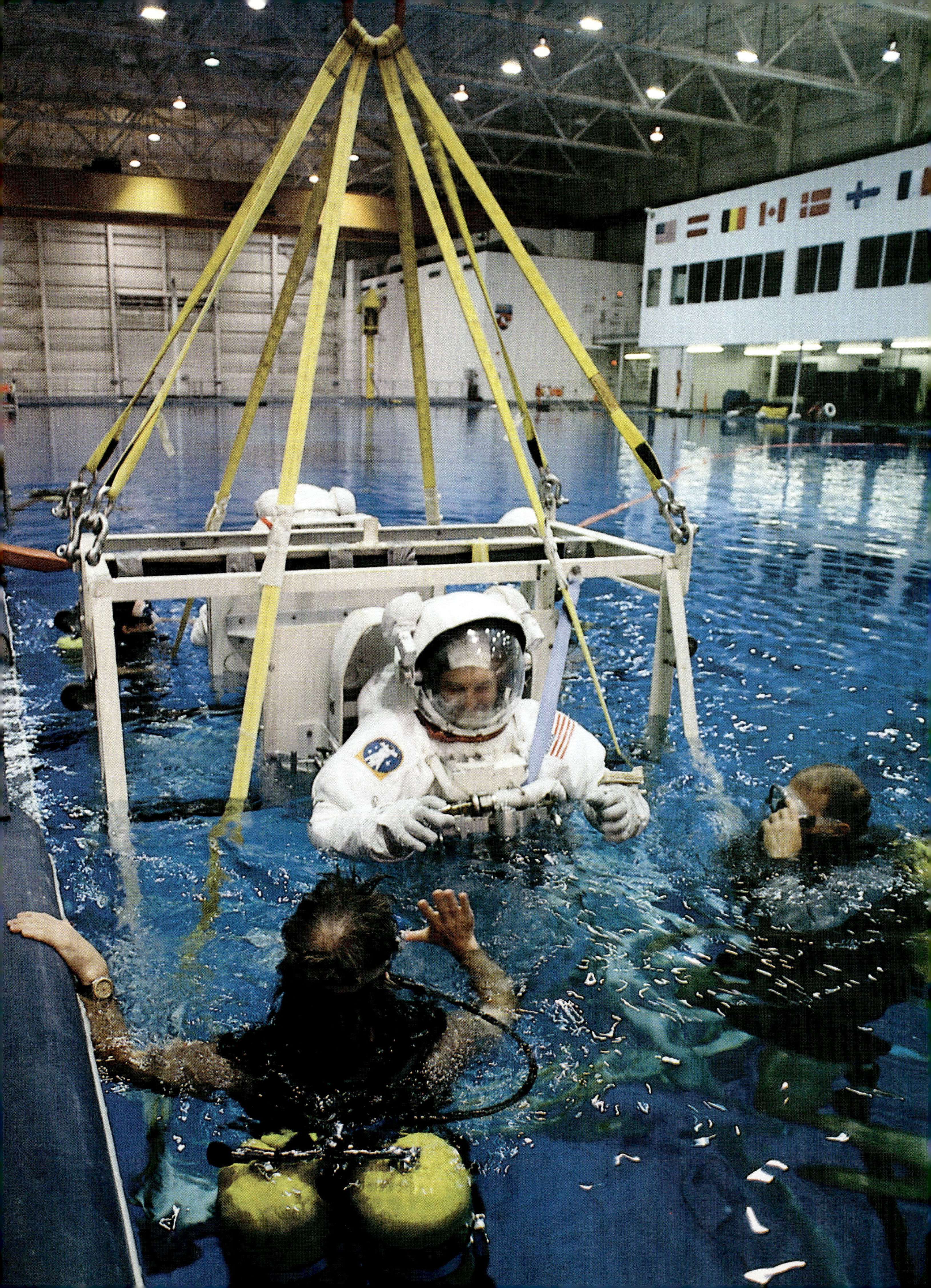

```
                                    000:00:04:26-
        WALLOPS UHF LOS     133:16:28:00+
        BERMUDA UHF LOS     000:14:39-
                             000:15:12-
```

```
1  GNC 1041: ITEM (03) EXEC              SSP096         SPECS    v01.02.00
2  GNC 1041: RESUME                                                        S
3  BFS    0: ITEM (03) EXEC                                                S
4  BFS    0: RESUME                                                        S
                                                                           S
133/16:55:47    1 GNC   1041 ITEM (03) EXEC
133/16:55:33    3 BFS      0 ITEM (03) EXEC
133/16:55:01    1 GNC   1041 RESUME
133/16:52:49    4 BFS      0 RESUME
133/16:51:50    1 GNC    990 FAULT
133/16:51:42    1 GNC   1041 I/O RESET   EXEC
133/16:51:38    1 GNC    510 RESUME
133/16:47:42    3 BFS      0 SYS SUMM
133/16:47:22    4 BFS      0 ITEM (02) EXEC
133/16:47:13    4 BFS      0 ITEM (16) EXEC
133/16:47:11    3 BFS      0 RESUME
133/16:46:52    1 GNC    510 ITEM (39) EXEC
```

```
                SSP096     Onboard Fault Summary  v1.02.00
      PASS Faults (GNC Auto)              GPC     Time (GMT)
 S    18     FCS CH         1             12 4    133/16:51:46.62
      17     DISPLAY SW     R             12 4    133/16:51:45.64
      16     BCE STRG 2     MLS           12 4    133/16:51:44.69
      15     BCE STRG 1     NSP           12 4    133/16:51:44.69
      14     BCE STRG 1     MLS           12 4    133/16:51:43.74
      13     MPS CMD        C             12 4    133/16:42:56.69
```

LAT = -40.5   ALT = 212
LON= -124.9 RNC = 51.6

-150 -120 -90 -60

TRAJECTORY   FDO

on Control Center
T-HOLD
CLOSE
esa
NASDA
TDRS-275
GUIDANCE/NAVIGATION
(GNC)
Mission Control Center

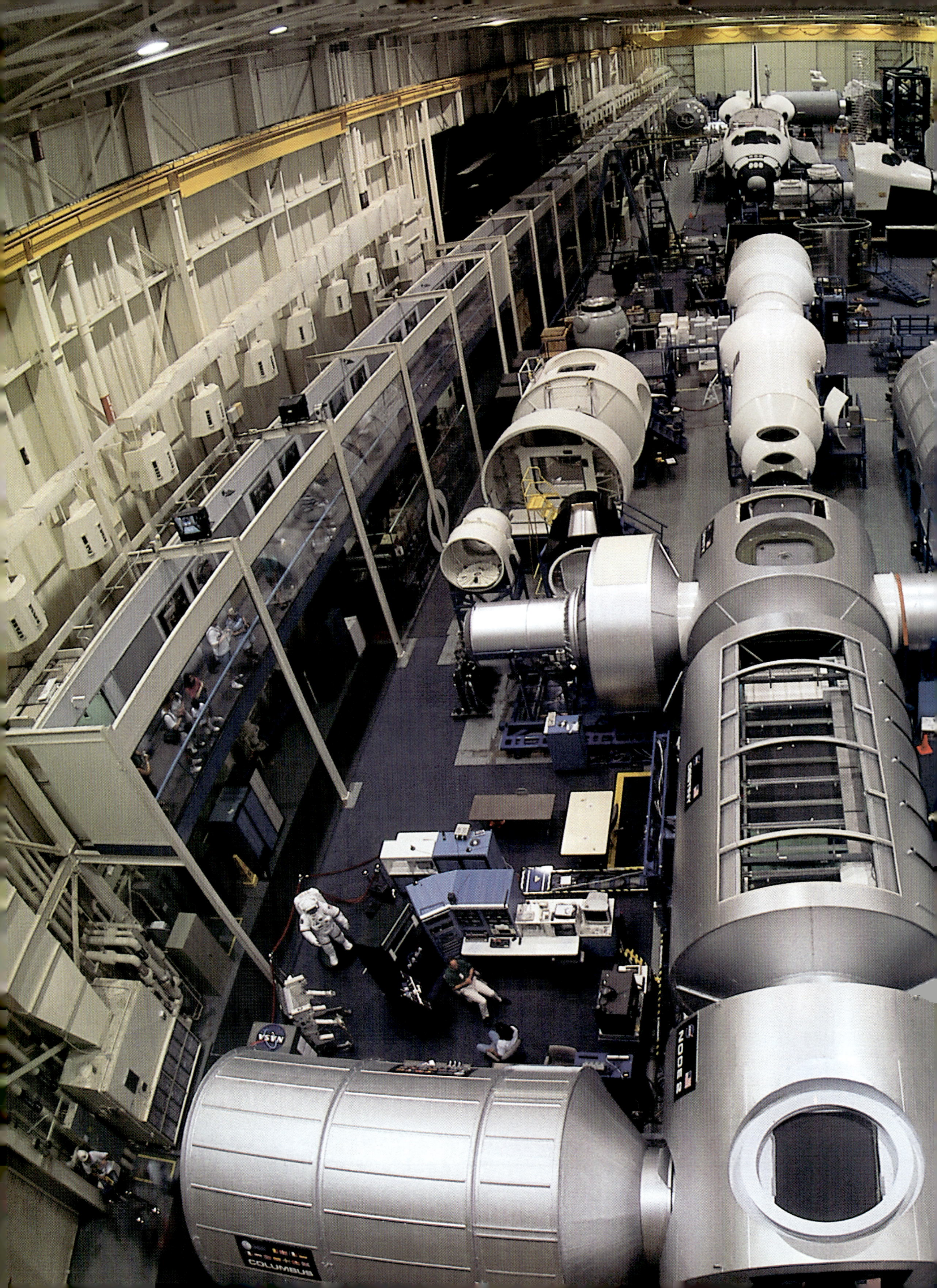
COLUMBUS
NODE 2

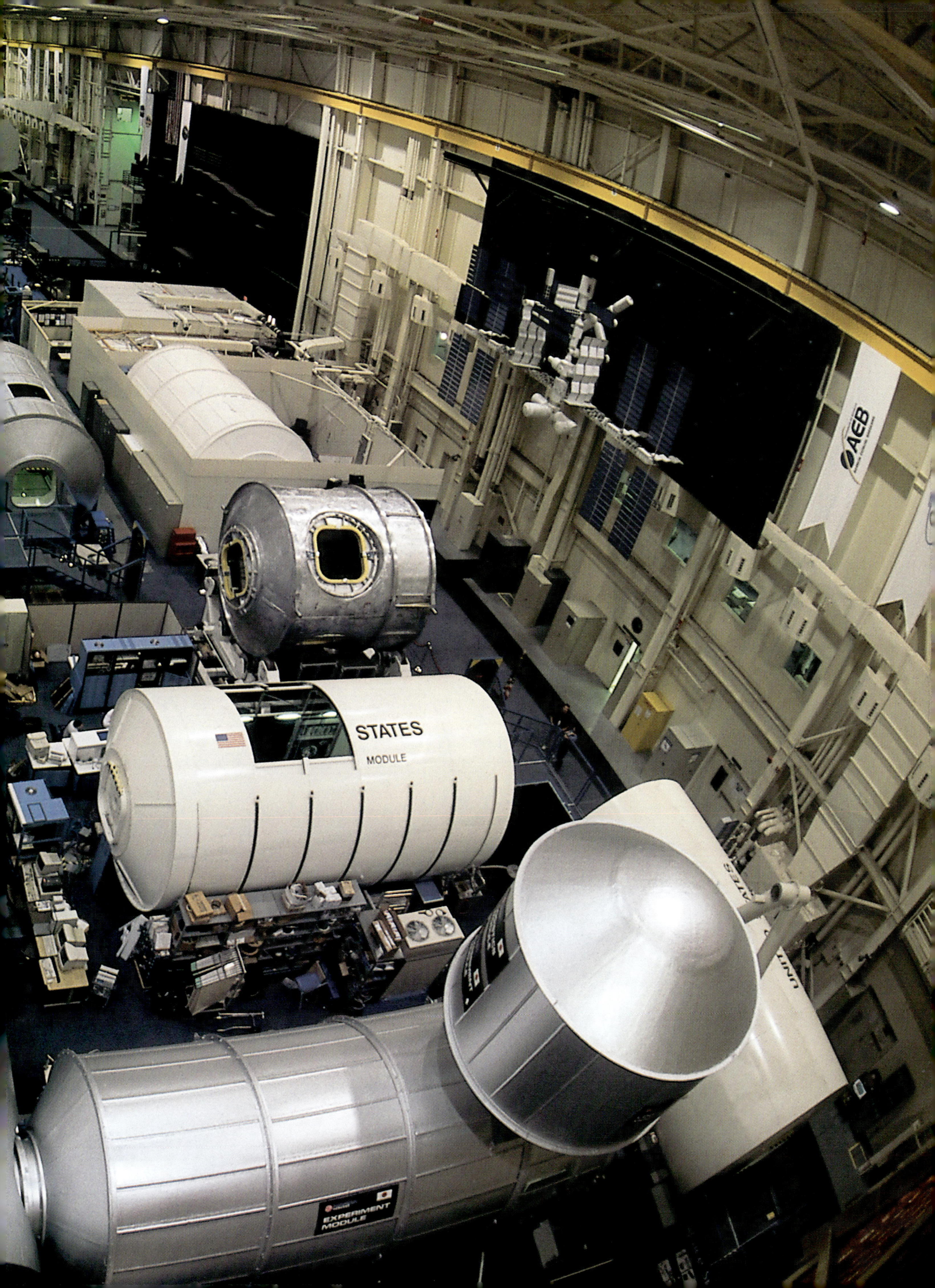
STATES
MODULE
AEB
EXPERIMENT
MODULE

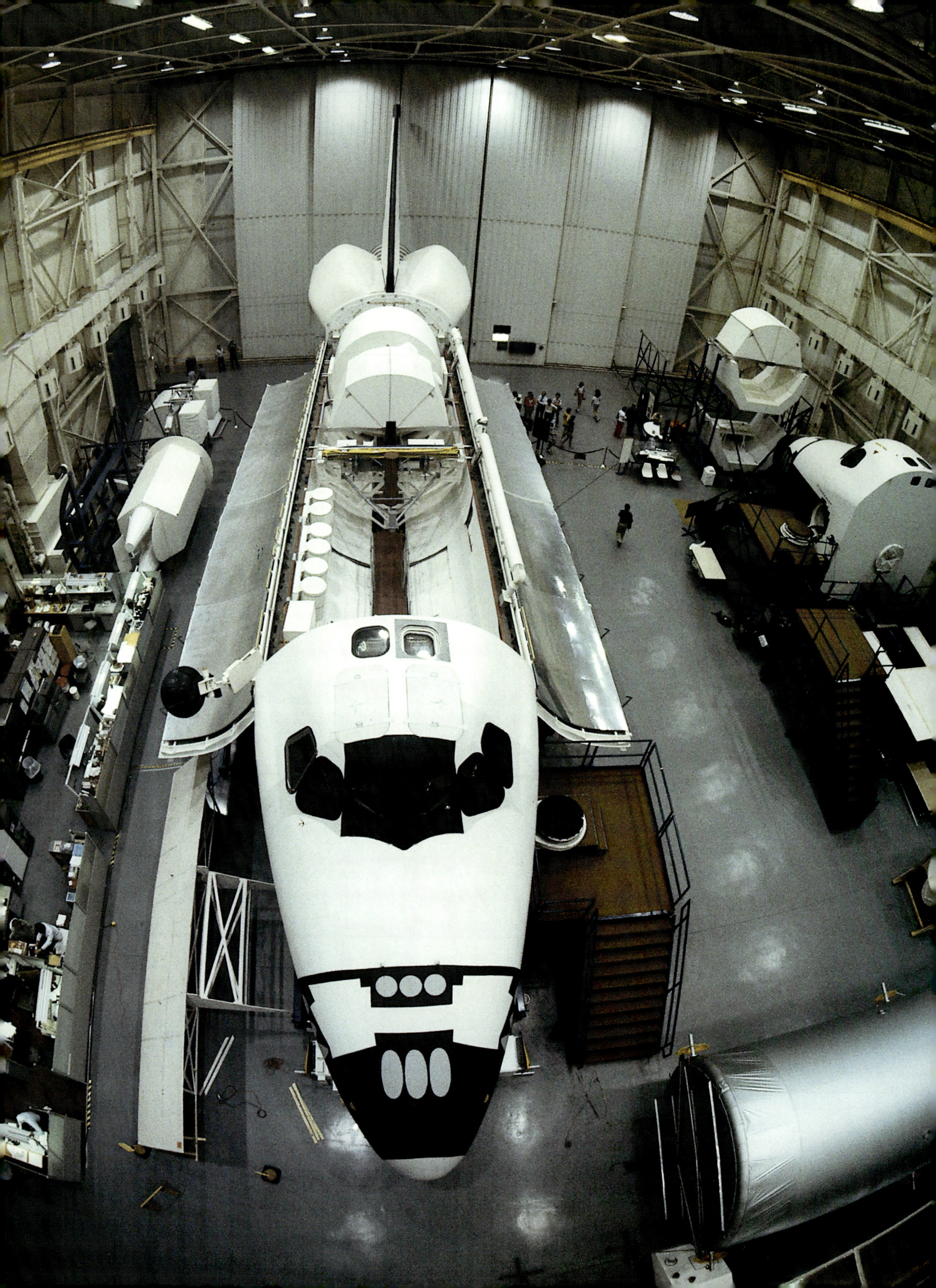

HOUSTON ★ People ★ Opportunity ★ Success

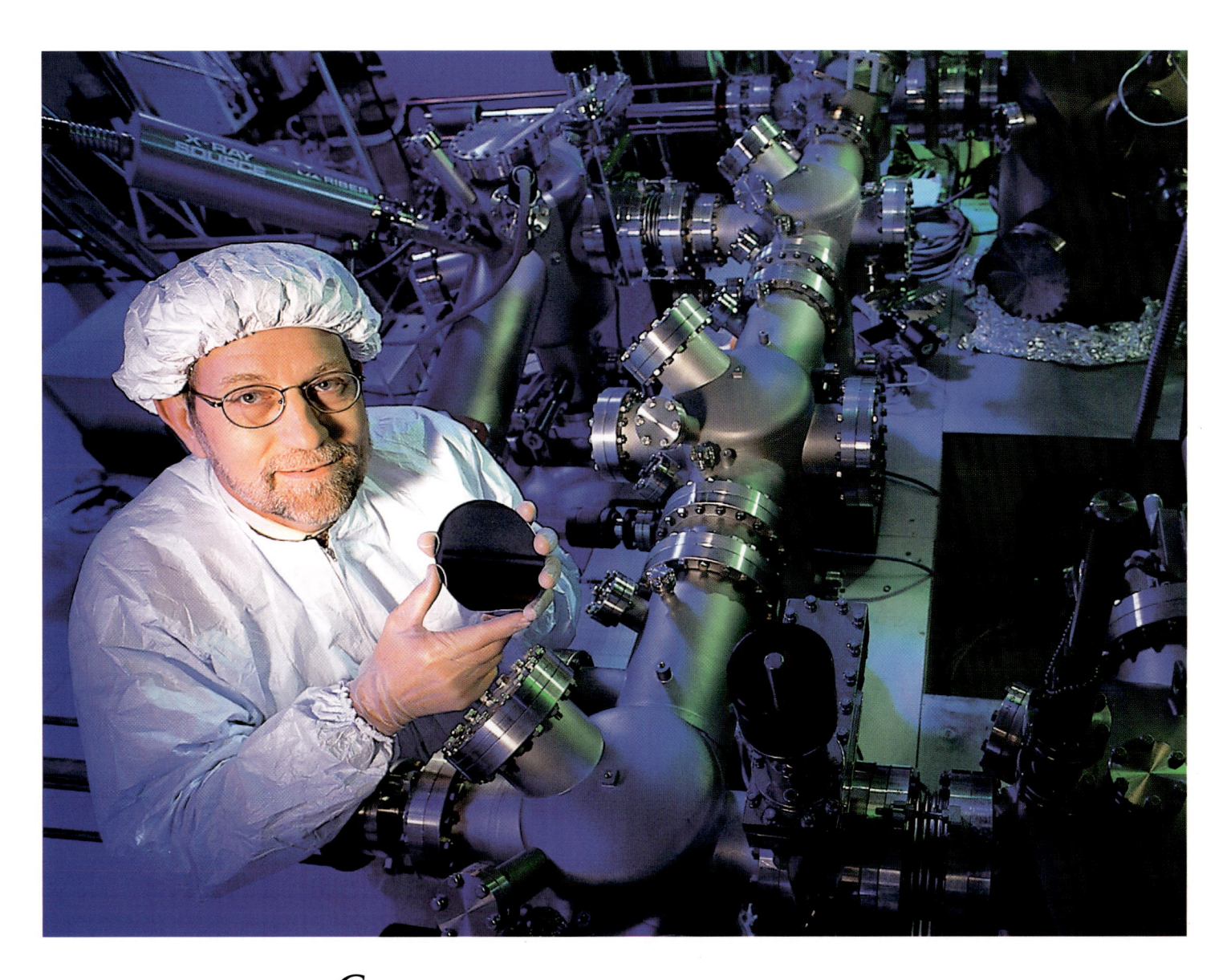

Capitalizing on Space. Dr. Alex Ignatiev (above) holds a sample of thin film materials in his lab at the Space Vacuum Epitaxy Center at the University of Houston. The NASA Commercial Space Center is using the pure vacuum of space to conduct scientific research in the development of new materials. The thin film materials technology developed could some day lead to applications such as faster electronics components for computers. ★ Using a full scale mock-up of the Space Shuttle (left), astronauts familiarize themselves with procedures for conducting all scientific, medical and engineering research projects, including storing and launching research projects and satellites from the shuttle's cargo bay.

HOUSTON ★ People ★ Opportunity ★ Success

For All Mankind. Astronaut Eugene Cernan (above), the last man to walk on the moon, remains active in the U.S. space program as chairman of Johnson Engineering. The Houston-based NASA contractor provides engineering, design and development services in support of the space shuttle, space station and future space flight projects. The command module that flew Cernan and the Apollo 17 crew to the moon in 1972 is on display at Space Center Houston, the official visitors center of NASA'S Johnson Space Center. ★ Rocket Park (right) on the grounds of NASA's Johnson Space Center is a favorite attraction for visitors who want to see full-size rockets like the ones used in the early years of the U.S. space program.

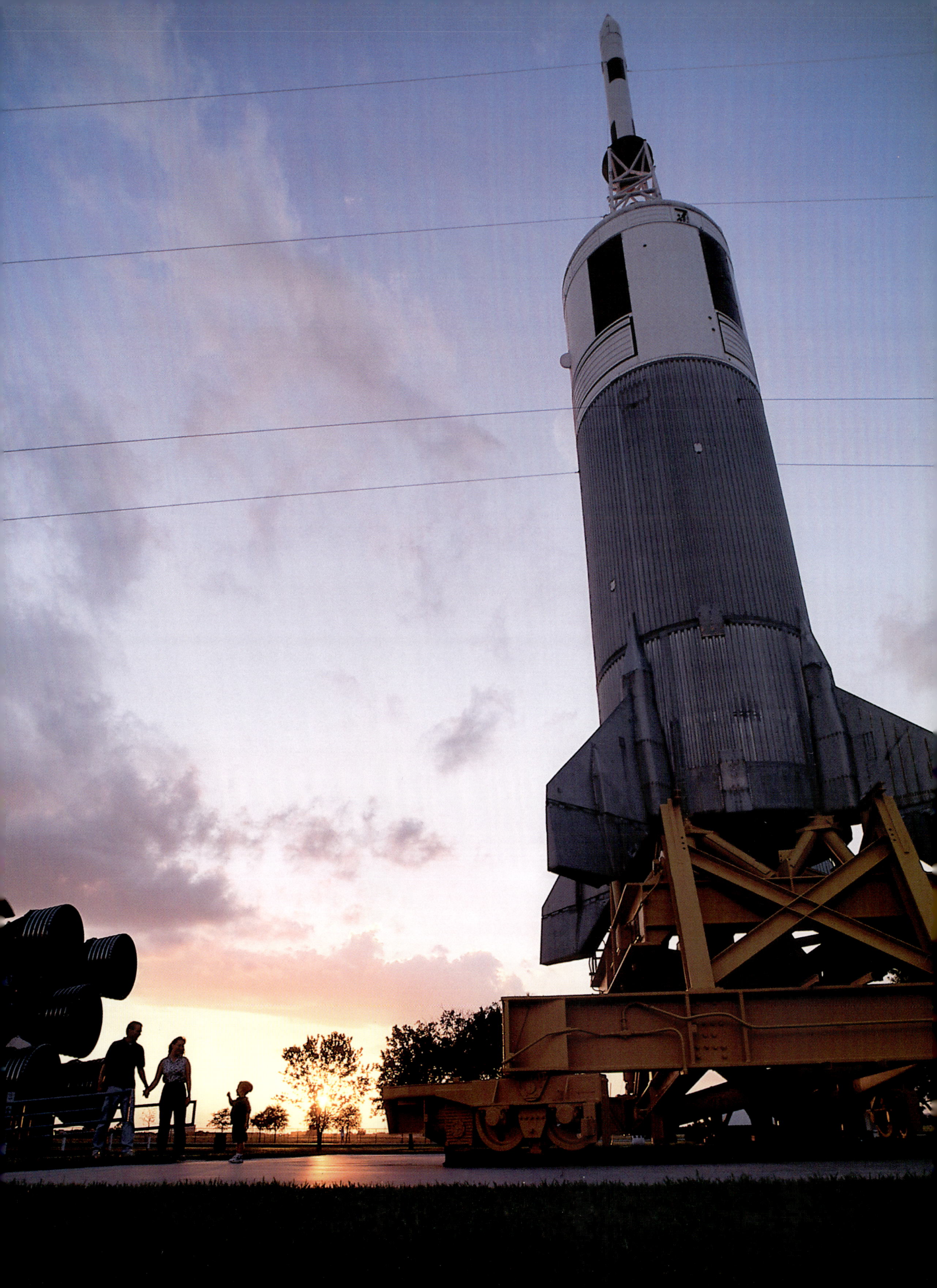

HOUSTON ★ People ★ Opportunity ★ Success

Technology

Mention new technology and most people will immediately think of a half dozen silicon valleys, cities, forests or areas. Yet it's hard to imagine a city with a more diverse portfolio of technology interests and resources than Houston.

Think about it: where else at the beginning of the new millennium would you be able to find researchers, scientists and engineers within 50 miles of each other who are involved in everything from geotechnology to nanotechnology, supercomputing to superconductivity, aerospace and planetary exploration to deepwater offshore exploration, biosciences to agrisciences, new materials research to digital signal processing, cancer research and the development of artificial hearts?

Altogether, Houston is home to more than 150,000 researchers, scientists, doctors and engineers exploring new ideas in eight general areas of technology applications: energy, chemicals, materials, space, medicine, biosciences, computer hardware and software technology.

Houston can trace its technology lineage primarily back to the wildcatter era at the beginning of the 20th century. Back then, everything that was needed to drill an oil well had to be invented or made from scratch. The list included drill bits, blowout preventers, wireline technology, offshore drilling platforms and more. Today, the energy industry in Houston is a major force in research and technology development. Using 3-D seismic visualization technology and a host of technologically-enhanced equipment, energy companies can now find oil and gas in extremely challenging and complex locations, and then pump oil and gas from wells drilled 30,000+ feet in rough waters that are more than two miles deep.

The creation of the Texas Medical Center in the middle of the century gave Houston its second major platform for research and development of new technologies, especially those aimed at finding the causes, cures and/or means of preventing disease. Again, while Houston has been known in the medical field primarily for the pioneering work done here in cancer and cardiac research and treatment, the reality is that Houston doctors and scientists are involved in virtually every major area of medical research. At the beginning of the millennium, Houston doctors and researchers are involved in more than $300 million of research annually.

With the creation of NASA's Johnson Space Center in the early 1960s, Houston entered a new and unique area of research and development. Thousands of Houston engineers and scientists helped develop the technology that put a man on the moon, and later went on to train and prepare more than 500 astronauts and coordinate research and experiments on more than 75 space shuttle missions. Now, Houstonians are helping build and launch the single largest research laboratory ever developed by humans: the International Space Station.

While the energy, medical and space industries have accounted for the bulk of Houston's research funds and efforts during the past century, the region's major universities will likely play a pivotal role in research and development of new technologies in the coming century. The University of Houston, for example, conducts more than $50 million in research each year and is the home of cutting edge research in superconductivity, space vacuum epitaxy and advanced molecular computation. Rice University, with $40 million in annual research funds, already has two Nobel Prize winners in chemistry for the discovery of fullerenes and has leading research programs in gene therapy, tissue engineering, computer science, space physics, nanoscale science and technology.

When combined with the pioneering medical and biomedical research and development programs at Baylor College of Medicine, the University of Texas M.D. Anderson Cancer Center and the University of Texas Health Science Center as well as other area colleges, the Houston region boasts more than $500 million of research and development activity each year.

On the private sector side of the R&D equation, Houston also is home to dozens of companies with major research and development programs in a variety of disciplines. Shell, Texaco, Exxon and Chevron, for example, have major energy research centers in Houston while Compaq Computer, BMC Software and Texas Instruments have significant programs in computer hardware, software and digital signal processing technologies.

While it is impossible to predict which area of technology will be the most promising or will play a defining role in the world economy of the coming century, given Houston's diverse mix of research and development resources – coupled with the city's ingrained spirit of exploration and discovery – it's a safe bet that Houston and Houstonians will play a leading role in the development of new technologies throughout the 21st century. ■

Technology Leaders. Dr. Paul Chu studies the effects of a superconducting material in his lab at the Texas Center for Superconductivity at the University of Houston. The center is recognized as one of the world's leading multidisciplinary centers for the study of materials leading to the full-scale commercialization of high temperature superconductivity. ★ Ranked as one of the world's largest computer companies, Compaq Computer Corporation (pages 62-63) is Houston's leading technology company. At its 1,000-acre campus-style headquarters in northwest Houston, Compaq's 10,000 area employees are responsible for research, engineering, design, development, marketing, distribution and manufacturing of its full line of personal computers. ★ Houston-based BMC Software (pages 64-65) is one of the world's largest independent software companies, providing management solutions that ensure the availability, performance and recovery of business-critical software applications.

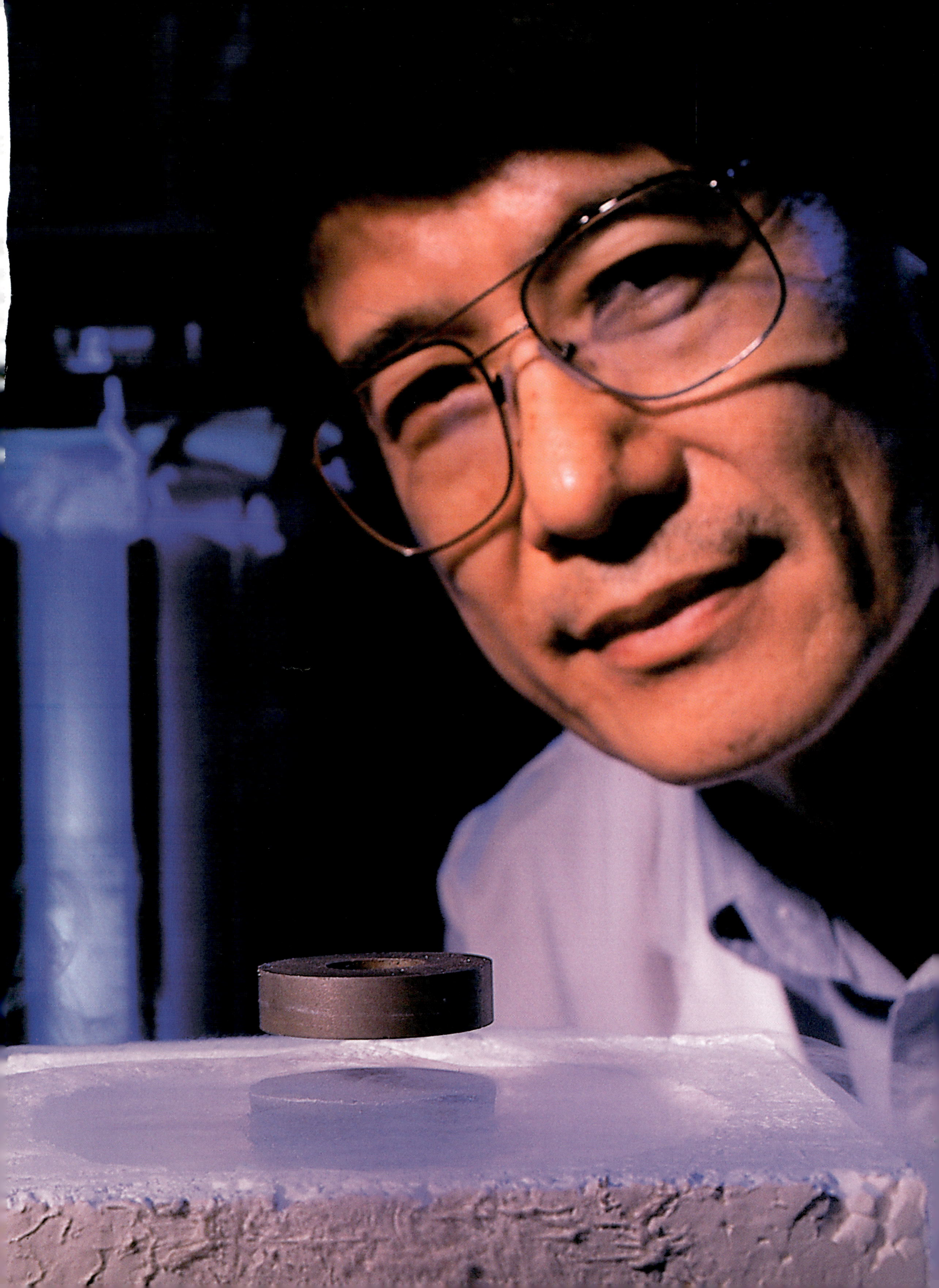

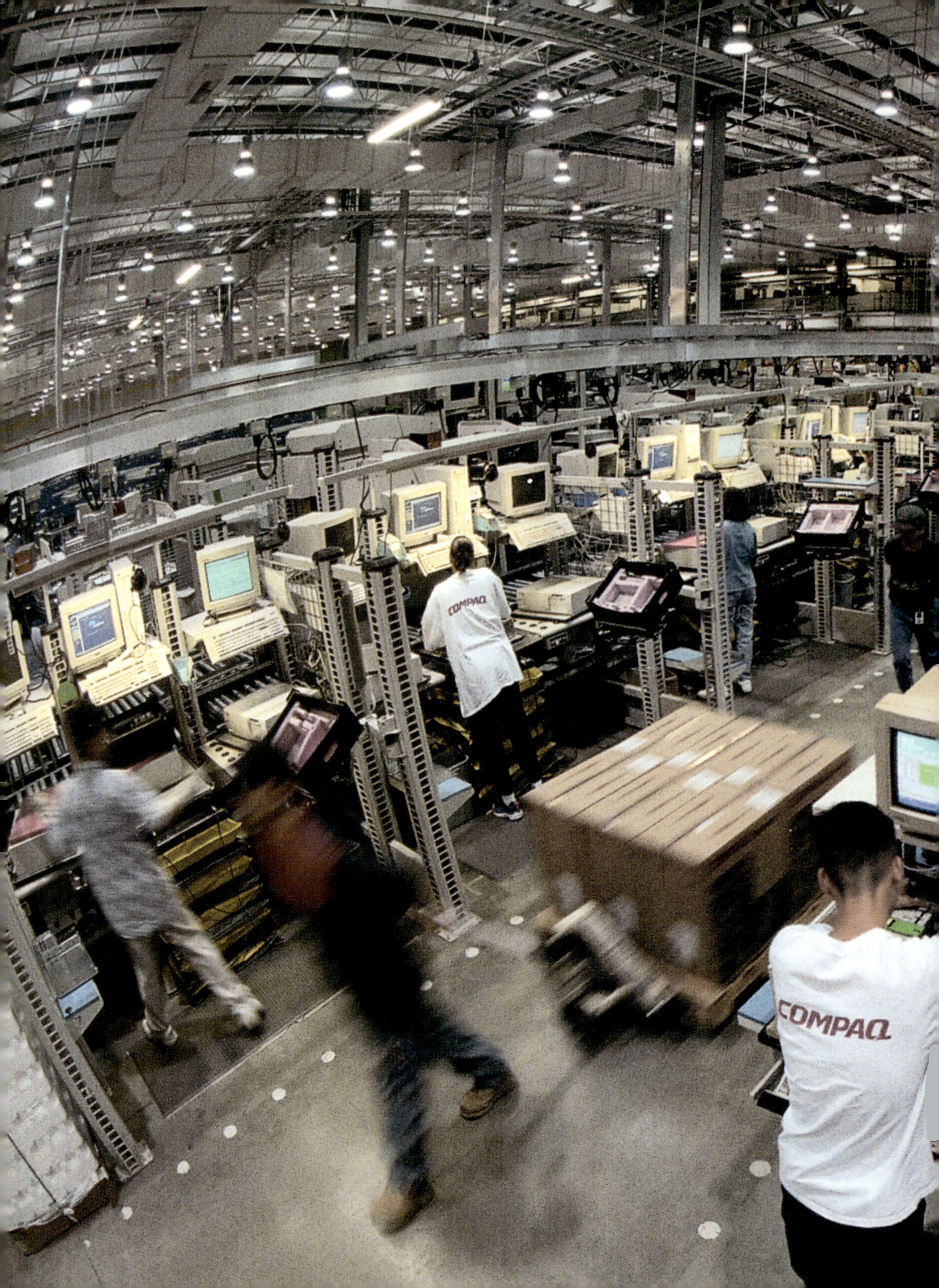
COMPAQ
COMPAQ

NOTICE
Safety glasses are required anytime unit is energized with chassis cover removed.
COMPAQ

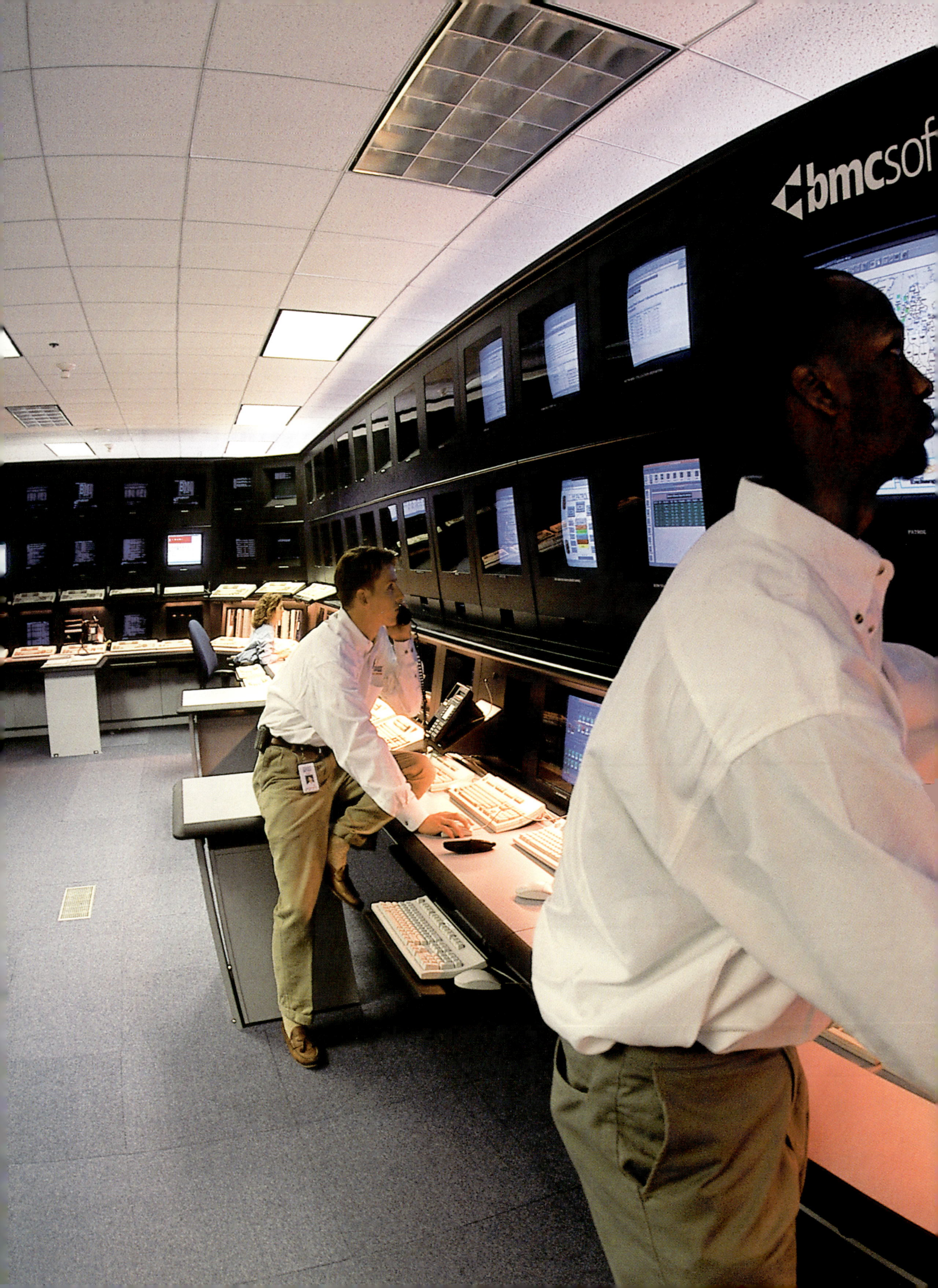
bmcsof

CONCORD WEB REPORTING CONCORD NETWORK HEALTH

BEST 1 NETWORK ASSOCIATES SNIFFER

ALERT SYSTEM PATROL DEVELOPMENT

HOUSTON ★ People ★ Opportunity ★ Success

Exploring the Potential of Biotechnology. Based on research initially conducted in Houston at Baylor College of Medicine, Tanox, Inc. (above) is focusing its product development efforts on therapeutics in three broad areas: immunology (asthma/allergy and autoimmune diseases), infectious diseases and oncology. Houston is home to more than 80 companies engaged in research, development and commercialization in the biotechnology and biosciences industries. Many of the companies are direct results of the $2 billion in research conducted over the past five years at the Texas Medical Center. ★ DNA samples (right) are loaded into a sequencer machine at Baylor College of Medicine's Human Genome Sequencing Center, one of only six large-scale sequencing programs initially funded by the National Human Genome Research Institute. The machine is designed to unravel the DNA code by determining the order in which bases, or chemicals, appear on strands of DNA. In a typical month, Baylor will run 65,000 sequencing reactions, run 1,368 sequencing gels, process 16 gigabytes of trace data and submit 1.5 million bases of sequence as part of the international effort to discover all the 80,000 to 100,000 human genes and to determine the complete sequence of the 3 billion DNA bases.

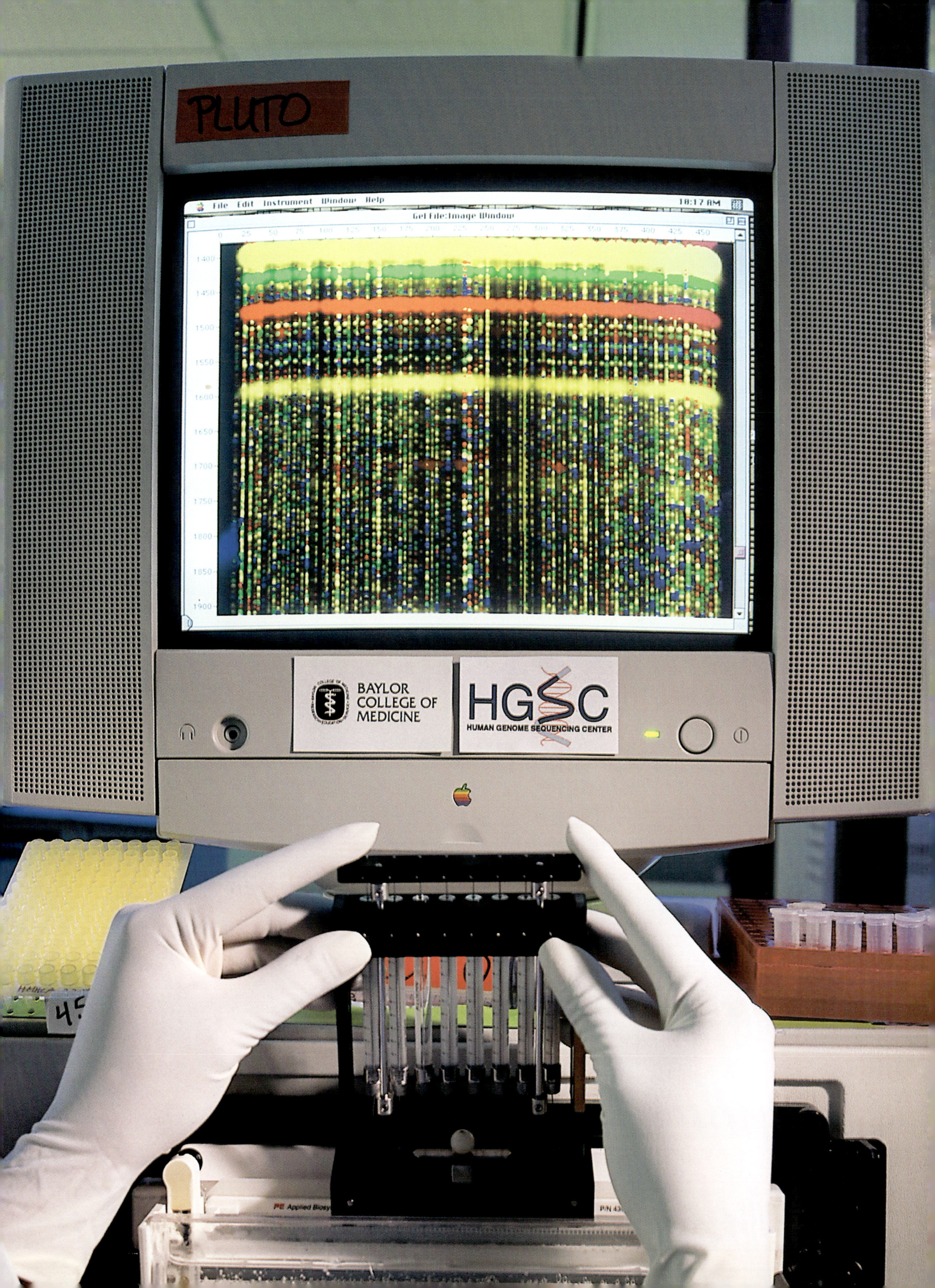
PLUTO
File Edit Instrument Window Help
Gel File:Image Window
BAYLOR
COLLEGE OF
MEDICINE
HGSC
HUMAN GENOME SEQUENCING CENTER

HOUSTON ★ People ★ Opportunity ★ Success

Photo: David Nance, Courtesy Exxon Chemical Company

Corporate Research Centers. *Researchers at Exxon Chemical Company's Baytown Polymer Center (above) are industry leaders in developing and commercializing metallocene catalysts, a technical breakthrough that is revolutionizing the polyolefins industry. The catalysts enable products such as thermoplastics used in the automotive, appliance and other industries to be made with greater purity and strength.* ★ *Many Shell Oil Company products have resulted from research at the company's Westhollow Research Center (right) in west Houston. These include polymers for carpet and textiles, auto components, electrical connectors, industrial pipe and liners, industrial fibers and packaging.*

Photo Courtesy Shell Oil ▶

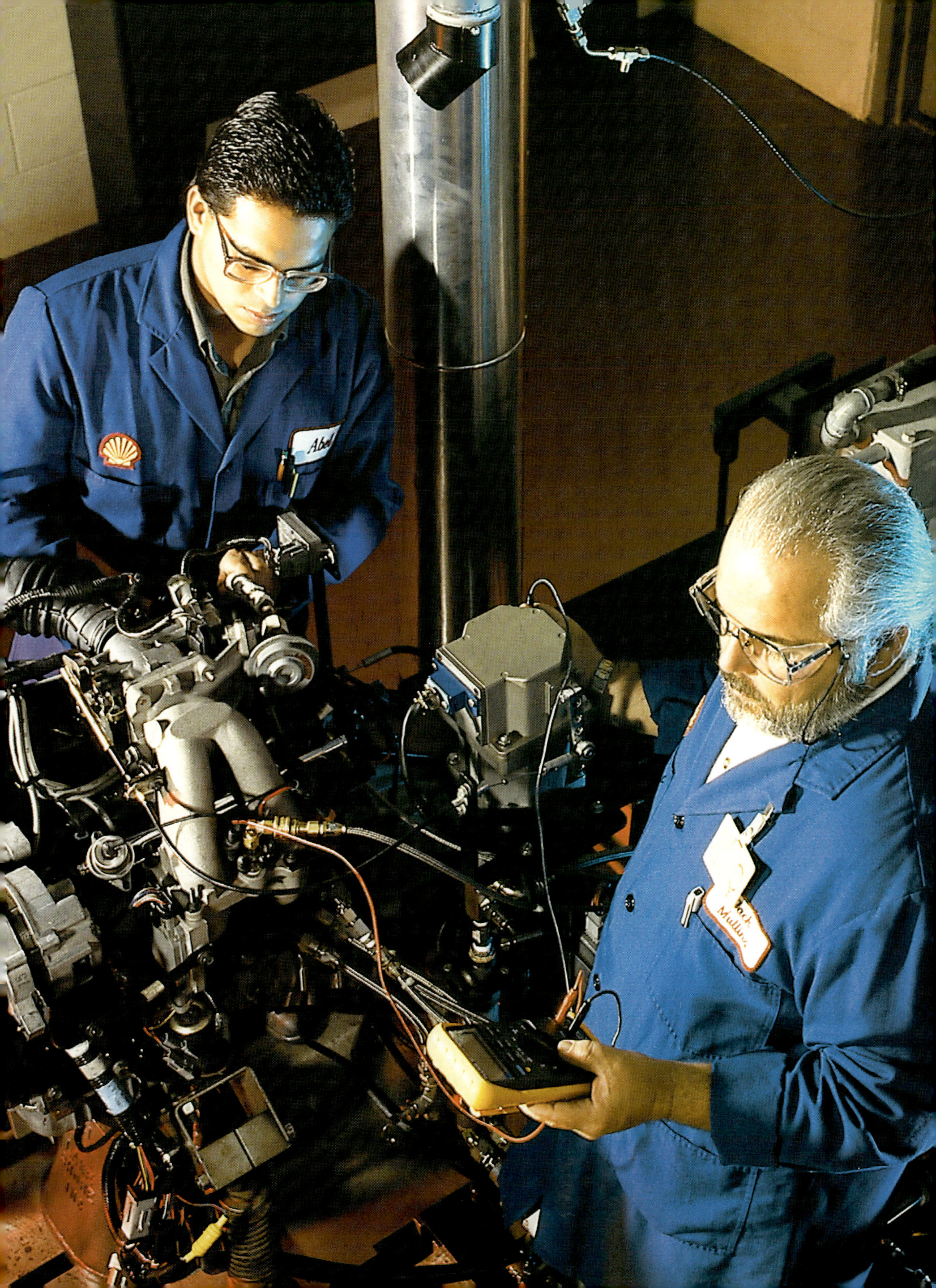
Abel

HOUSTON ★ People ★ Opportunity ★ Success

Trade and Transportation

Look at any great city through the ages and you will discover that, at their height on the world stage, virtually every one was a major hub for trade and commerce. For most, their roles as trade centers were the result of the natural confluence of rivers and the seas or other geographic advantages.

Houston had none of the natural prerequisites to becoming a major center for trade. Houston, after all, is not located on the coast and is not situated on a major river. Yet, from the earliest days of its founding, Houston aspired to be a world-class center for trade. To ensure that its dreams became reality, Houston has continuously invested in every form of modern transportation: the Port of Houston, the Houston Airport System, highways and freeways, and rail.

The fact that Houston has succeeded is a testament to the people, their vision and their determination throughout the century. It was Houstonians, for example, who dreamed of turning a sleepy, shallow bayou into a major artery for international shipping. Today, the Port of Houston is one of the largest ports in the world. In addition, their vision has helped create a city bustling with manufacturing plants, warehouses and distribution centers that serve markets across the country and around the world.

In many respects, the history of Houston in the 20th century is integrally tied to the Port of Houston and the 50-mile Houston Ship Channel, the city's original link to international trade. In fact, the Port of Houston is widely recognized as "the port that helped build the city of Houston" because of its dramatic impact on the growth and development of the city.

Throughout the century, Houston repeatedly invested in maintaining and expanding that vital link. Those investments have paid large dividends as the Port of Houston grew to become the largest U.S. port for foreign tonnage, the second largest U.S. port for total tonnage and the eighth largest port in the world. An average of 6,400 ships and 100,000 barges carrying 170 million tons of cargo move annually through the Houston Ship Channel.

In addition to the Port and Houston Ship Channel, the region's early role as a trade center was fueled in part by the railroads. In fact, as the 20th century began, Houston was known as "the city where 17 railroads meet the sea," and trade and commerce flowed along the steel rails. Today, two of the largest railroad systems in the country serve the Houston region, with an average of 120 trains passing through daily, providing an important complement to the Port of Houston and the area's trucking industry in serving the needs of Houston area businesses, industrial plants, warehouses and distribution centers.

From the earliest days of aviation, the importance and the potential of air service was not lost on Houstonians. Houston's formal air service began in 1935 with air passenger service to Houston at what is today Hobby Airport.

By the 1960s, Houston business leaders recognized that Houston would need a larger, more comprehensive airport system if it were to compete successfully against other major cities in the "jet age." Houston business leaders played a key role in building Houston Intercontinental Airport (now Bush Intercontinental Airport) by helping the city acquire the land for the airport. Since its opening in 1969, the airport has consistently set annual records for both passenger and air freight volume, handling more than 31 million passengers and 600 million pounds of air freight annually.

To address future air traffic needs, Houston is beginning the millennium by investing $1.7 billion in the Houston Airport System, including construction of a new runway, expansion of terminal facilities and new state-of-the-art air cargo facilities.

A significant part of the growth in Houston's air transportation sector has been international passenger traffic, which now accounts for more than 4.5 million passengers annually. In fact, one in nine Houston air passengers is traveling internationally. And those international passengers are flying to and from an expanding list of international cities. While 11 carriers offer non-stop service to over 40 international markets in 18 countries, the list of foreign destinations recently grew as Continental Airlines launched new service from Houston to Tokyo and Caracas, Venezuela, and won approval to begin new nonstop service from Houston to São Paulo, Brazil.

Today, Houston's extensive network of interstate highways and roadways are key components in the region's transportation infrastructure. More than $500 million is spent annually to expand and upgrade Houston's 575 miles of highways, freeways and toll roads.

Looking forward to new trade routes during the next century, Houston is aggressively working to create a new NAFTA highway, Interstate 69. The new interstate will provide a new direct trade link for Houston with Mexico, the industrial heartland of the Midwest and Canada. Coupled with the region's comprehensive transportation infrastructure, the new trade highway will further cement Houston's role as a world-class manufacturing and international distribution center. ■

A Transportation Hub. More than 600 truck lines serve the Houston region, including common carriers that operate daily scheduled service between Houston and cities across the United States and special-commodity carriers that haul oilfield equipment as well as gasoline and other petroleum products. ★ Eleven airlines offer non-stop service between Houston and 40 international markets in 18 countries from George Bush Intercontinental Airport/Houston (IAH) (pages 72-73). Overall, more than 31 million passengers travel through the city's largest airport on 23 airlines on direct or nonstop flights between Houston and more than 150 destinations worldwide.

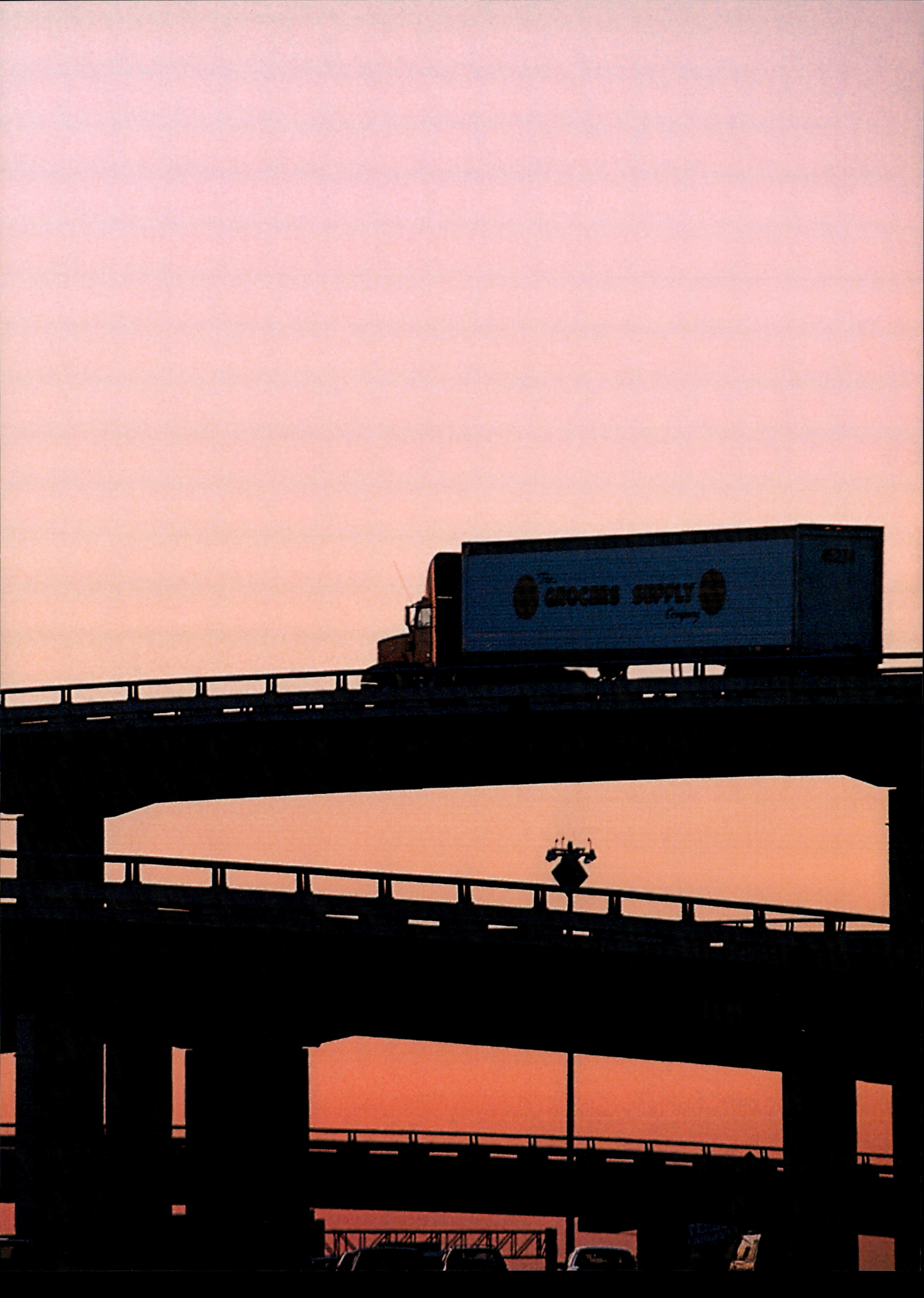
GROCERS SUPPLY

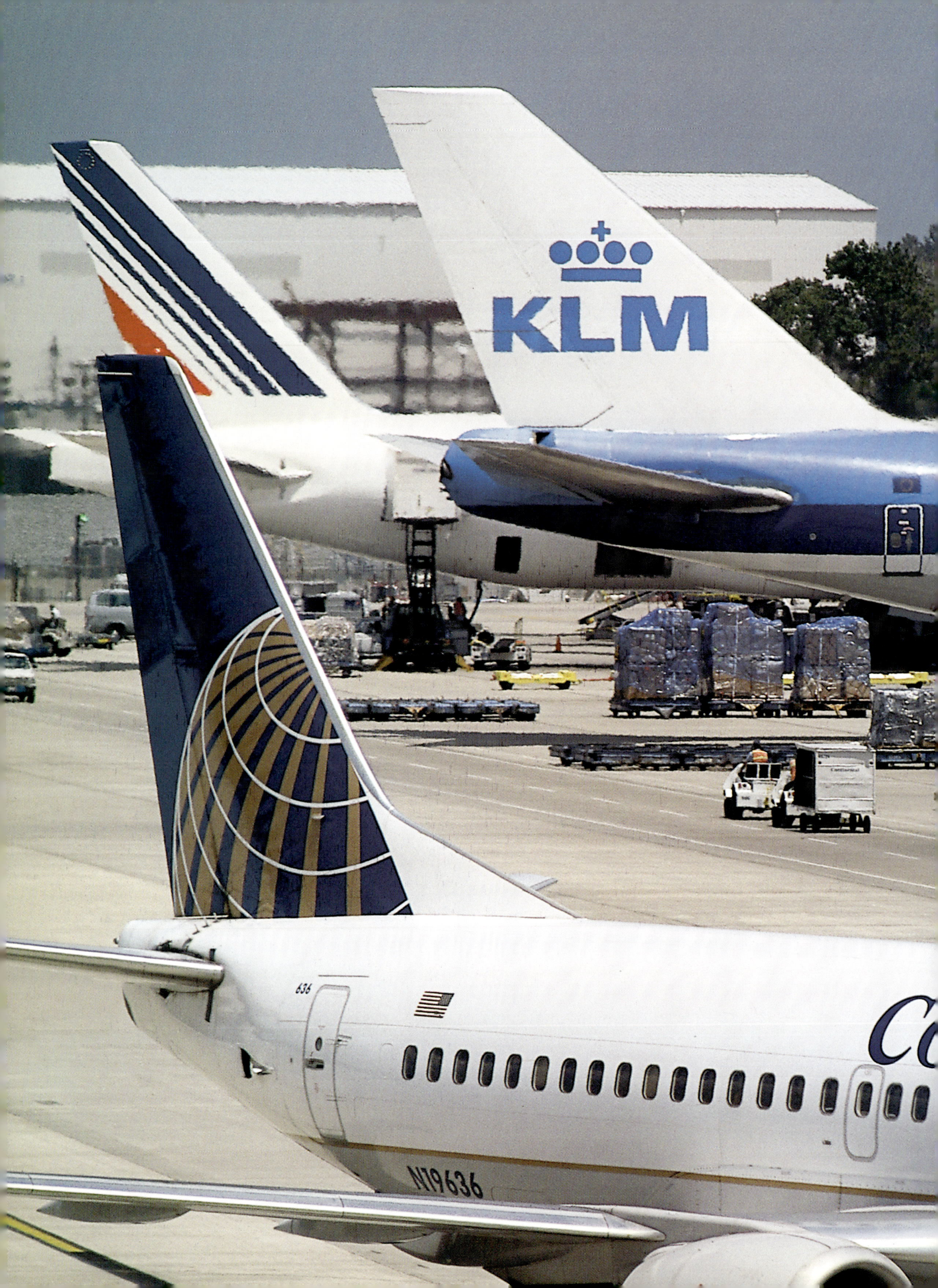
KLM
636
N19636

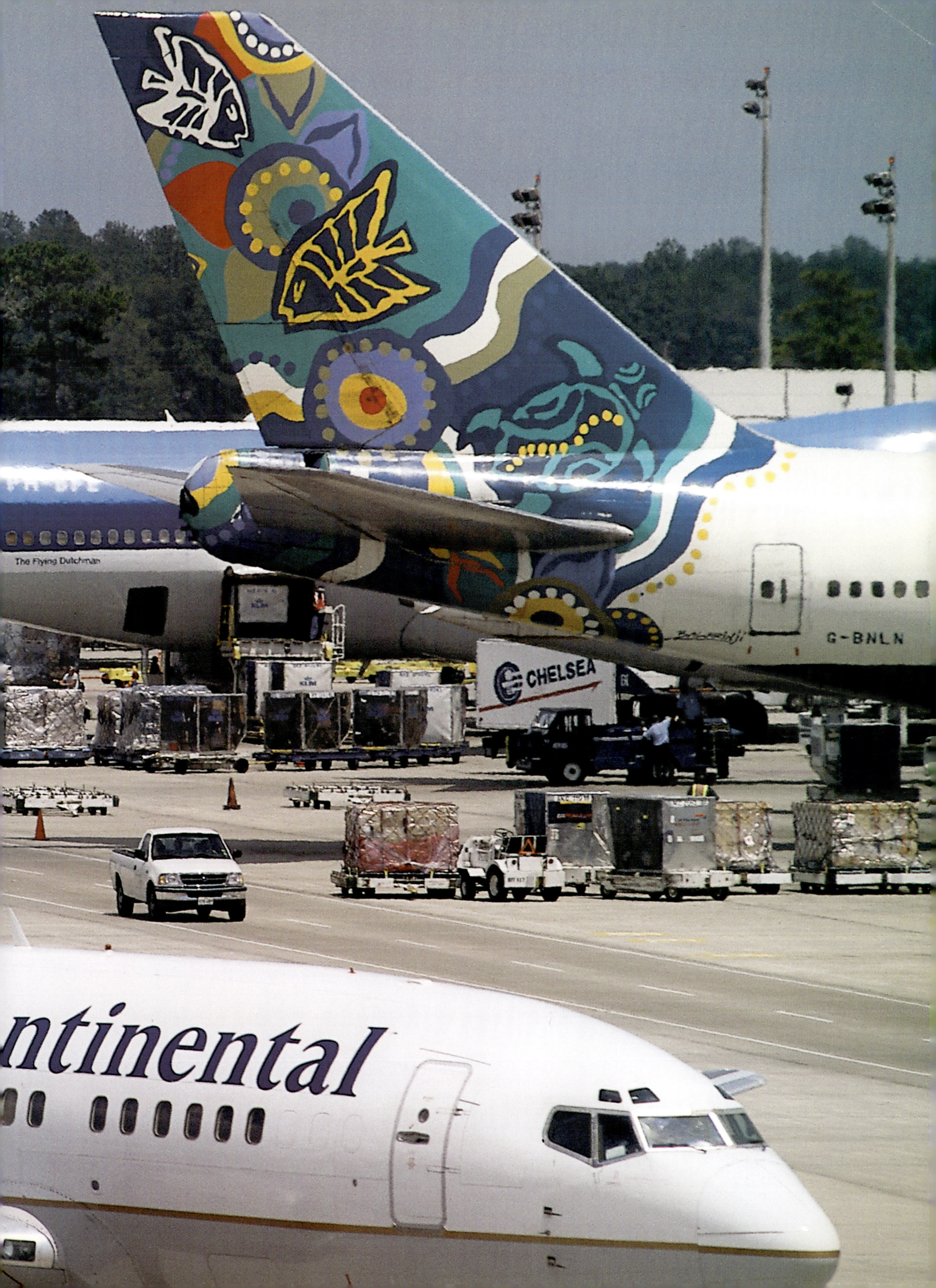
The Flying Dutchman
G-BNLN
CHELSEA
ntinental

On the Move. Located just nine miles from downtown Houston, Hobby Airport (above) is a major hub for Southwest Airlines and is served by eight other airlines. More than 9 million passengers annually use Hobby for direct and nonstop flights between Houston and 71 cities throughout the United States. The airport also supports a major general aviation operation, including general aviation activity between Texas and Mexico. ★ Fourteen all-cargo airlines and more than 500 freight forwarders move more than 600 million pounds of freight each year through George Bush Intercontinental Airport/Houston (right). In addition to more than 500,000 square feet of public and private warehouse space, the airport features an Air Cargo Distribution Center with a 24-hour, seven-day-a-week air mail facility, a large-scale climate-controlled refrigeration and freezer warehouse, and a U.S. Customs Animal and Plant Health Inspection Station. ★ Union Pacific is one of the largest railroads serving Houston, providing service to major points throughout the western two-thirds of the United States and links to both Mexico and Canada The company's Englewood yard (pages 76-77) in northeast Houston uses a network of 64 switching tracks to process more than 1,500 cars a day. ★ The Port of Houston's Barbours Cut Container Terminal (pages 78-79) is the largest and most modern container terminal along the Gulf Coast. The 230-acre facility features six berths, 6,000 feet of quay space and 12 wharf cranes, and can accommodate more than 23,400 containers, 532 refrigeration containers and 4,000 wheeled containers.

75

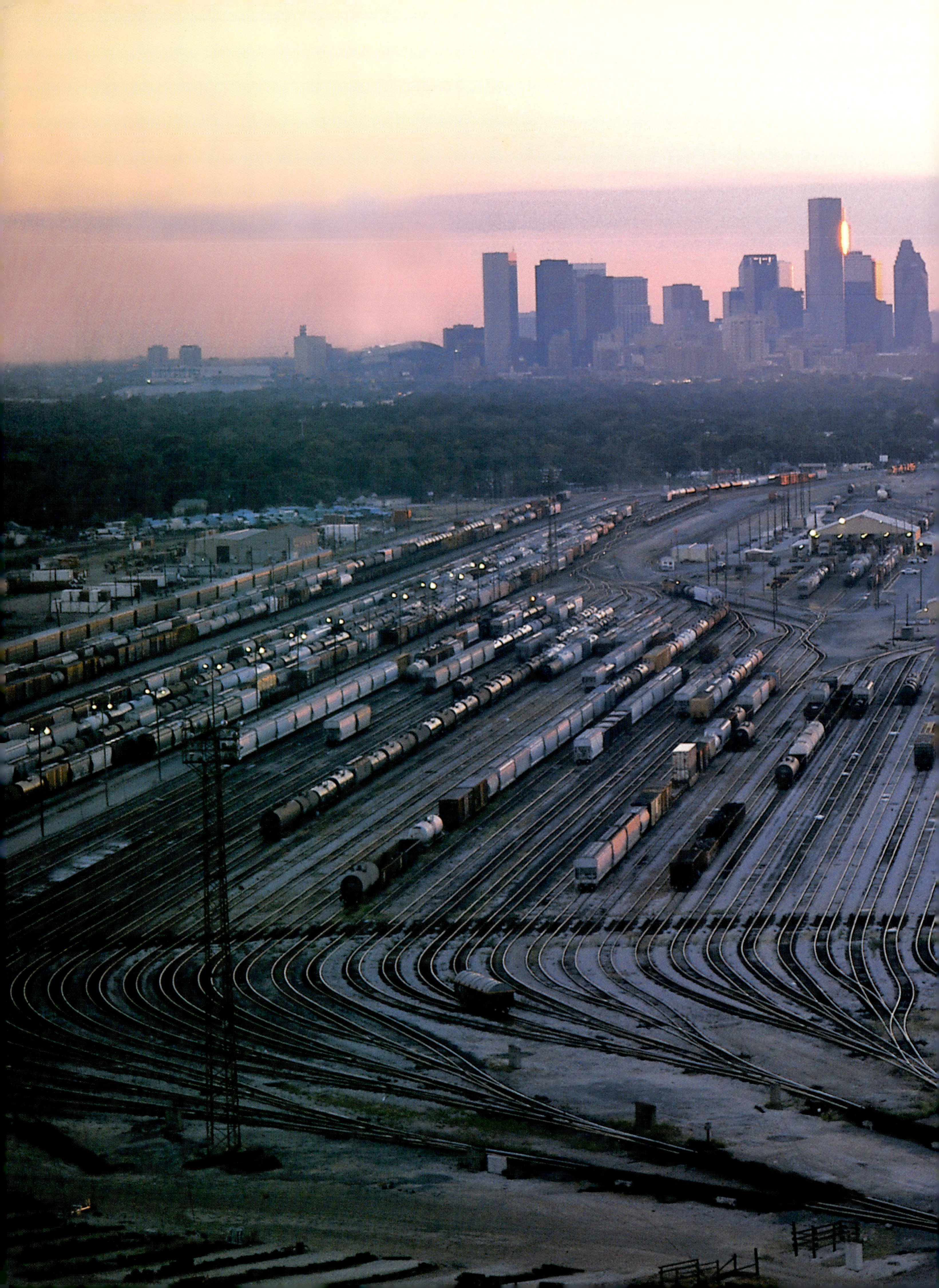

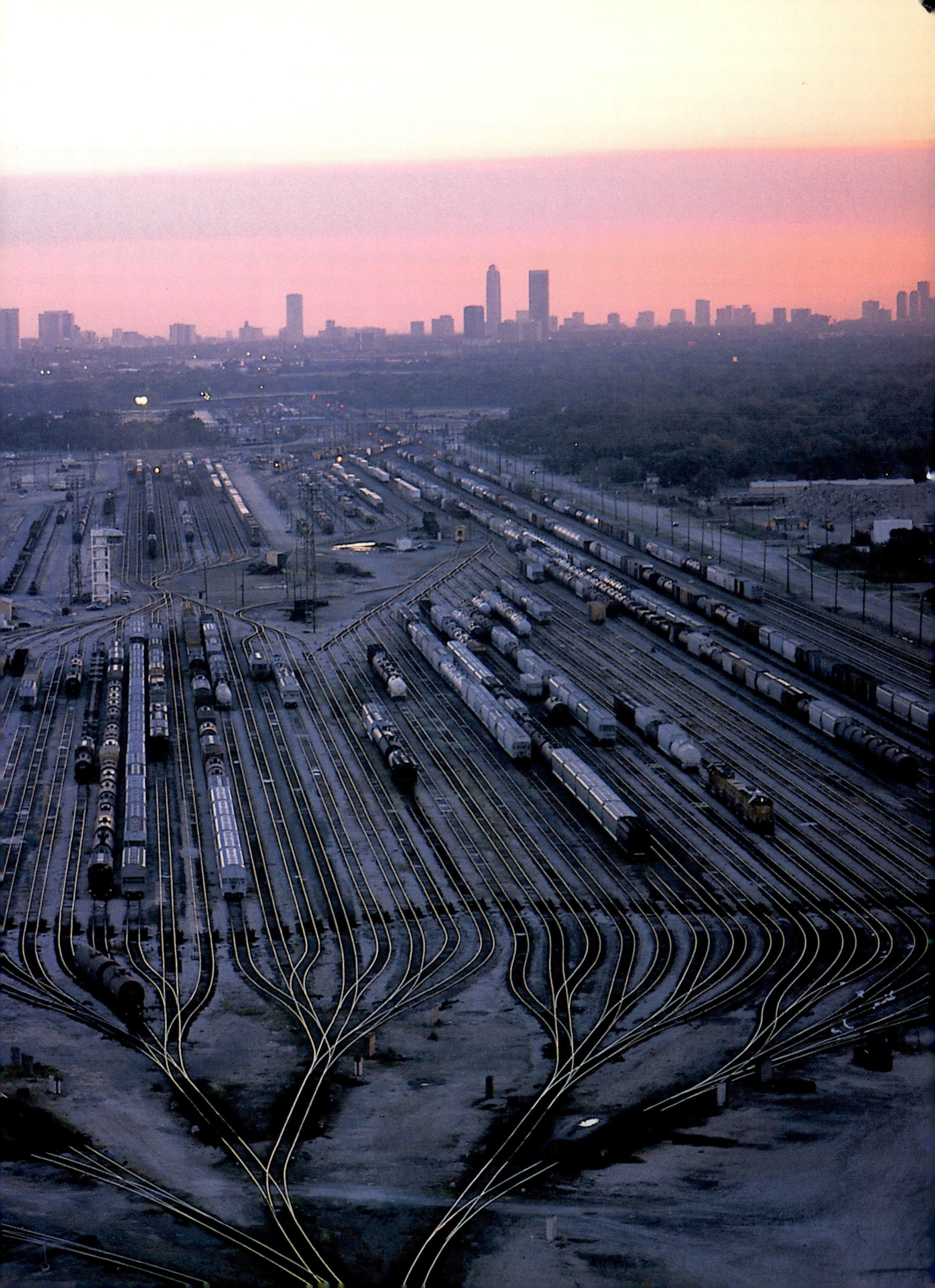

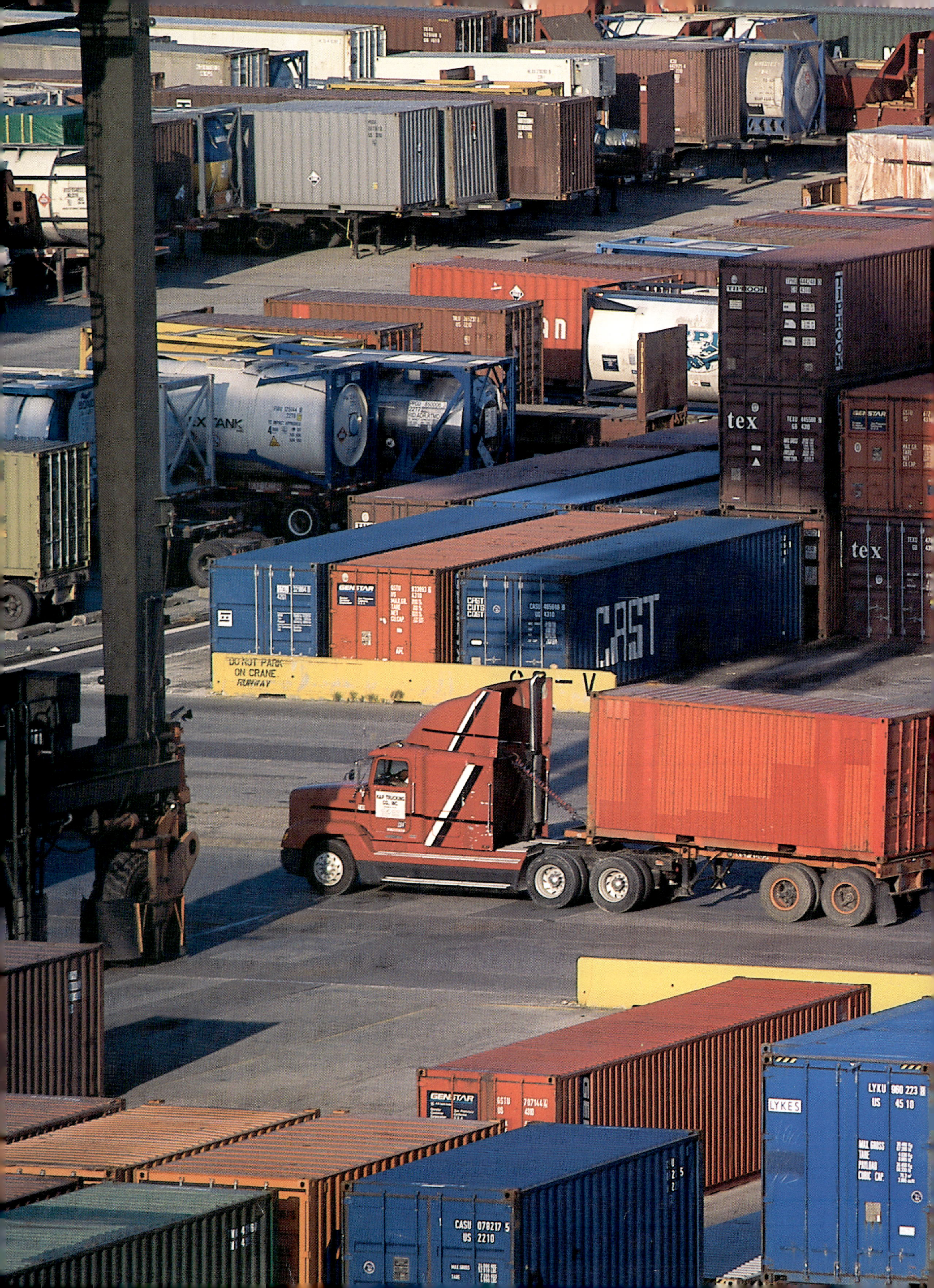
DO NOT PARK
ON CRANE
RUNWAY
CAST
tex
tex
LYKES

PACECO TRANSTAINER 30 LONG TON
PORT OF HOUSTON
GENSTAR
Hapag-Lloyd

HOUSTON ★ People ★ Opportunity ★ Success

Cruising into the Future. A new kind of ship now calls weekly on Houston as cruise lines have discovered the convenience – and passenger interest – in sailing from Houston to destinations in Mexico and the Caribbean. Norwegian Cruise Line (above) offers seven-day cruises to the western Caribbean from the Port of Houston Authority's Barbours Cut Terminal. The "Texaribbean Cruise" offers tourists stops in Calica/Cancun and Cozumel, Mexico, as well as the small private island of Roatan, Bay Islands, off Honduras' Caribbean Coast. ★ The Fred Hartman Bridge (right) over the Houston Ship Channel provides a scenic new gateway to Houston as well as a valuable link for motorists and industries in southeast Harris County. The $120 million bridge is one of many significant new investments in Houston's transportation infrastructure.

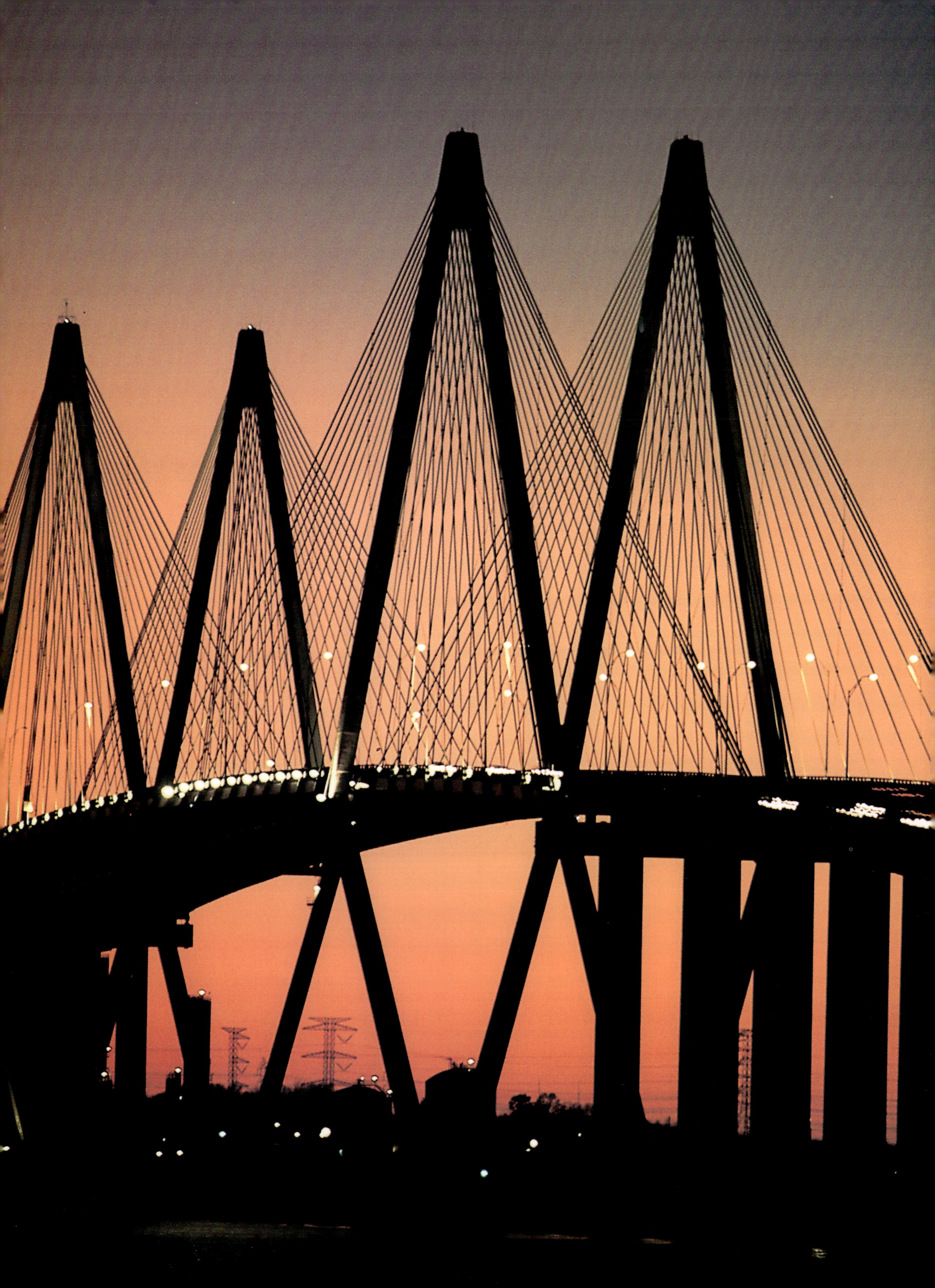

HOUSTON ★ People ★ Opportunity ★ Success

***K**eeping Houston Moving. Unlike other major cities, Houston has reduced traffic congestion as a result of spending almost $1 billion a year since 1982 on a comprehensive regional mobility plan that included expansions of freeways and arterial streets as well as construction of new tollways, transitways and high-occupancy vehicle lanes.* ★ *In a futuristic command center, Houston Transtar (right) operates one of the first high-tech transportation and emergency management centers in the United States. The $13 million facility is a unique joint project of the Texas Department of Transportation, the Metropolitan Transit Authority, the City of Houston and Harris County. Using state-of-the-art telecommunications systems and cameras mounted on special sites on area highways, Transtar officials can monitor traffic conditions, coordinate police and emergency dispatches, and provide traffic reports through electronic message boards and private traffic reporting services.*

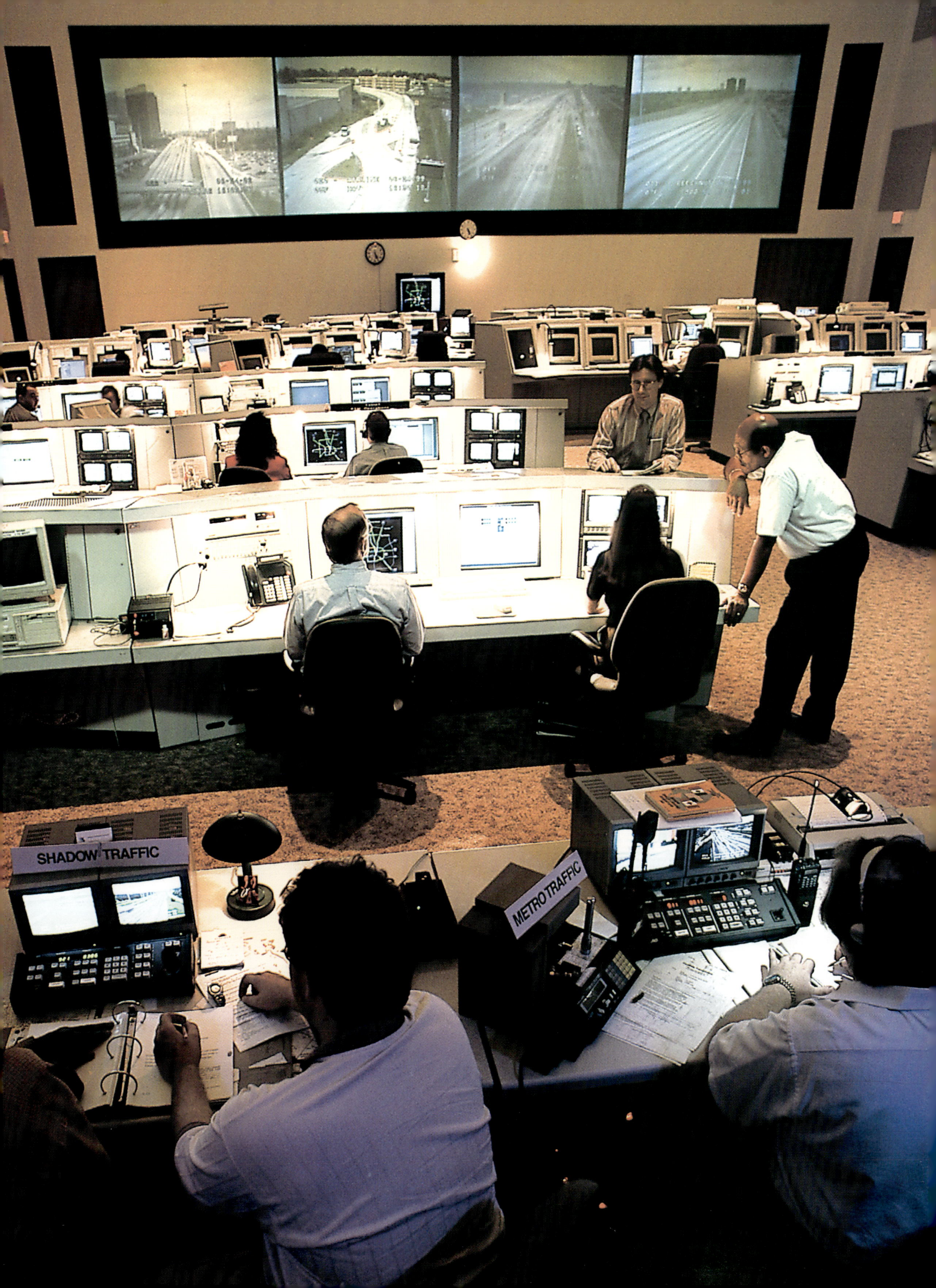
SHADOW TRAFFIC
METRO TRAFFIC

Business Climate

To understand the dramatic growth of Houston during the 20th century, one first must understand the area's business climate. While many other cities talk about having a pro-business climate, Houston, as the saying goes, walks the walk.

Dozens of other cities in Texas and the Southwest were both larger and better-positioned for economic growth at the beginning of the century. Even within the region, other cities could have capitalized on the discovery of oil and supplanted Houston's rise as the capital of the energy industry during the century.

Today, Houston is the envy of many cities. As the fourth largest city in the United States, Houston boasts 13 Fortune 500 companies, a workforce of more than 2 million (25 percent of whom have completed at least fours years of college), competitive wage rates, low local taxes and no personal income tax.

Houston's growth and success is a direct result of the pro-business climate that Houston leaders fostered and nurtured throughout the century. Even today, when companies and their CEOs are asked to rank cities, "pro-business attitudes" is one of the most important criteria that they use. And Houston is consistently rated highly for its positive business environment. In a recent survey by *Fortune*, 94 percent of the nation's CEOs who responded ranked Houston's pro-business attributes as excellent.

Throughout the 20th century, Houston and its business and civic leaders have consistently pursued projects and programs that would benefit the entire region and not just specific areas. At the same time, Houston's elected leaders have consistently pursued policies that complemented and facilitated those efforts while keeping the burden of taxes and regulation to a minimum. As a result, Houston has dozens of examples of how the public and private sectors can work constructively together on programs that benefit the entire region.

Perhaps the most telling early example was the concerted efforts by Houston business leaders to transform a quiet bayou into a bustling channel for international trade. In many respects, the 1914 opening of the Houston Ship Channel, creating a deepwater port 50 miles inland, marked the coming of age of Houston as a major city, and has paid economic dividends – in terms of money, jobs, trade and diversity – every year since. In 2000, for example, the Port of Houston will account for more than 205,000 jobs and have an annual economic impact of more than $7.7 billion in the region.

But the Port of Houston isn't the only example. The same foresight and innovation by Houston business and civic leaders helped create the Texas Medical Center, secure NASA's Johnson Space Center, build Bush Intercontinental Airport and create dozens of other projects, programs and institutions.

In addition to its position as one of the top cities for business in the United States, Houston has assumed an important role in the international business community. Sparked by the global needs of the energy industry and reinforced by the international trade infrastructure available in Houston through its port and airport systems, Houston has become one of the world's leading cities for international business.

Today, international business and trade account for about a third of all jobs in the region. More than 4,000 companies in Houston are engaged in international business, including more than 600 foreign firms with manufacturing facilities, distribution centers or offices in the Houston region.

To facilitate trade and address the needs of those foreign companies – as well as the 700,000 foreign-born residents of the region – Houston hosts 70 consulates, ranking it as the largest consular corps in Texas and the Southwest and fourth largest in the nation.

In international banking and finance, Houston leads the Southwest United States with 28 foreign banks from 10 nations. In addition, 18 local or U.S. banks operate international departments to serve the financial needs of their worldwide clients in Houston. Houston also is home to one of only six regional offices of the Export-Import Bank of the United States (Ex-Im Bank), an independent U.S. government agency that helps finance the overseas sales of U.S. goods and services.

Throughout the 20th century, Houston's success in promoting trade around the world has enabled it to become the seventh largest metropolitan exporter in the nation, handling approximately $18 billion in exports. Mexico is Houston's top trading partner through the Port of Houston, with a combined total of $3.5 billion and 26 million tons of imports and exports. The port's other top trade partners include Algeria, Belgium, Brazil, Colombia, Germany, Saudi Arabia, Spain, the United Kingdom and Venezuela. For international air cargo, Houston's top trade partners include France, Germany, Italy, Mexico, the Netherlands, Saudi Arabia and the United Kingdom. ■

Houston: A Bustling, Metropolitan Business Center. Houston is a city built for business. While the energy industry still accounts for a significant part of the region's economy, Houston today has a more diversified economy shaped by its entrepreneurial spirit and international trade and business opportunities. ★ Downtown Houston (pages 86-87) is home to 3,500 companies including Fortune 500 companies such as Continental Airlines, Cooper Industries, Dynegy, El Paso Energy, Enron, Lyondell Chemical Company and Reliant Energy.

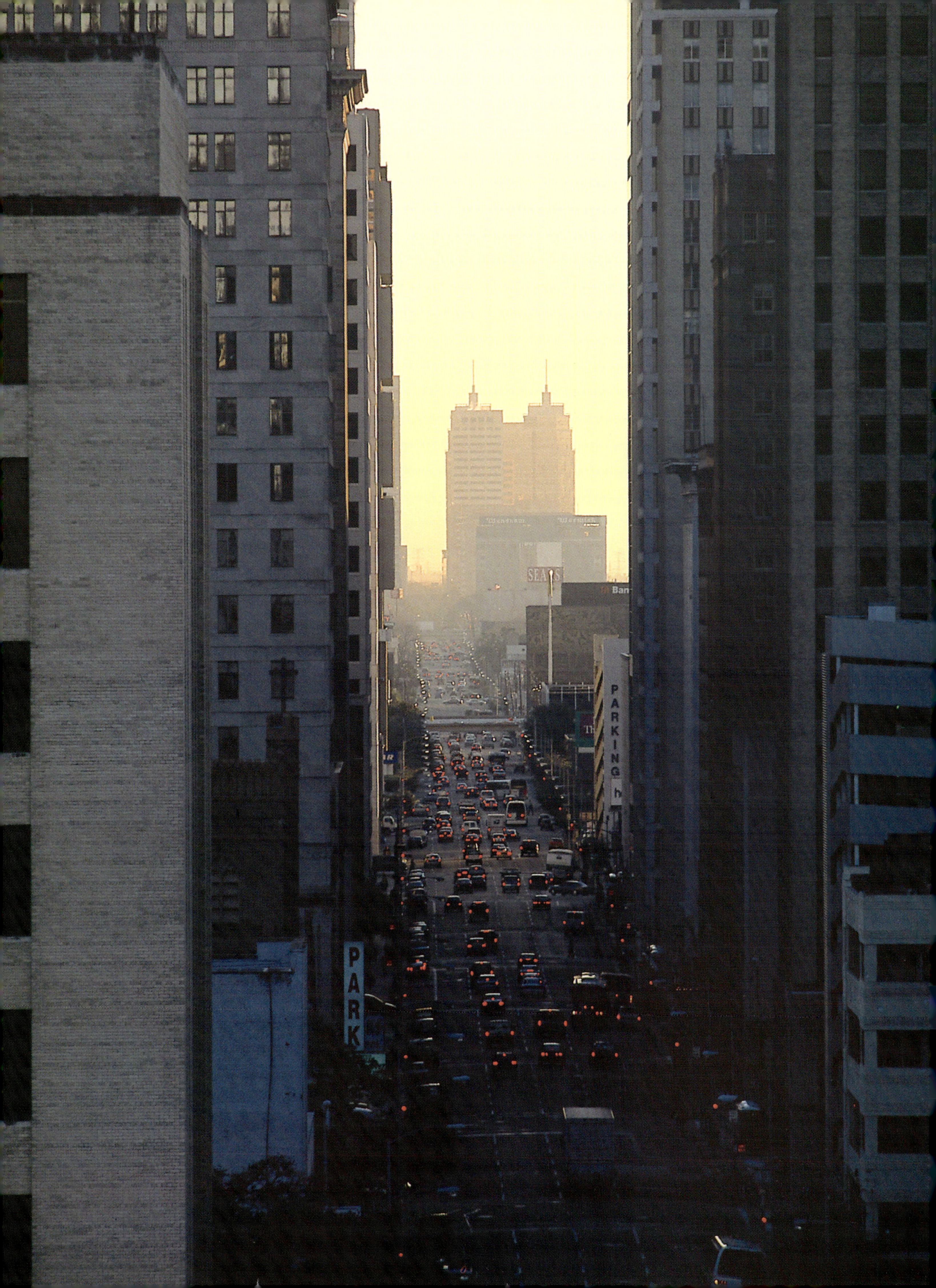
PARKING
PARK

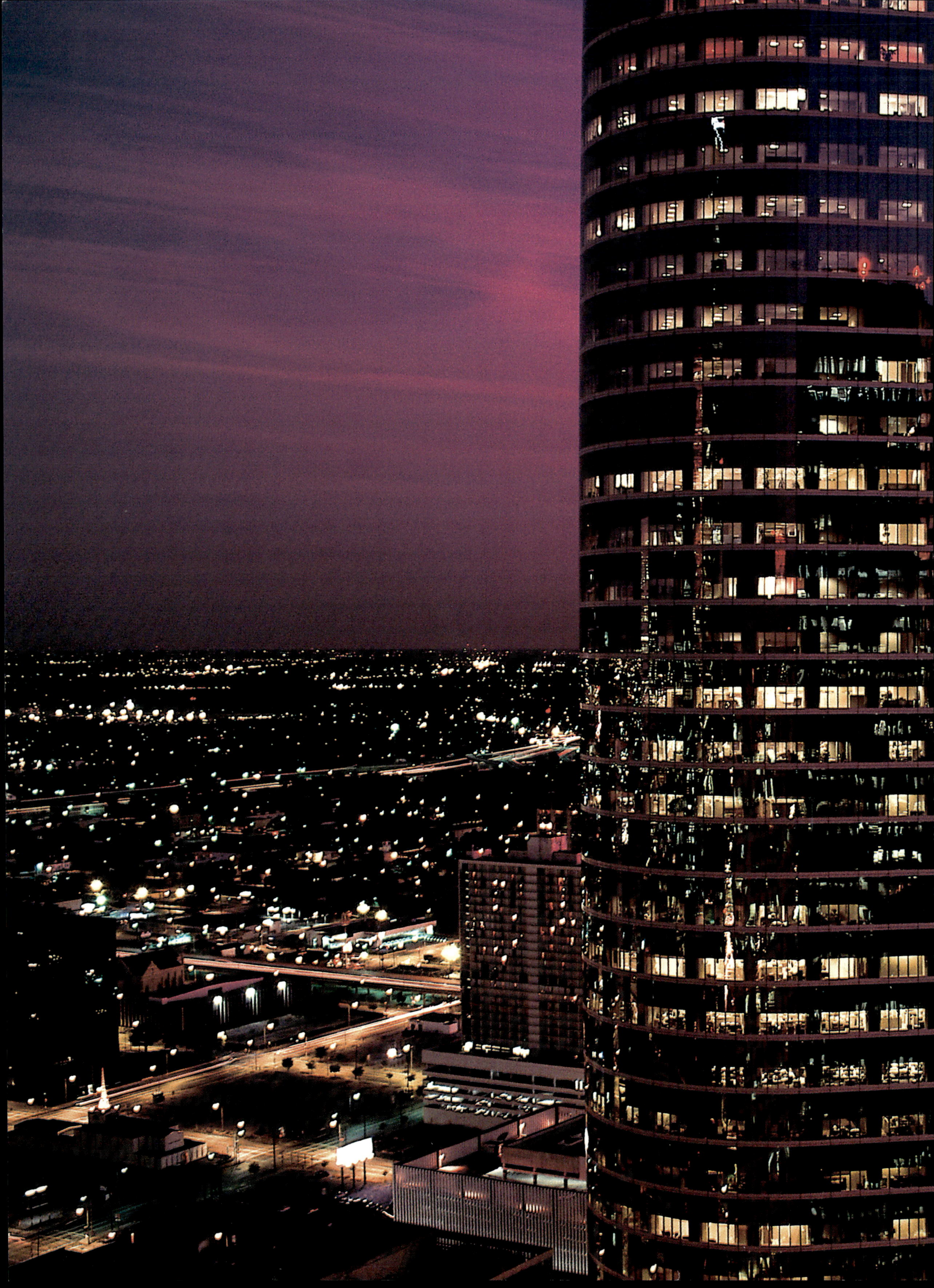

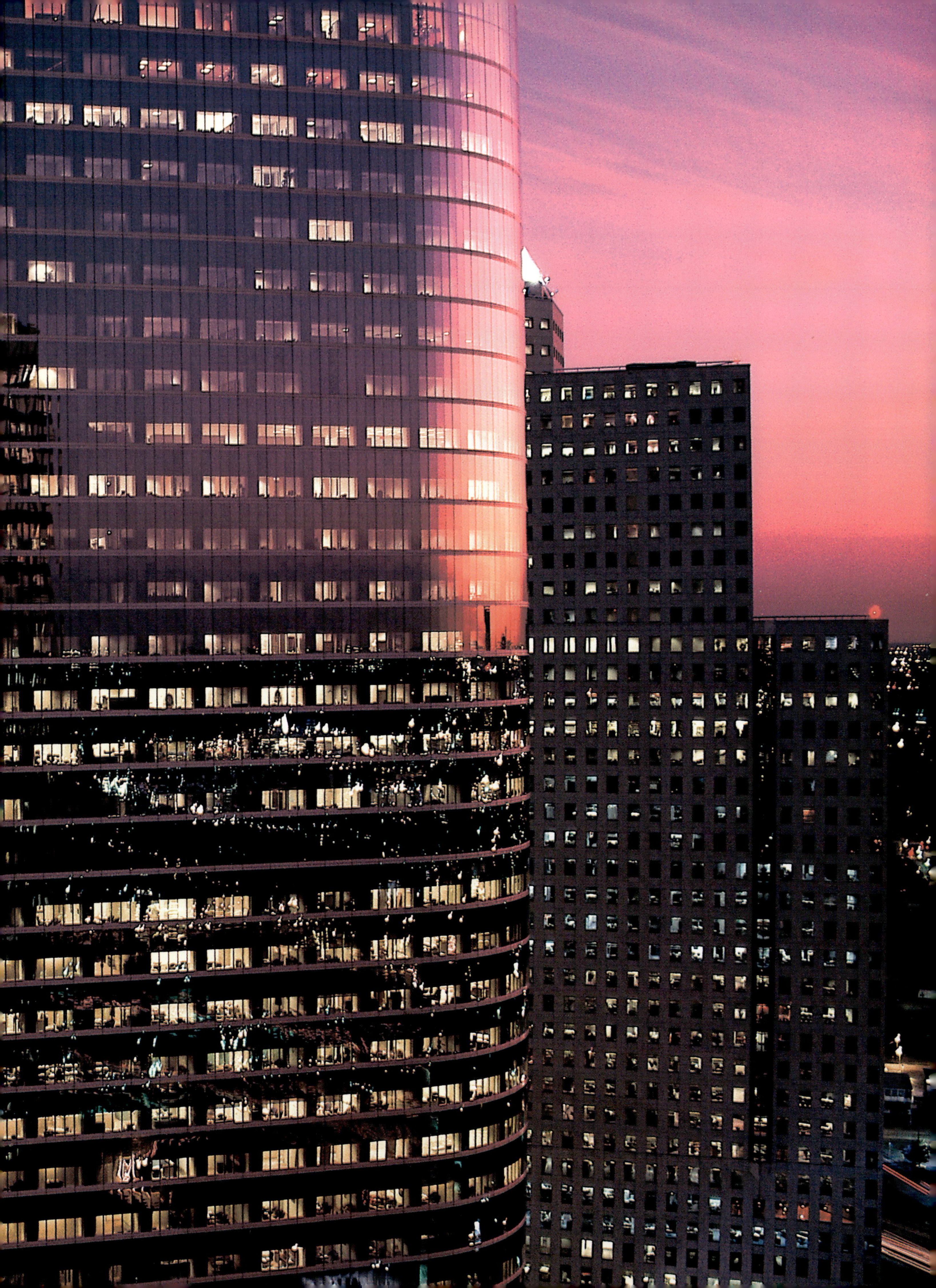

HOUSTON ★ People ★ Opportunity ★ Success

Fast-Growing Companies. Combining the power of the Internet with the entrepreneurial zeal and technological talent of Houston's workforce, Telescan Inc. (above) has quickly emerged as an industry leader in providing Internet services to financial and publishing service companies, as well as proprietary analysis and content to individual investors. ★ Since opening its forklift manufacturing, assembly and distribution facility in Houston during the past decade, Mitsubishi Caterpillar Forklift America (right) has experienced significant growth and expansion. Workers at the international joint-venture company represent more than two dozen countries. The company's forklifts are sold and distributed throughout the United States, Canada, Mexico and South America.

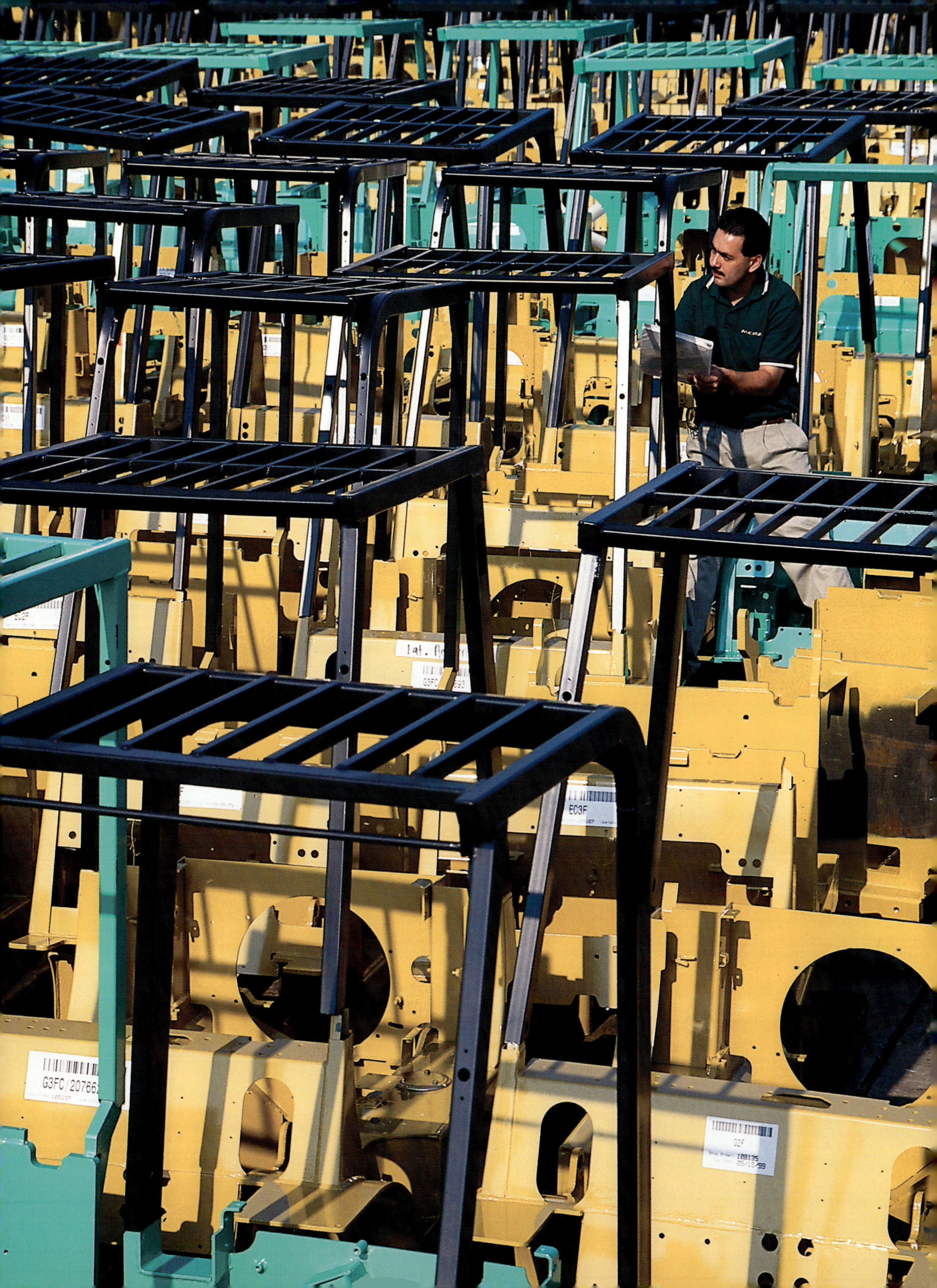
G3FC / 20766
EC3F
G2F
108135

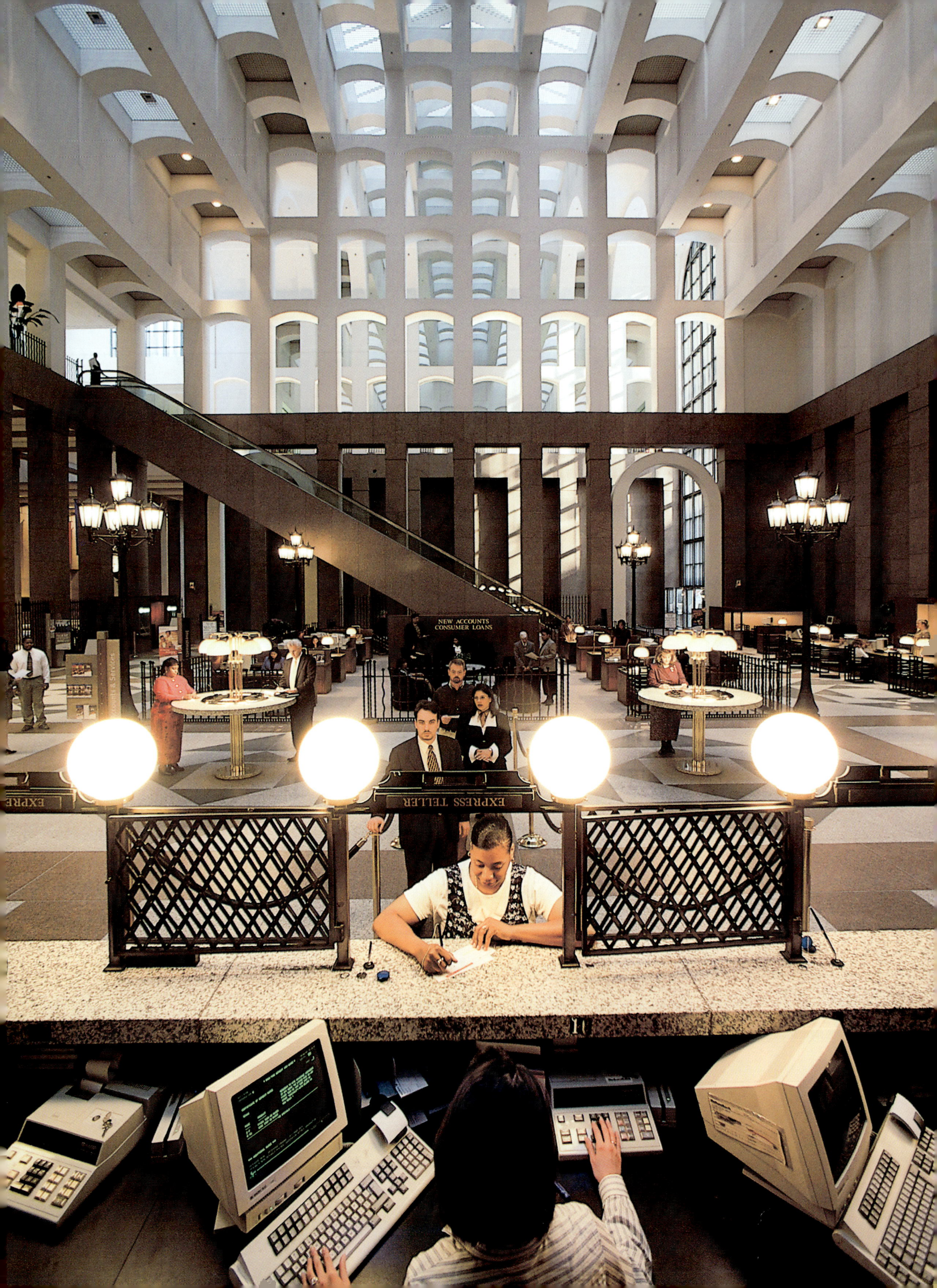
NEW ACCOUNTS
CONSUMER LOANS
EXPRESS TELLER

HOUSTON ★ People ★ Opportunity ★ Success

From Wall Street to Main Street. With more than $121 billion in assets under management and more than 2,100 employees worldwide, Houston-based AIM Funds (above) maintains a bustling trading floor in Greenway Plaza. The home-grown company offers a full, diversified line of retail mutual funds and investment products for investors at all levels of risk tolerance. AIM also serves many of the largest banks in the U.S. through trusts, pension funds, profit-sharing plans, securities lending programs, and other custodial relationships. ★ The elegant and spacious Bank of America building (left) in downtown Houston is home to the bank's regional headquarters. The financial needs of Houston's growing business community are served by each of the major U.S. banks, several local and regional banks and 28 foreign banks from 13 countries.

HOUSTON ★ People ★ Opportunity ★ Success

A Manufacturing and Distribution Center. Sysco, a Houston-based Fortune 500 company, uses the latest computer scanning technology to keep track of the thousands of food service products in its massive 380,000-square-foot warehouse and distribution center in east Houston. Sysco is the largest marketer and distributor of food service products in North America, providing products and services to nearly 300,000 restaurants, hospitals, schools, hotels and industrial caterers. ★ One of Houston's oldest companies, Stewart & Stevenson Inc. (right), started the 20th century in Houston as a "carriage repair and horseshoeing parlor." Today, the 98-year-old company is a leading manufacturer and distributor of industrial and energy-related equipment.

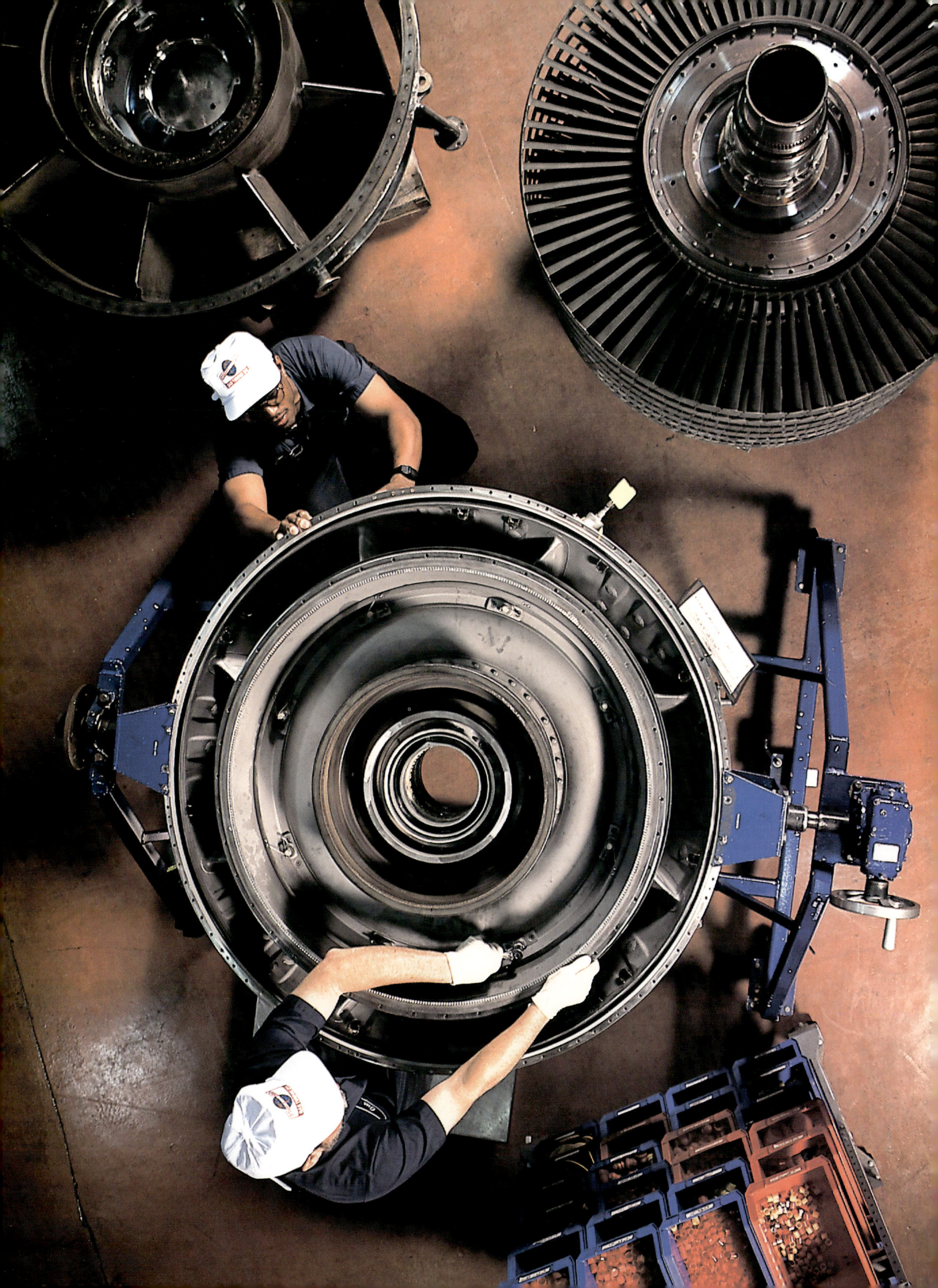

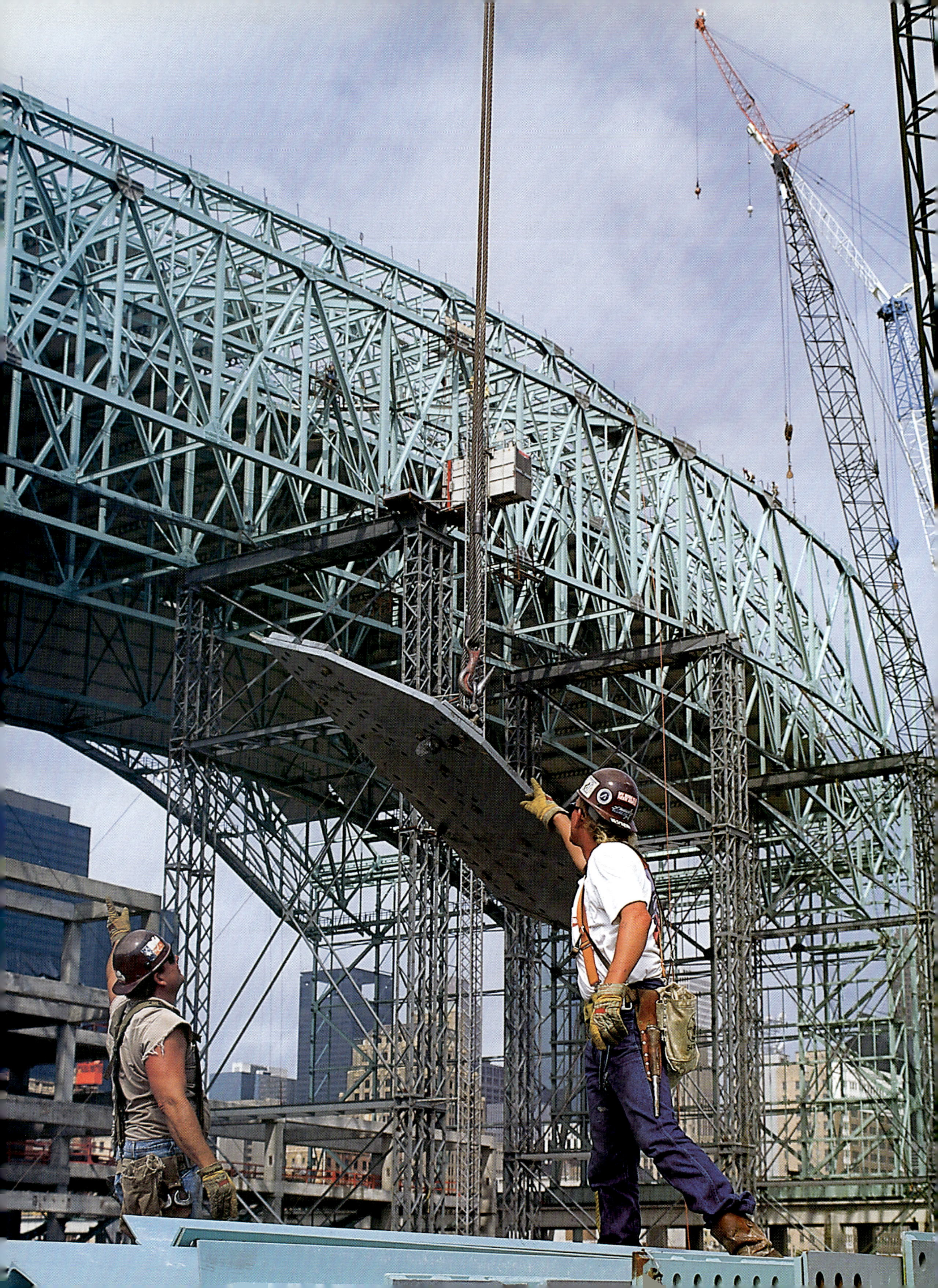

HOUSTON ★ People ★ Opportunity ★ Success

Building a New Houston. Symbolizing the bright long-term outlook for the city, Houston began growing again in the late 1990s. Spurred in part by the renovation of the Rice Hotel and the construction of Enron Field, downtown Houston and the surrounding area are witnessing a resurgence in the construction of new housing, restaurants and clubs. ★ Workers at Enron Field (left), the new home of the Houston Astros, moved swiftly to meet the goal of having the new stadium in downtown Houston ready for the 2000 season of Major League Baseball.

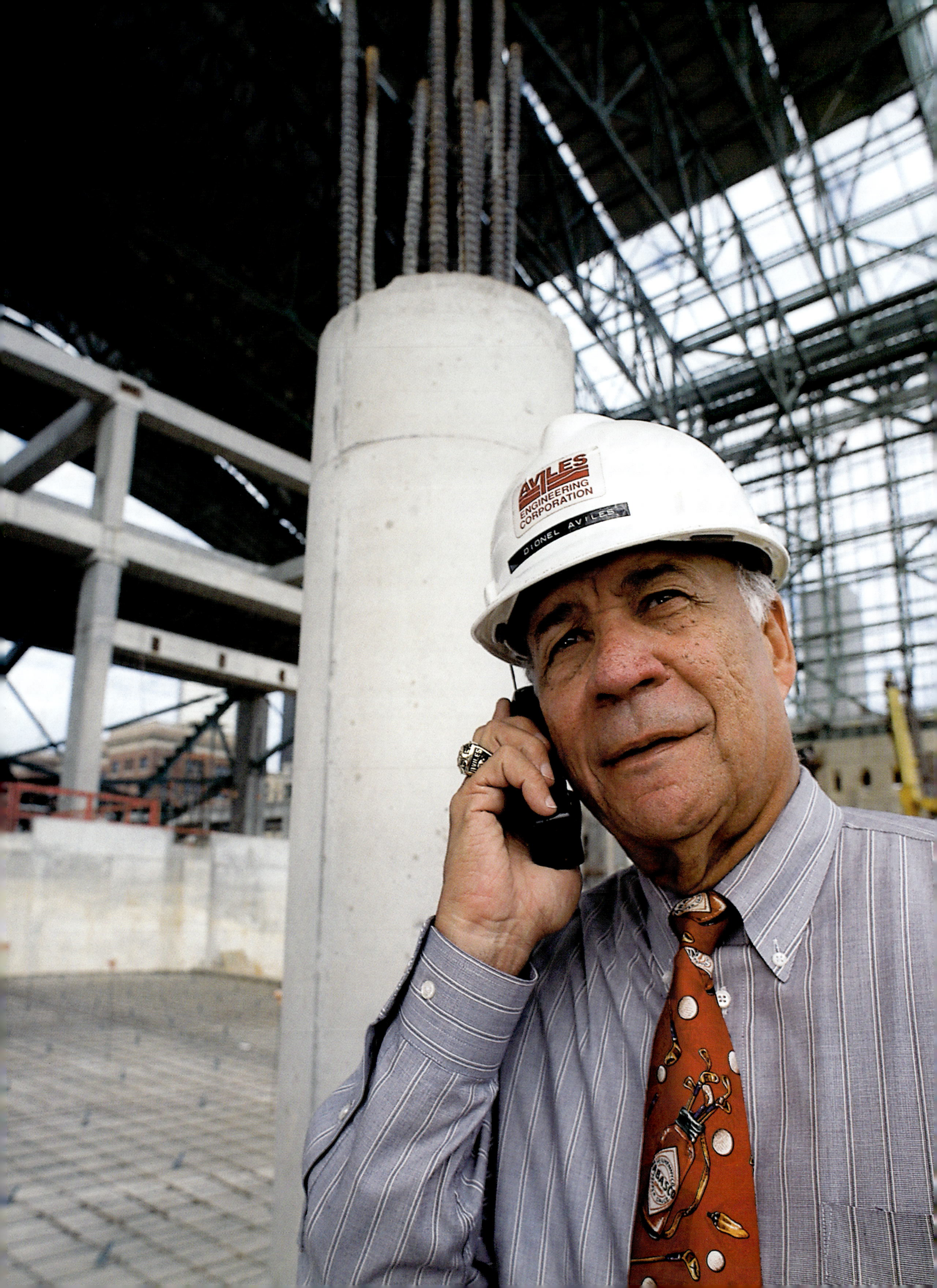
AVILES
ENGINEERING
CORPORATION
DIONEL AVILES

HOUSTON ★ People ★ Opportunity ★ Success

Creating Opportunities. Since founding MetroBank in 1987 to meet the banking needs of Houston's various ethnic communities, Chairman Don Wang (above) has helped the bank grow to 11 Houston locations and more than $620 million in assets, ranking it as one of the top independent banks in the region. ★ For 18 years, Dionel Aviles, (left) founder and president of Aviles Engineering Corp., has been conducting engineering tests for major construction projects all around Houston, from runways at Bush Intercontinental Airport to government buildings in downtown Houston. The firm's largest and most recent assignment: testing the concrete and welding used to build the new Enron Field in downtown Houston.

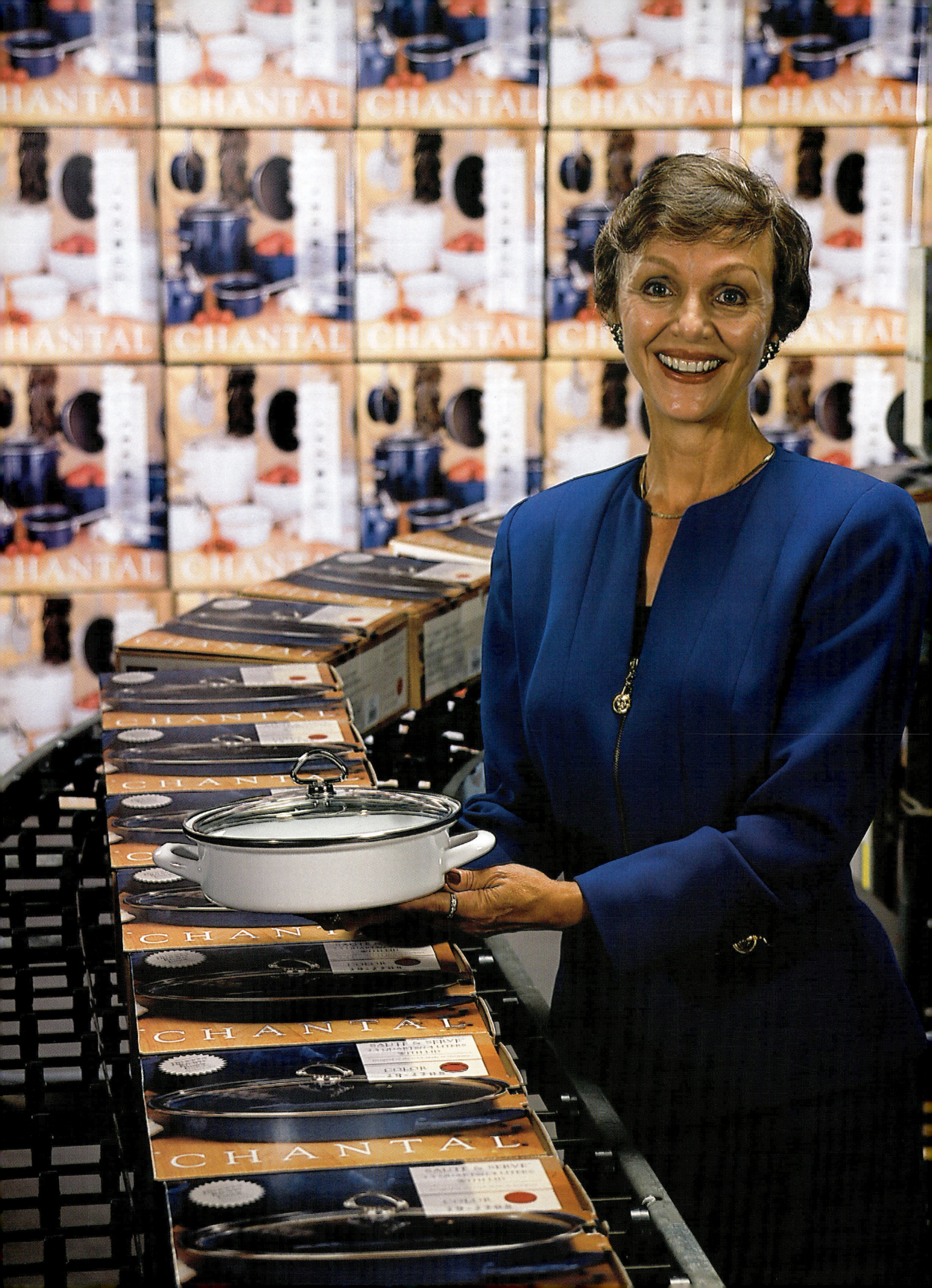
CHANTAL

HOUSTON ★ People ★ Opportunity ★ Success

Wired In and Cooking. *Capitalizing on a keen interest in technology, entrepreneur Geary Broadnax (above) is at the heart of Houston's Internet community. In establishing one of the first Internet service providers in the area, Broadnax saw his company, Insync Internet Services, Inc., shoot to the top ranks of Houston's fastest growing private companies.* ★ *Chantal Cookware Corp. founder and President Heida Thurlow (left) holds 18 design and utility patents from the United States and Germany for the company's enamel-on-steel cookware products. Drawing upon suppliers from around the world, Chantal completes final assembly, quality control and packaging at the company's headquarters in Houston.*

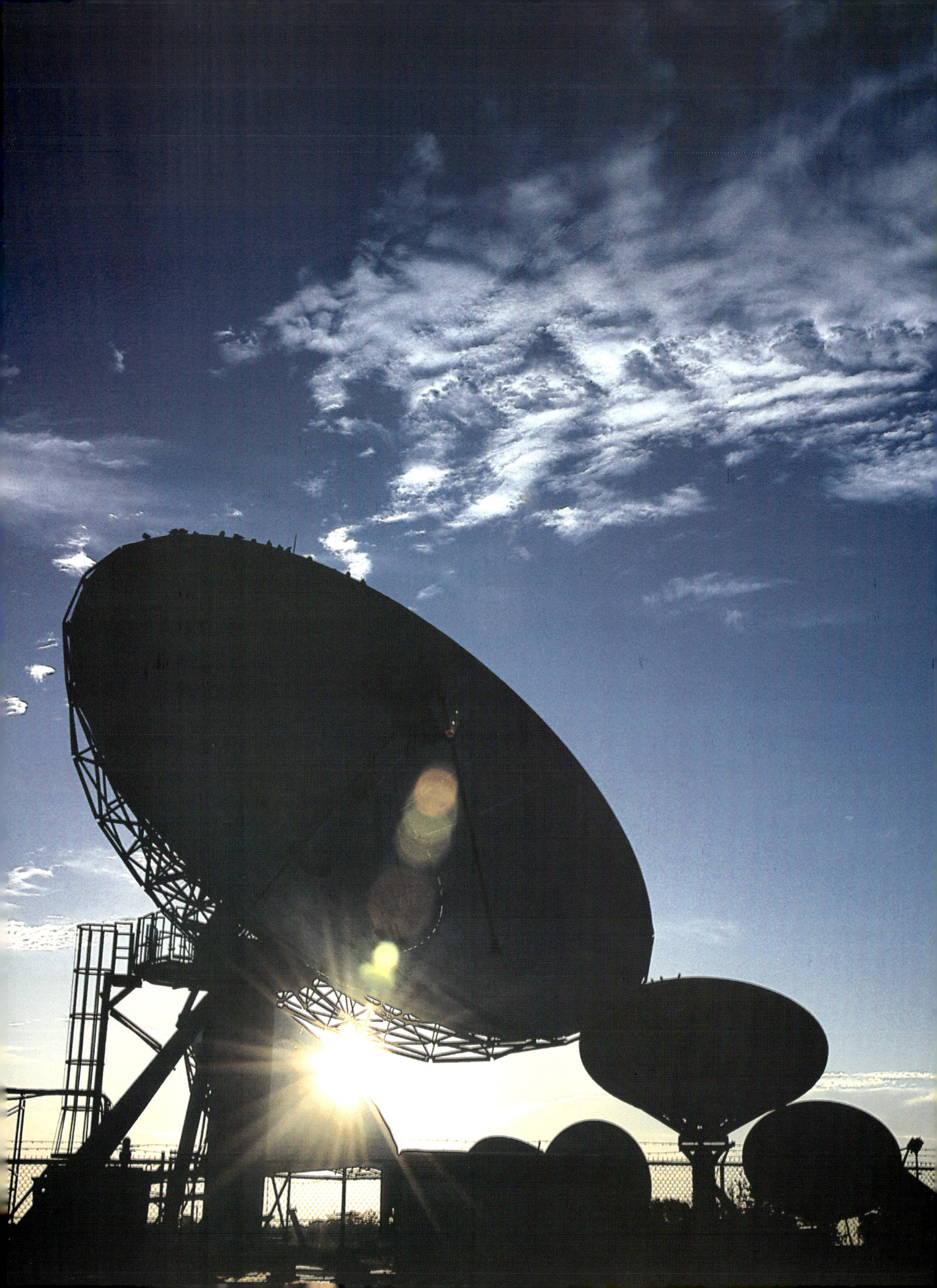

HOUSTON ★ People ★ Opportunity ★ Success

The Power of Houston. Providing electricity for 1.6 million customers, Reliant Energy HL&P is one of Houston's oldest companies. The company placed its first arc light into operation in 1882, only about three months after Thomas Edison directed completion of the country's first electric plant. Today, Reliant Energy HL&P's 12 domestic power plants have a generating capacity of nearly 14,000 megawatts. At the company's energy control and data center, Reliant workers monitor electric usage and demand in a 5,000-square-mile region 24 hours a day, 365 days a year. ★ Whether via wired or wireless telecommunications (left), Houston is well equipped to move voice, data and audio across town and around the world. In addition to more than 2 million access lines from Southwestern Bell, Houston is served by 31 cellular telephone companies and several other local service providers and cable operators. ★ Water supply now available or under development at Lake Houston (pages 102-103), together with nearby Lake Conroe and Lake Livingston, will meet Houston's projected needs through 2035.

◄ *Photo: Ray Viator*

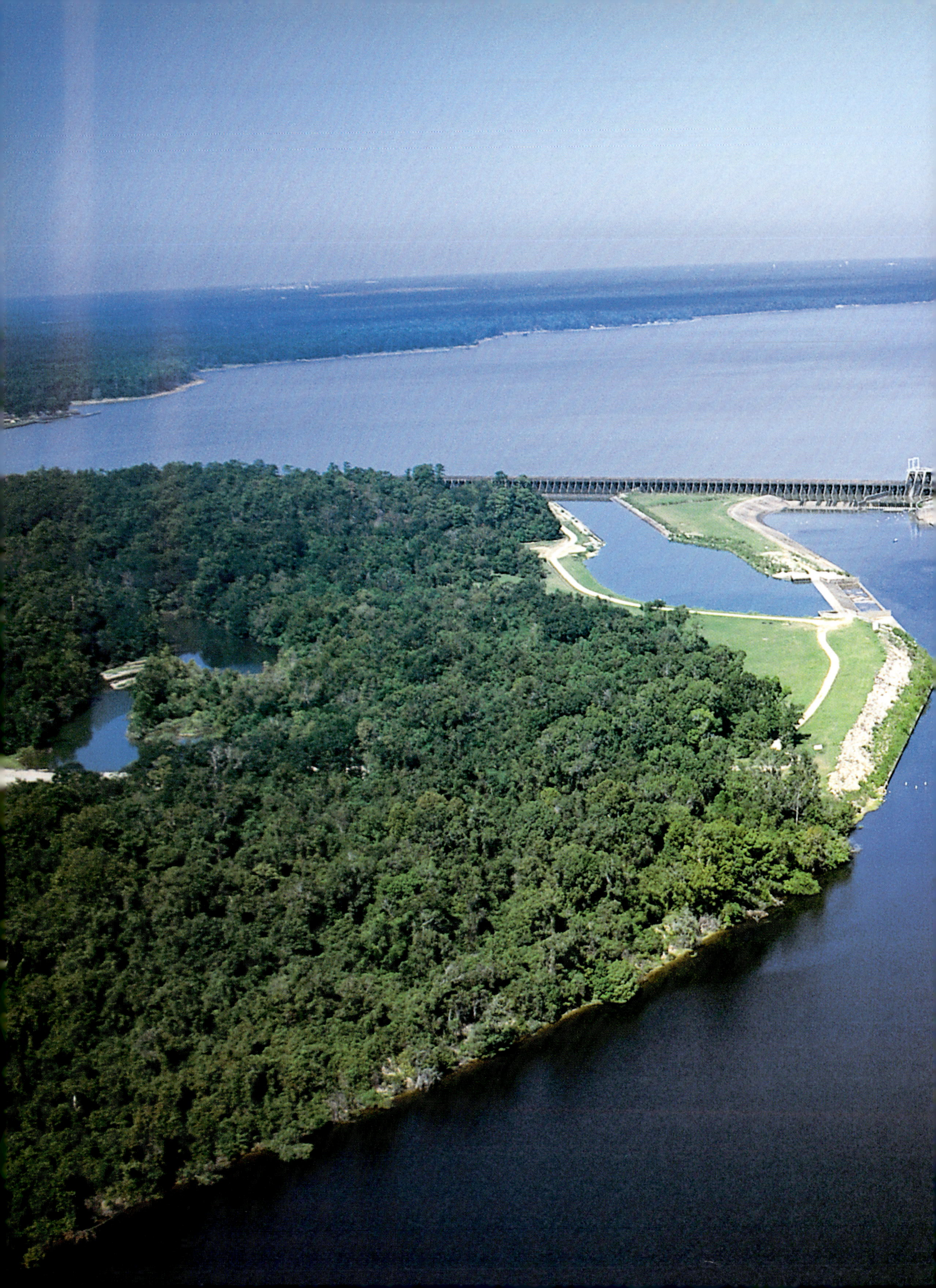

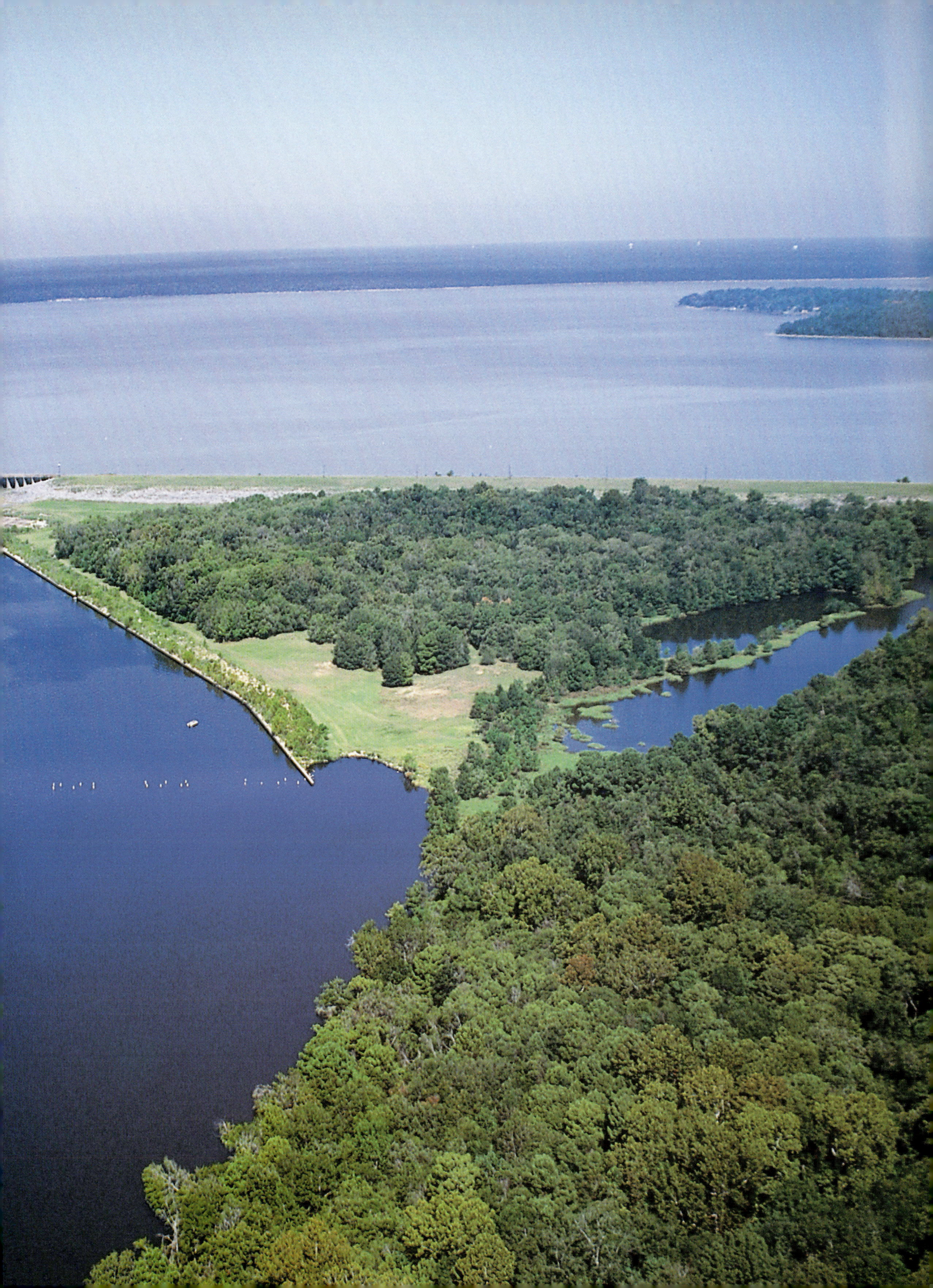

HOUSTON ★ People ★ Opportunity ★ Success

*C*onverging on Houston. *More than 400 major conferences, conventions and trade shows draw 2 million visitors to Houston each year. With 1.7 million square feet of exhibit and conference room space, Houston has the second largest amount of convention space in the country for major exhibitions.* ★ *Downtown Houston offers some of the most competitive and affordable office lease rates of any major city in the country.*

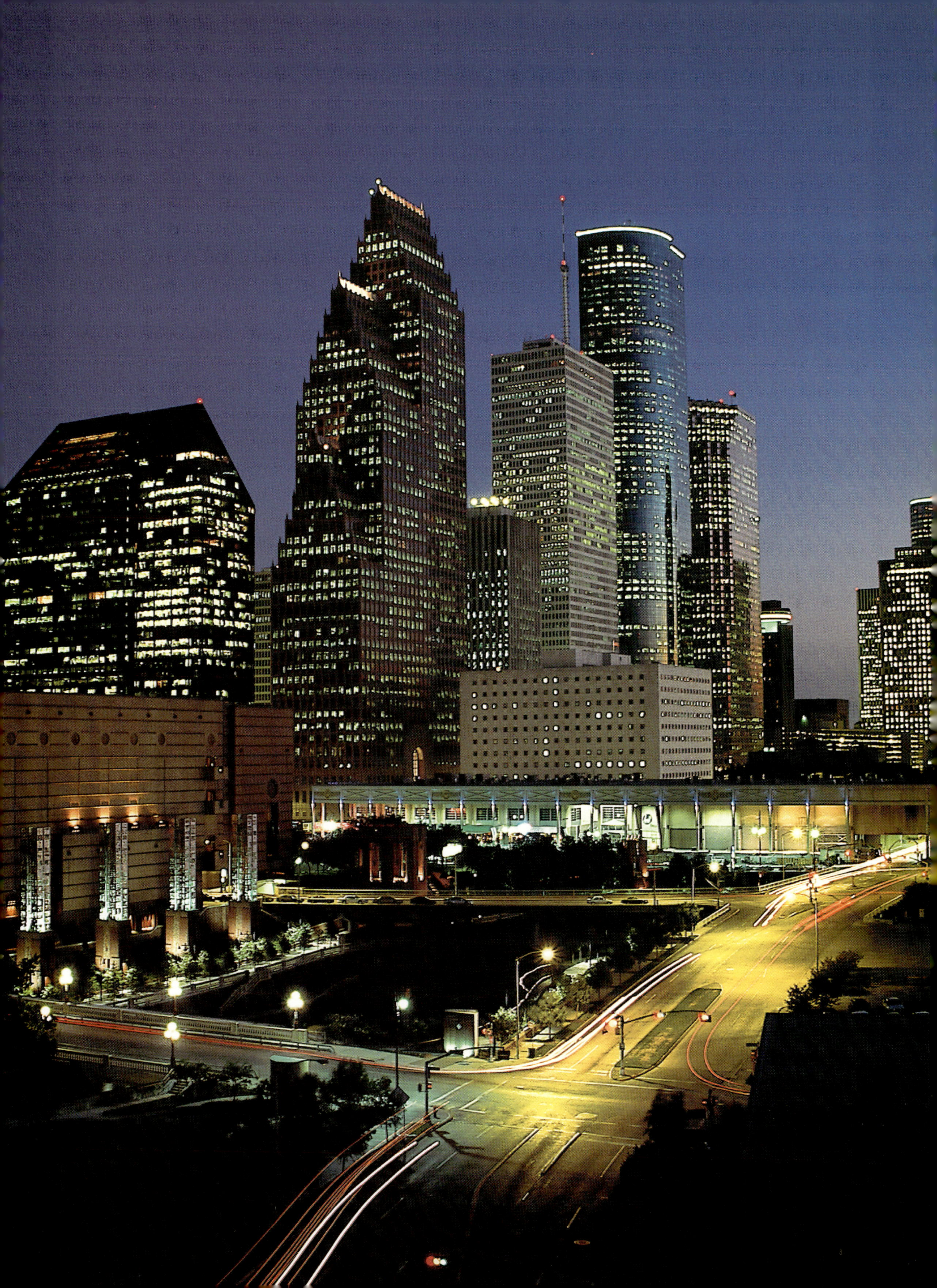

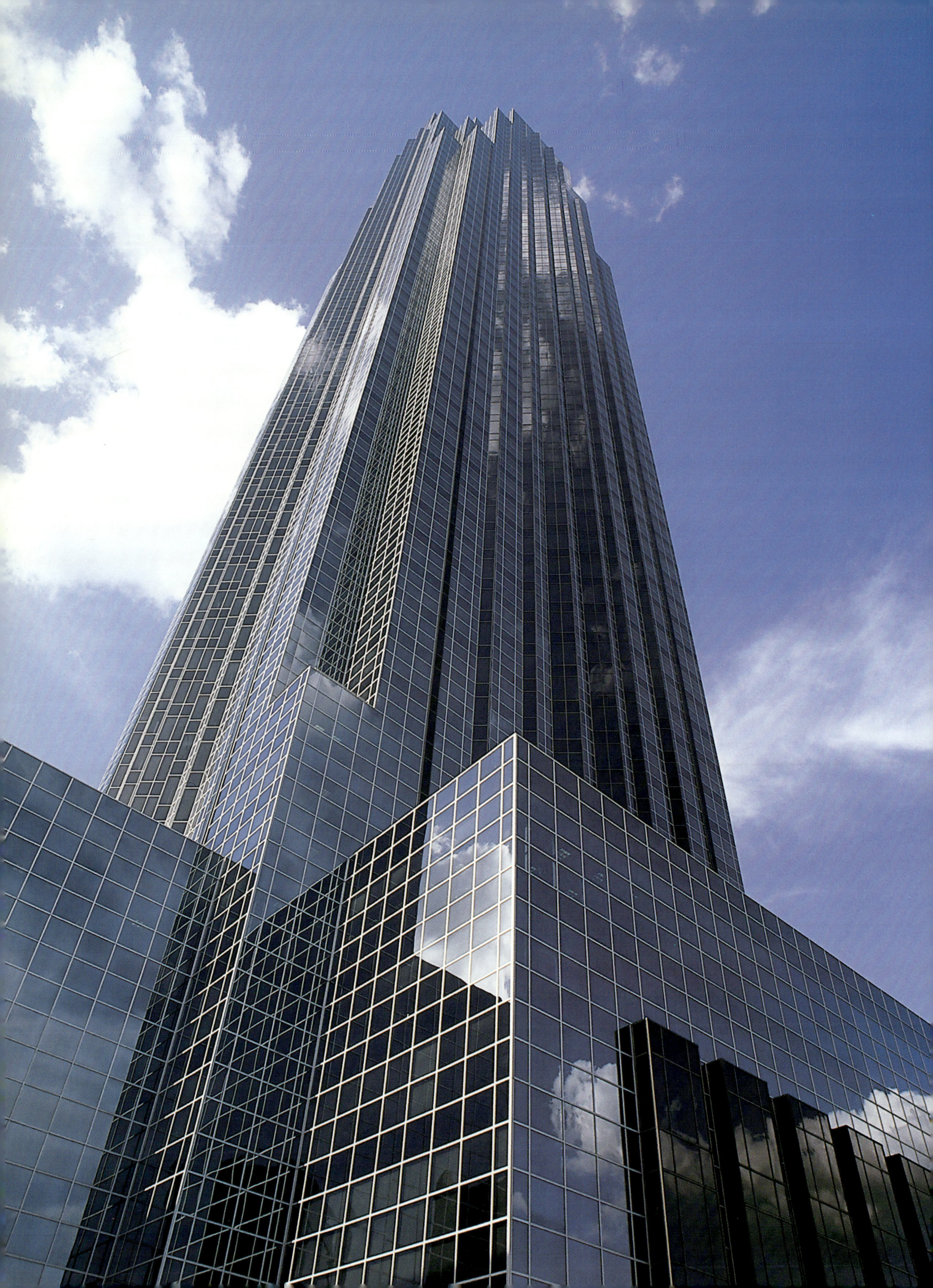

HOUSTON ★ People ★ Opportunity ★ Success

Photo Courtesy Conoco, Inc.

***O**ffice Options.* In addition to downtown, Houston offers office options in several major activity centers throughout the region. Nestled beside a lake and landscaped grounds, the world headquarters for Conoco, Inc. (above) provides the energy company's employees with a campus-style environment in the Energy Corridor in west Houston. ★ At 64 floors and 1.5 million square feet, Williams Tower (left) near The Galleria anchors the Uptown Houston area and is the tallest building in the United States outside a central business district.

HOUSTON ★ People ★ Opportunity ★ Success

Quality of Life

One of Houston's greatest advantages is that it offers a seemingly boundless number of choices to meet the needs, interests and lifestyles of area residents. It is a city that tempts outsiders with a rich variety of cultural and recreational interests and then seduces them with a lifestyle and low cost of living that is almost impossible to walk away from.

In fact, most newcomers to Houston are pleasantly surprised and overwhelmed by the abundance and variety of arts and cultural institutions, sports and recreation, neighborhoods and housing options, schools and educational opportunities that abound in the Houston region.

The result is that Houston's biggest boosters and advocates are sometimes those who at first might have been skeptics about the quality of life that Houston offers.

The reality is that Houston has been nurturing and enhancing the quality of life in the region throughout the century. The fledgling Houston Symphony became a formal organization in 1913 and now enjoys an international reputation. Texas' first art museum, The Museum of Fine Arts, Houston, opened its doors in 1924. In 2000, it will complete a major expansion, doubling in size to more than 150,000 square feet of gallery space to showcase the 35,000 pieces of art work in its collection.

Those early efforts of Houston leaders set a solid cultural foundation for the new century in Houston set a precedent that has been nourished by community, government and business leaders throughout the century. As a result, Houston can proudly claim to be one of only a few cities in the country with permanent companies in each of the major performing arts: symphony, opera, ballet and drama. The Houston Symphony, Houston Grand Opera and Houston Ballet enjoy international reputations for their innovative programs and artists. Houston Grand Opera, for example, has produced 24 world premieres since 1973. The Alley Theatre, which received a 1996 Tony Award as the best regional theater in the country, and Theatre Under the Stars both have developed and produced plays and musicals that later went on to successful runs on Broadway.

But Houston's cultural and artistic interests extend far beyond just those groups. In fact, Houston boasts dozens of arts and cultural institutions and organizations that represent a diverse, international and eclectic range of interests. Houston's Museum District, for example, ranges from the comprehensive Museum of Fine Arts, Houston to the Contemporary Arts Museum, and from the Houston Museum of Natural Science to the Children's Museum of Houston and the Museum of Health & Medical Science, and from the Holocaust Museum to the internationally acclaimed Menil Collection.

Recreation and entertainment in the Houston area are just as rich and diverse. Options include neighborhood parks, Memorial Park and Hermann Park, more than 66 miles of jogging trails, over 200 baseball fields, more than 100 football/soccer fields, two arboretums, a velodrome, more than 60 public swimming pools, hundreds of public tennis courts and over 100 public and private golf courses.

On the professional level, Houston pioneered the concept of indoor baseball and football when the Astrodome – proclaimed as the "Eighth Wonder of the World" – opened in 1965. With the new century, the Houston Astros will again have a dramatic impact on Houston as the Major League Baseball team moves to the state-of-the-art Enron Field downtown. The team's commitment to its new retractable-roof stadium already has ignited an explosion of development and entertainment that is adding a new sparkle to downtown Houston.

Houston also is a city of champions. In fact, it's a city of back-to-back champions with the NBA Houston Rockets and back-to-back-to back champions with the WNBA Houston Comets.

In addition to the cultural, entertainment and recreational amenities, Houston offers residents a variety of housing options, from high-rise condominiums to garden apartments, from mansions on tree-lined streets to waterfront homes on area lakes and bays. Houston also has been a leader and innovator in residential development. The Woodlands, for example, was one of the first successful master-planned communities in the nation. Houston is now home to more than a dozen master-planned communities – in every quadrant of the region – that incorporate a variety of housing options along with schools, parks, pools, golf courses and retail businesses in a complementary environment.

When you put it all together, Houston offers an exceptionally high quality of life. In fact, a recent survey by The Gallup Organization found that Houstonians were substantially more satisfied with the region's quality of life than were residents in the other major cities surveyed, including Chicago, Philadelphia and Atlanta. ■

A Golfer's Dream. From the public courses at Hermann Park and Memorial Park to the Tournament Player's Course (site of the annual Shell Houston Open) at The Woodlands as well as Tour 18's sampling of the best golf holes in the United States, golfers can find a wide variety of options – and challenges – on more than 100 golf courses in the region. ★ *Houston is home to dozens of master-planned residential communities such as First Colony (pages 110-111), The Woodlands, Kingwood, Clear Lake City and others.*

Photo (pages 110-111) Courtesy American Golf Country Clubs ▶▶

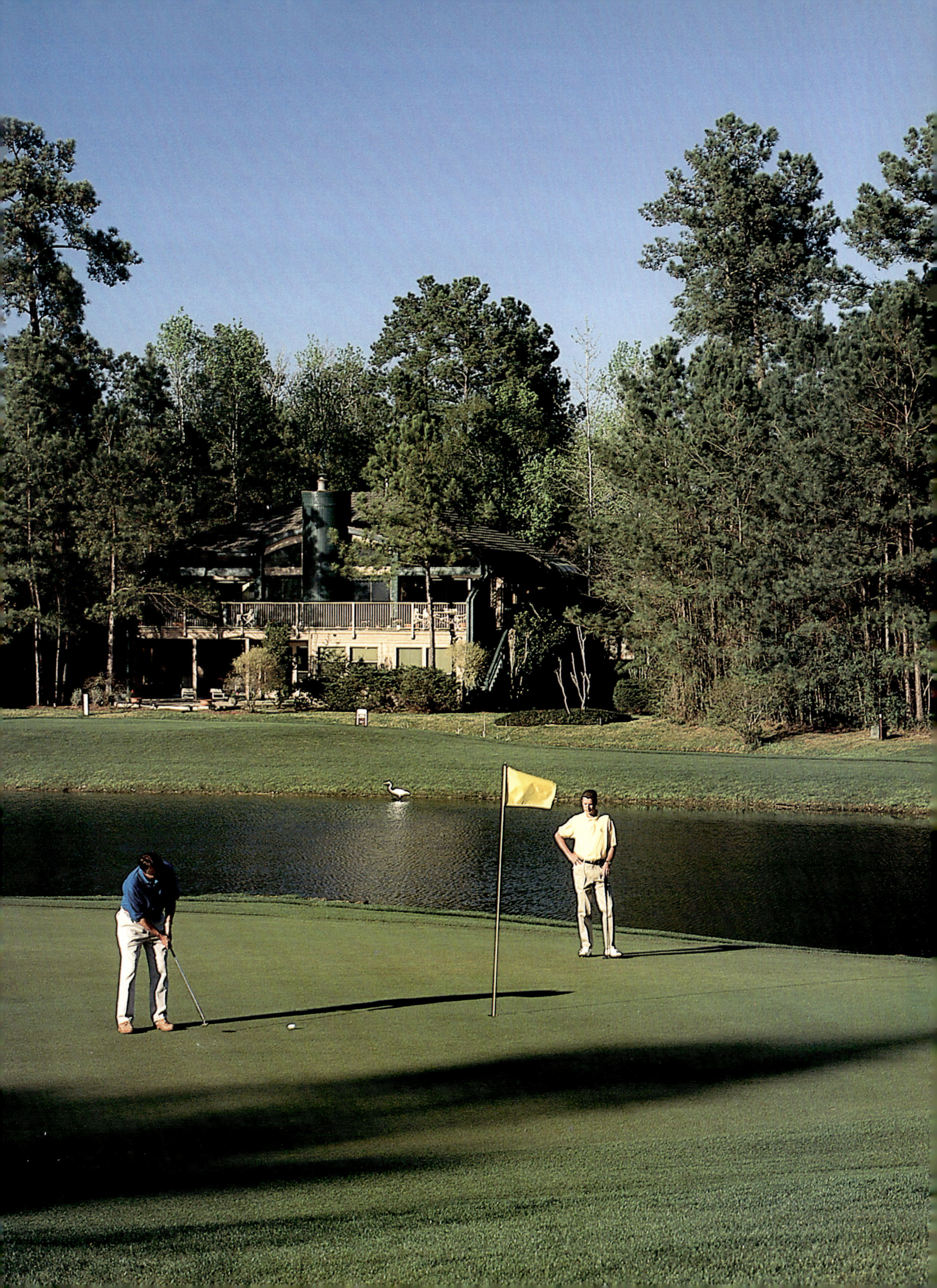

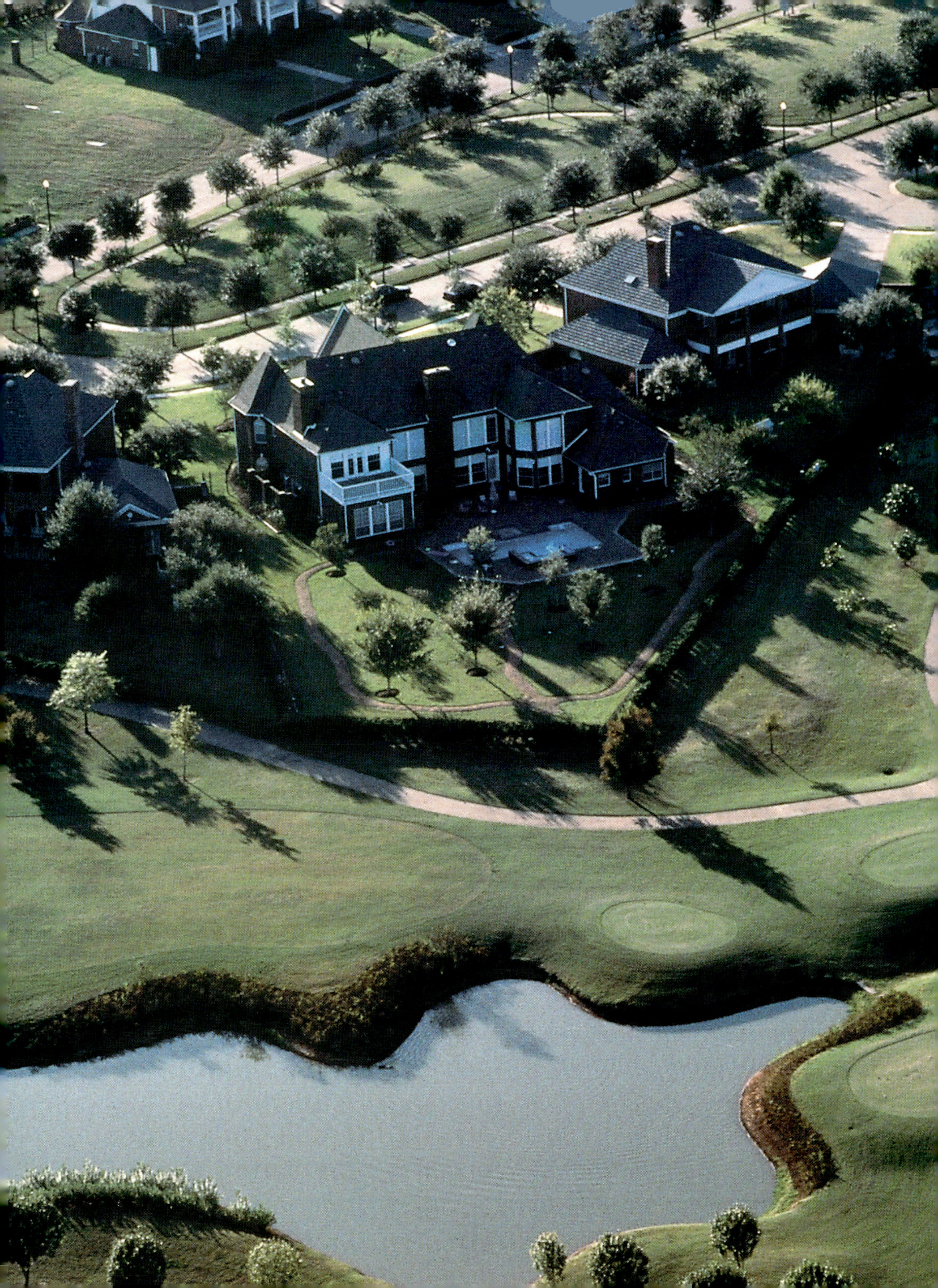

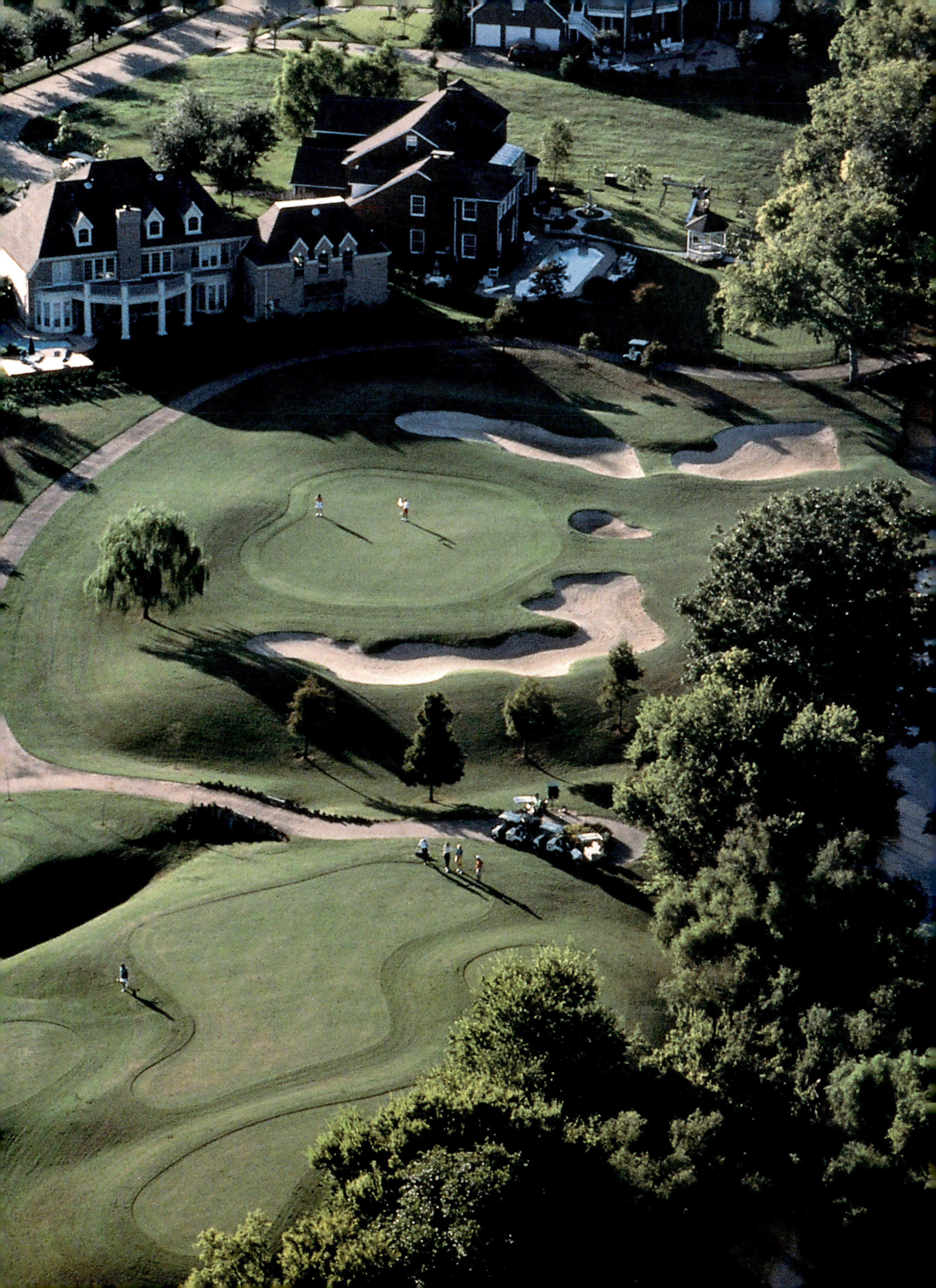

HOUSTON ★ People ★ Opportunity ★ Success

Upscale and Classic Neighborhoods. River Oaks (above) was Houston's first upscale neighborhood when it was developed in the 1920s by lawyer William C. Hogg, who thought his planned residential community would provide a model for the rest of the city to follow. Many of the neighborhood's prized homes were designed by John F. Staub. ★ Drawing its name from the fact that it boasts the highest elevation in the city of Houston, (23 feet higher than downtown Houston), the classic architectural design of many homes in the Heights area (right) harkens back to simpler times when the area was developed at the beginning of the 20th century.

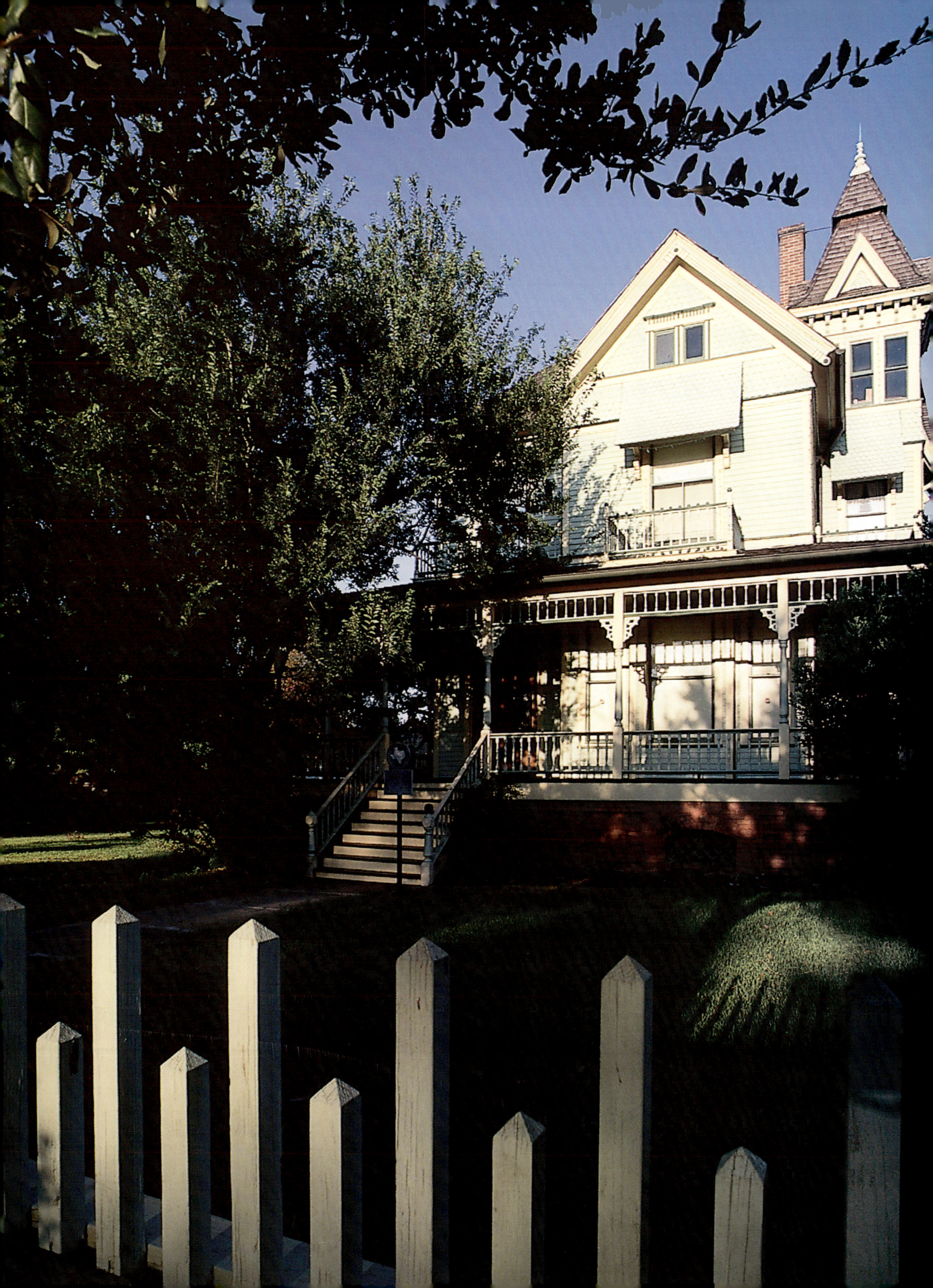

HOUSTON ★ People ★ Opportunity ★ Success

A Gardener's Heaven and a Sea Lover's Paradise. Houston offers homes in many price ranges and designs to fit different lifestyles. Houston's semi-tropical climate means that weekend gardeners can cultivate a variety of flowers, shrubs and trees. ★ The Clear Lake area south of Houston (right) features many waterfront homes with slips to keep boats ready for an excursion on Galveston Bay.

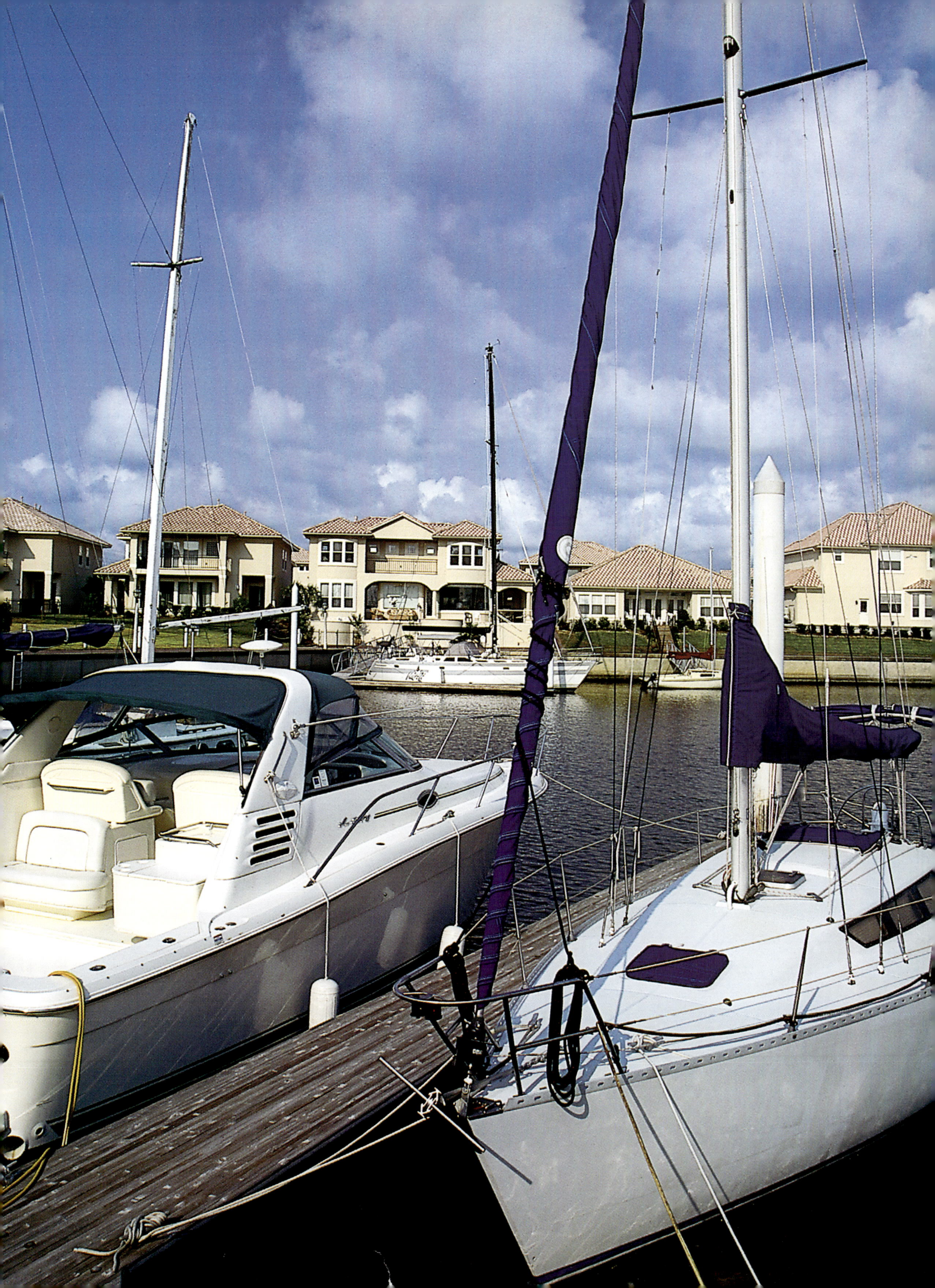

H O U S T O N ★ P e o p l e ★ O p p o r t u n i t y ★ S u c c e s s

A Home with a View. Houstonians are rediscovering the benefits of living in the heart of Houston, with easy access to work and a thriving theater and entertainment district. ★ With more than 450,000 apartments and other multi-family housing units, the Houston area offers residents a wealth of options in every price range.

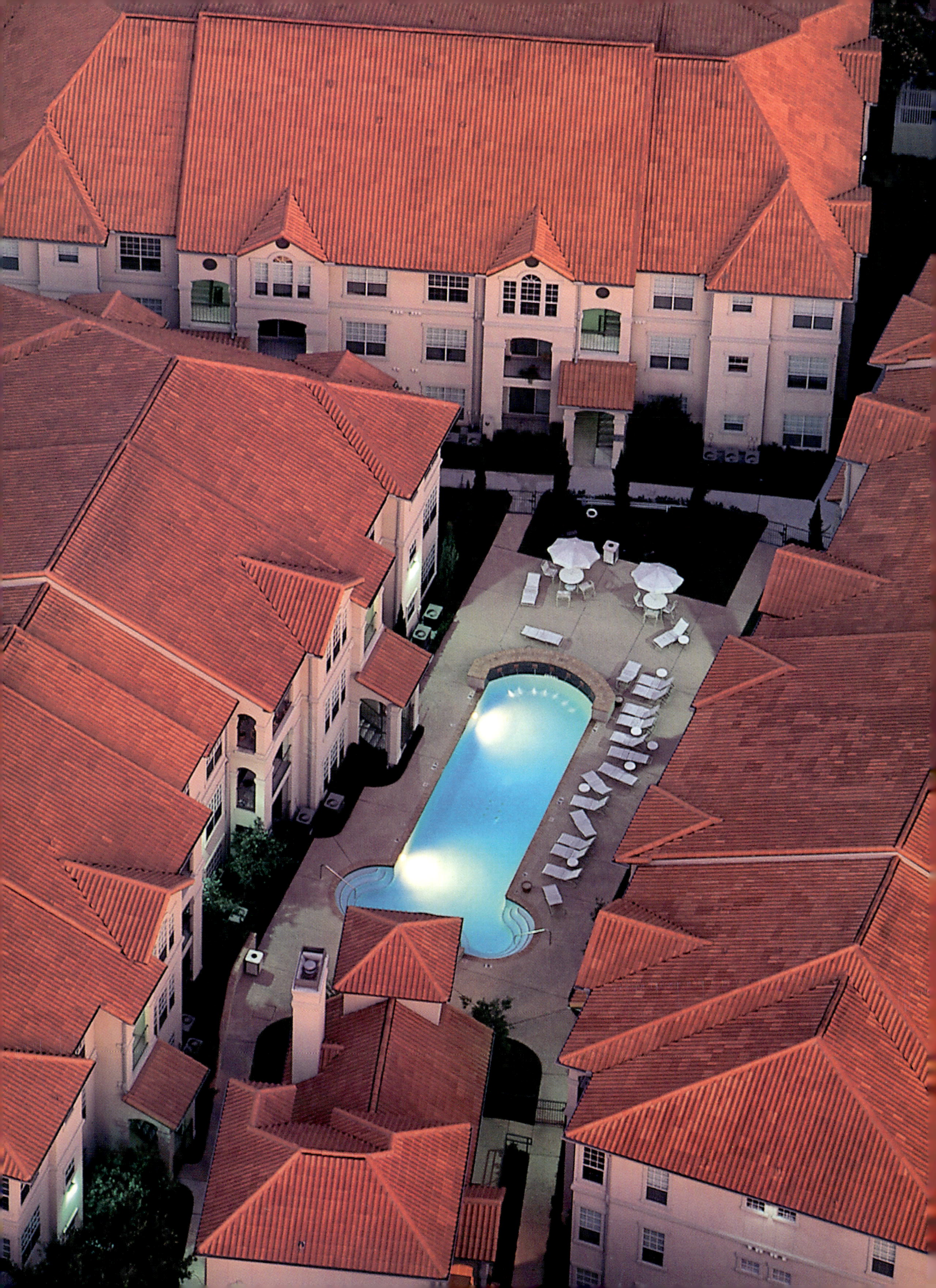

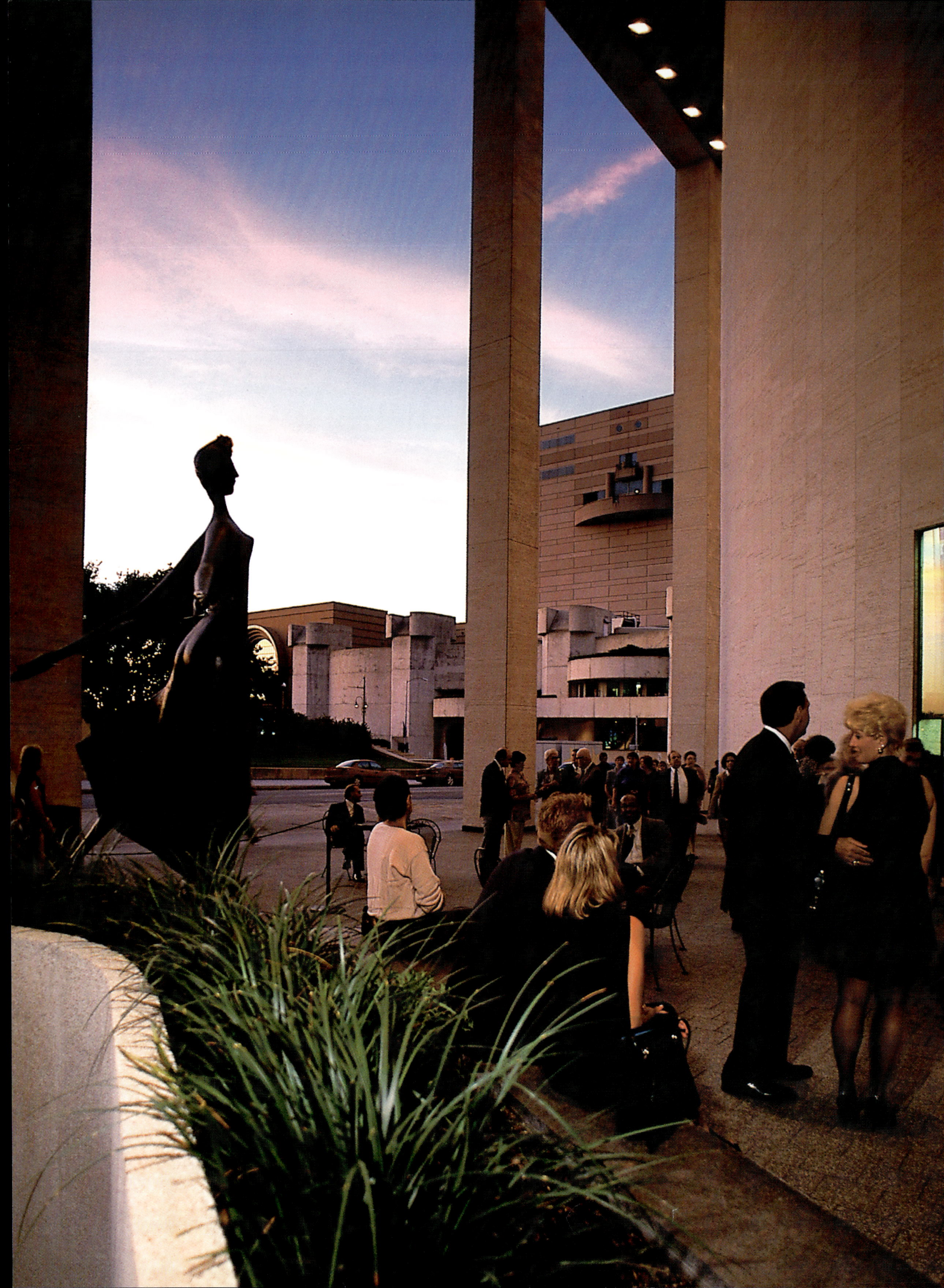

HOUSTON ★ People ★ Opportunity ★ Success

Photo: Jim Caldwell, Courtesy Houston Grand Opera

World-Class Performing Arts. *Houston Grand Opera, founded in 1955, is the nation's fifth largest opera company and is the only one to win a Tony, two Grammy and two Emmy awards. One of Houston Grand Opera's most popular shows is Robert Carsen's spectacular production of Boito's* Mefistofele *(above).* ★ *Anchored by Jones Hall for the Performing Arts, the Alley Theatre and The Wortham Theater Center, Houston's Theater District (left) features a busy schedule of performances by the Houston Symphony, Houston Grand Opera, Houston Ballet and the Alley Theatre as well as other performing arts organizations and touring productions of Broadway plays.*

119

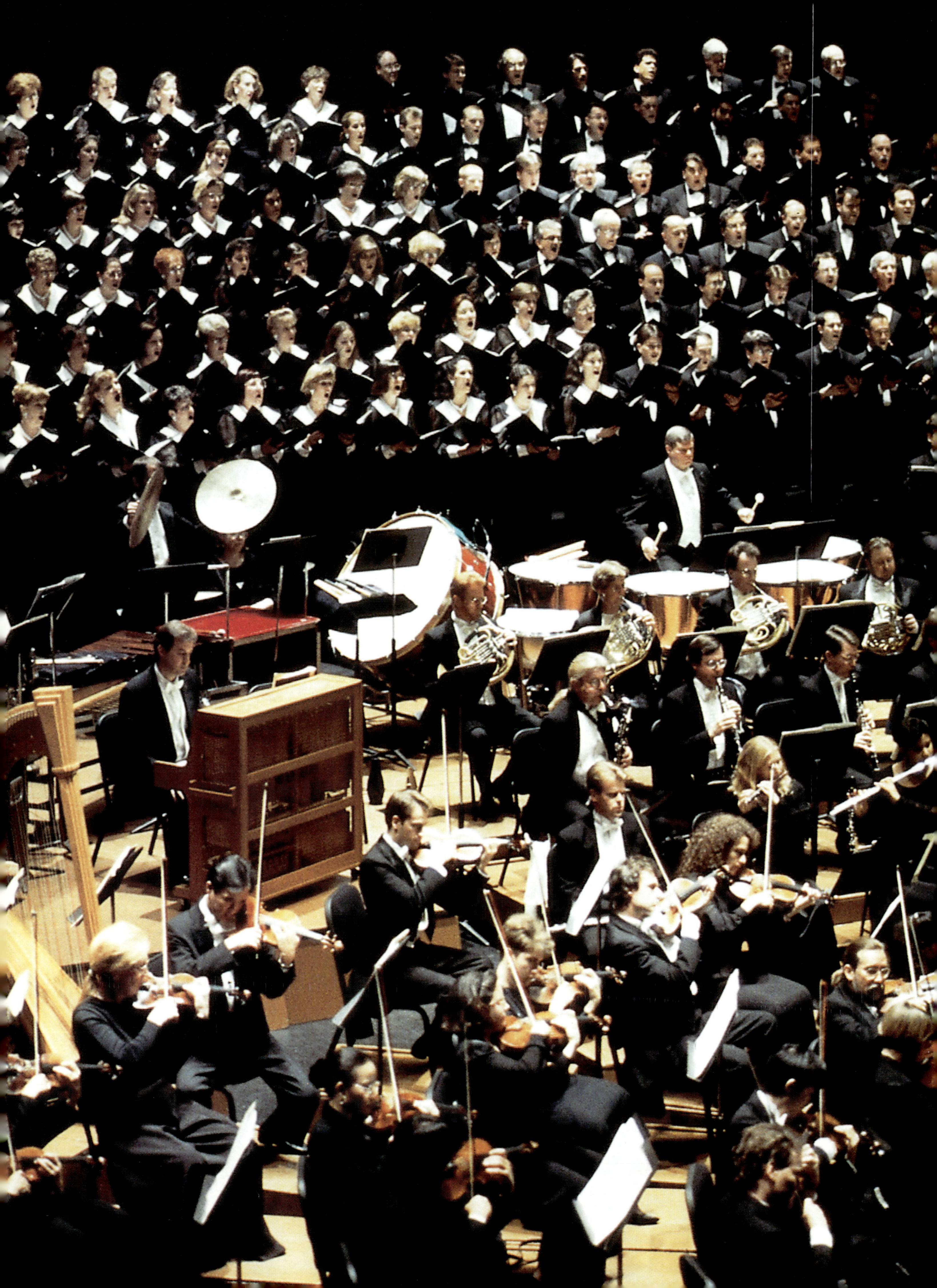

HOUSTON ★ People ★ Opportunity ★ Success

International Acclaim. *Winner of the 1996 Tony Award for outstanding regional theater, the Alley Theatre (above) is the nation's oldest continuously-operating resident theater company outside New York. From its modest beginnings in 1947 in a rented studio down an "alley" in downtown Houston, the Alley Theatre has emerged to become one of the nation's most innovative professional resident theatre companies, presenting world premieres, attracting international artists and staging new musicals that have found success on Broadway.* ★ *Founded in 1913, the Houston Symphony (left) is one of America's oldest performing arts organizations. Each season, 300,000 people attend more than 200 classical, pops, education and family concerts performed by the world-renowned orchestra's 97 full-time musicians. The Houston Symphony Chorus made its debut with the Houston Symphony in 1949.*

◀ *Photo: Ellis Vener, Courtesy Houston Symphony*

HOUSTON ★ People ★ Opportunity ★ Success

Photo: Drew Donovan, Courtesy Houston Ballet

***S**tirring Souls and Stimulating Minds.* Hailed by the New York Times as "one of the nation's best ballet companies," Houston Ballet (above) has toured extensively to critical praise throughout the United States and in Canada, Europe, the United Kingdom and Asia. Houston Ballet's world premiere production of Dracula, choreographed by artistic directory Ben Stevenson, featured Timothy O'Keefe and Susan Cummins. ★ Founded in 1924, The Museum of Fine Arts, Houston (right) houses 35,000 works from antiquity to the present and ranks as the largest collection in the Southwest. With the opening of the museum's new Audrey Jones Beck Building in 2000, the museum will rank sixth nationally in gallery space.

Photo: Thomas R. DuBrock, Courtesy The Museum of Fine Arts, Houston ▶

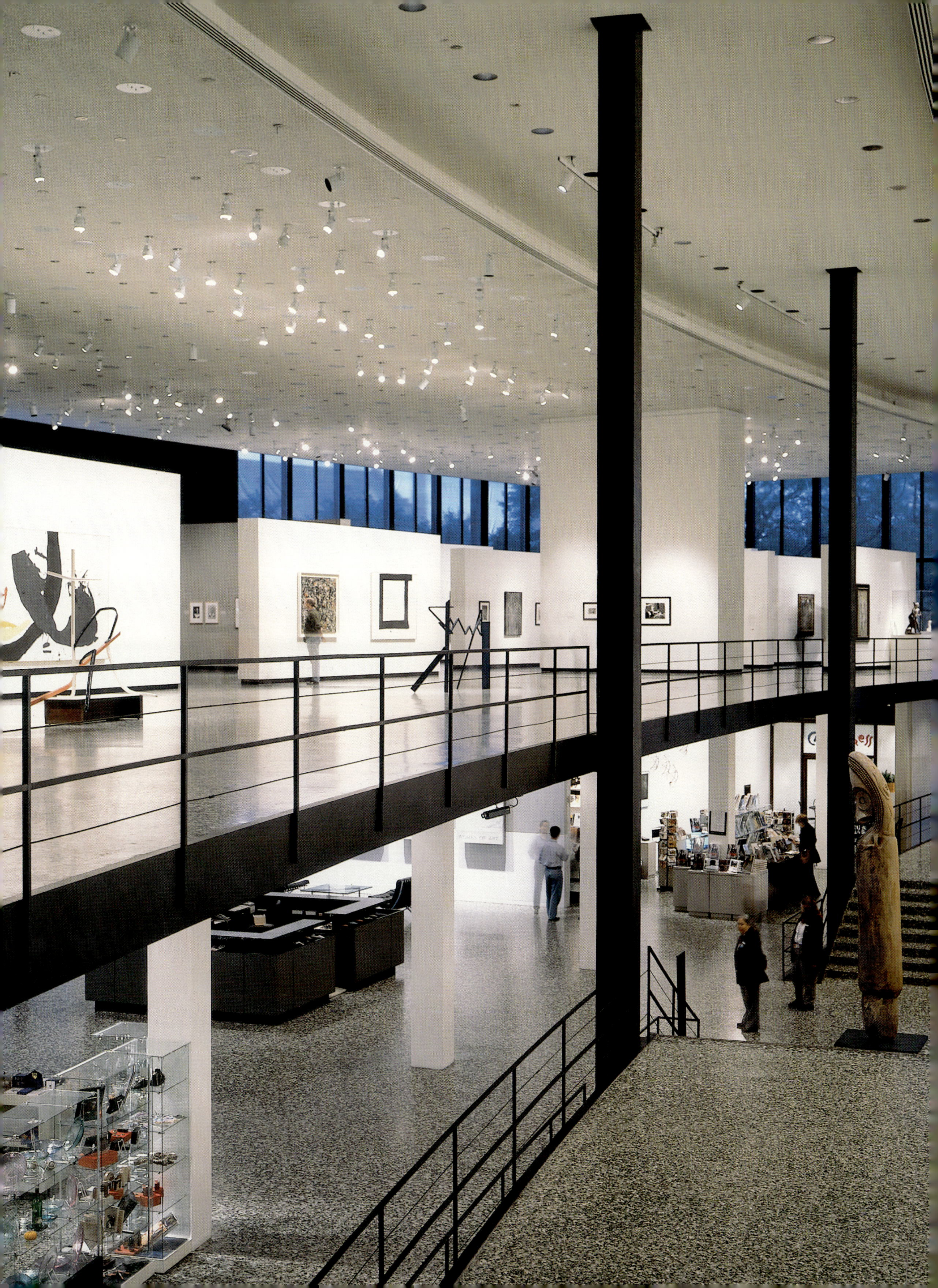

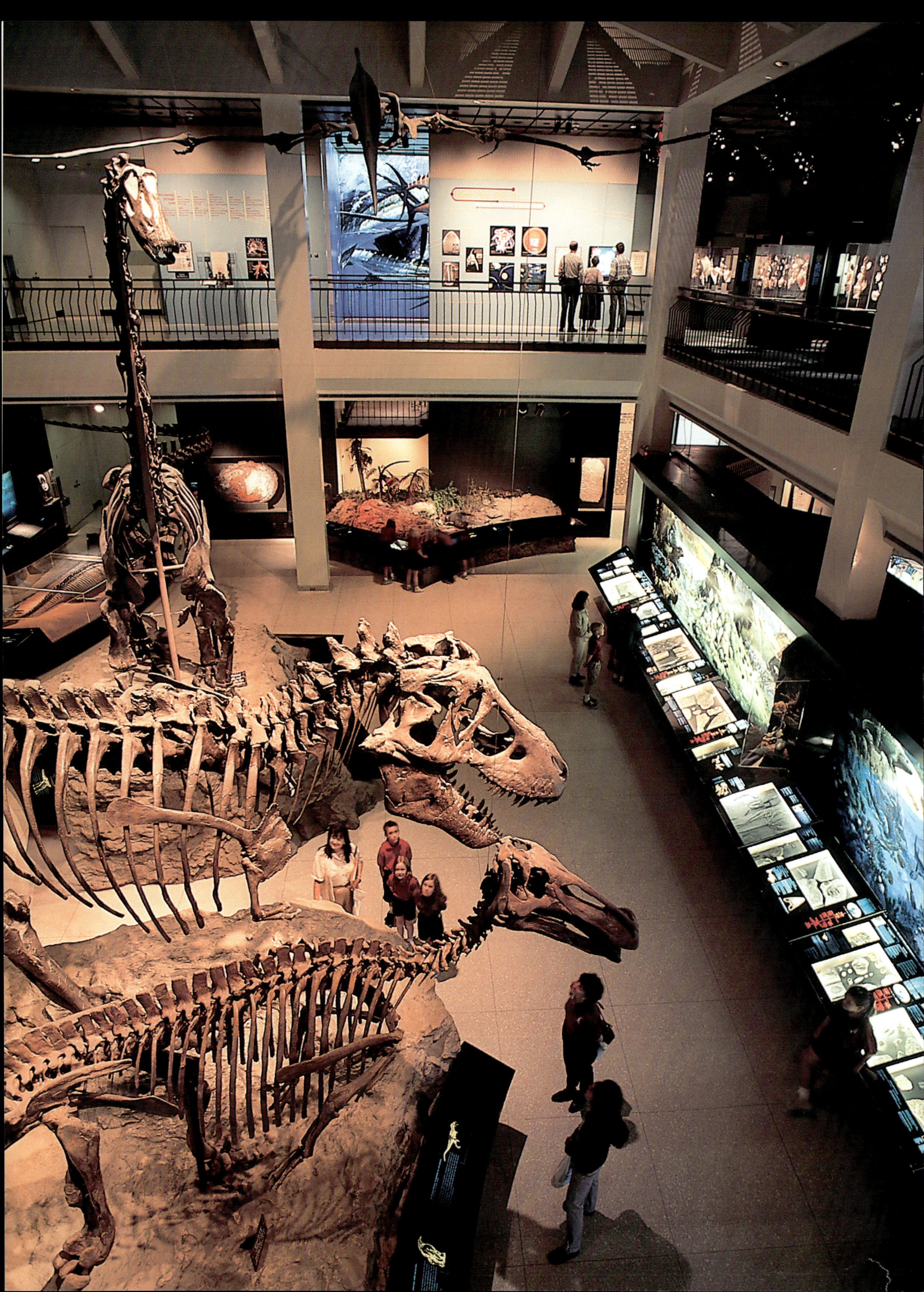

HOUSTON ★ People ★ Opportunity ★ Success

Offering Unique Perspectives. *Considered one of the most important privately assembled collections of the 20th century, The Menil Collection (above) opened in 1987 to preserve and exhibit the art collection of John and Dominique de Menil. The collection houses approximately 15,000 paintings, sculptures, prints, drawings, photographs and rare books. Exhibits include the tribal cultures of Africa, Oceania, and the American Pacific Northwest as well as masterpieces from antiquity, the Byzantine and medieval worlds, and the 20th century.* ★ *The Houston Museum of Natural Science (left) features more than 450 specimens of dinosaurs and other prehistoric animals as well as exhibits on malacology (seashells), gems and minerals, energy, chemistry and astronomy. Founded in 1909, the Houston Museum of Natural Science draws two million people annually, the largest number of visitors to any museum in Texas. The museum's complex includes the Burke Baker Planetarium, Cockrell Butterfly Center and Wortham IMAX Theatre.*

HOUSTON ★ People ★ Opportunity ★ Success

A Community Remebers. Opened in 1996, the Holocaust Museum Houston fosters Holocaust education, remembrance and understanding. The museum provides education about the uniqueness of this event and its ongoing lesson: that humankind must learn to live together in peace and harmony. The museum's permanent exhibit, "Bearing Witness: A Community Remembers," is unique in its emphasis on Houston-area Holocaust survivors. The museum's theater features the film, "Voices," a montage of oral histories of Houston-area Holocaust survivors.

HOUSTON ★ People ★ Opportunity ★ Success

Photo: Ray Viator

Museums for Everyone. *Documenting new directions in art through ever-changing exhibitions, the Contemporary Arts Museum (above) is a noncollecting museum for visual arts of the present and recent past. Founded in 1948, the museum believes the living artist is its greatest educational asset and seeks to bring artists and the public into contact in as many ways as possible.* ★ *The Amazing Body Pavilion of the Museum of Health & Medical Science (page 128) offers visitors a fantastic larger-than-life walking tour of the human body. Opened in 1996, the museum was founded by physicians of the Harris County Medical Society to create a free-standing health education facility for the community.* ★ *Serving more than 450,000 visitors annually, the Children's Museum of Houston (page 129) is one of the best attended youth museums in the country. The museum promotes learning by providing hands-on exhibitions in the areas of science and technology, history and culture, health and human development, and the arts.*

Photo (page 128) Courtesy Museum of Health & Medical Science ▶
Photo (page 129) Courtesy the Children's Museum of Houston ▶

127

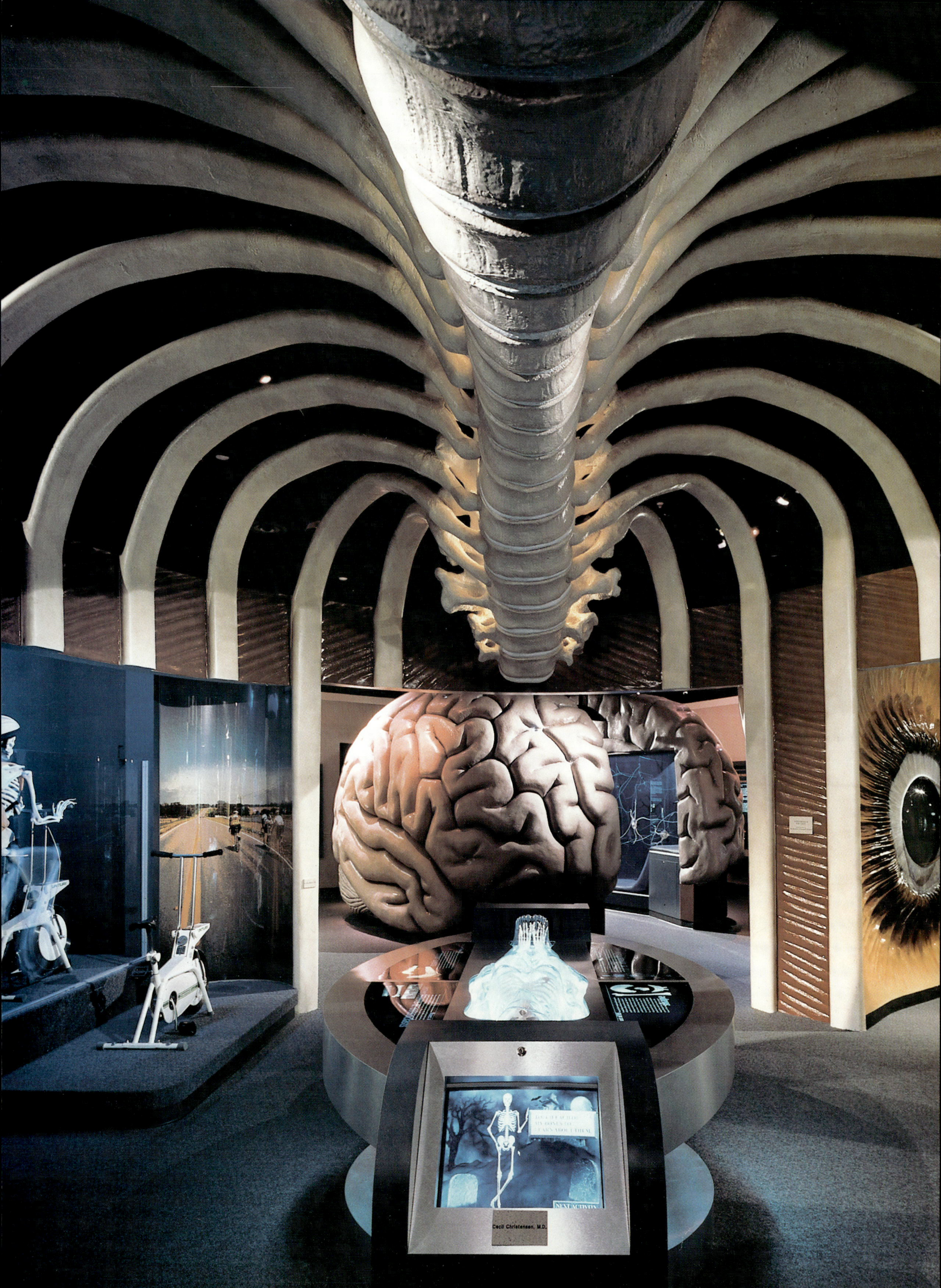
Cecil Christensen, M.D.

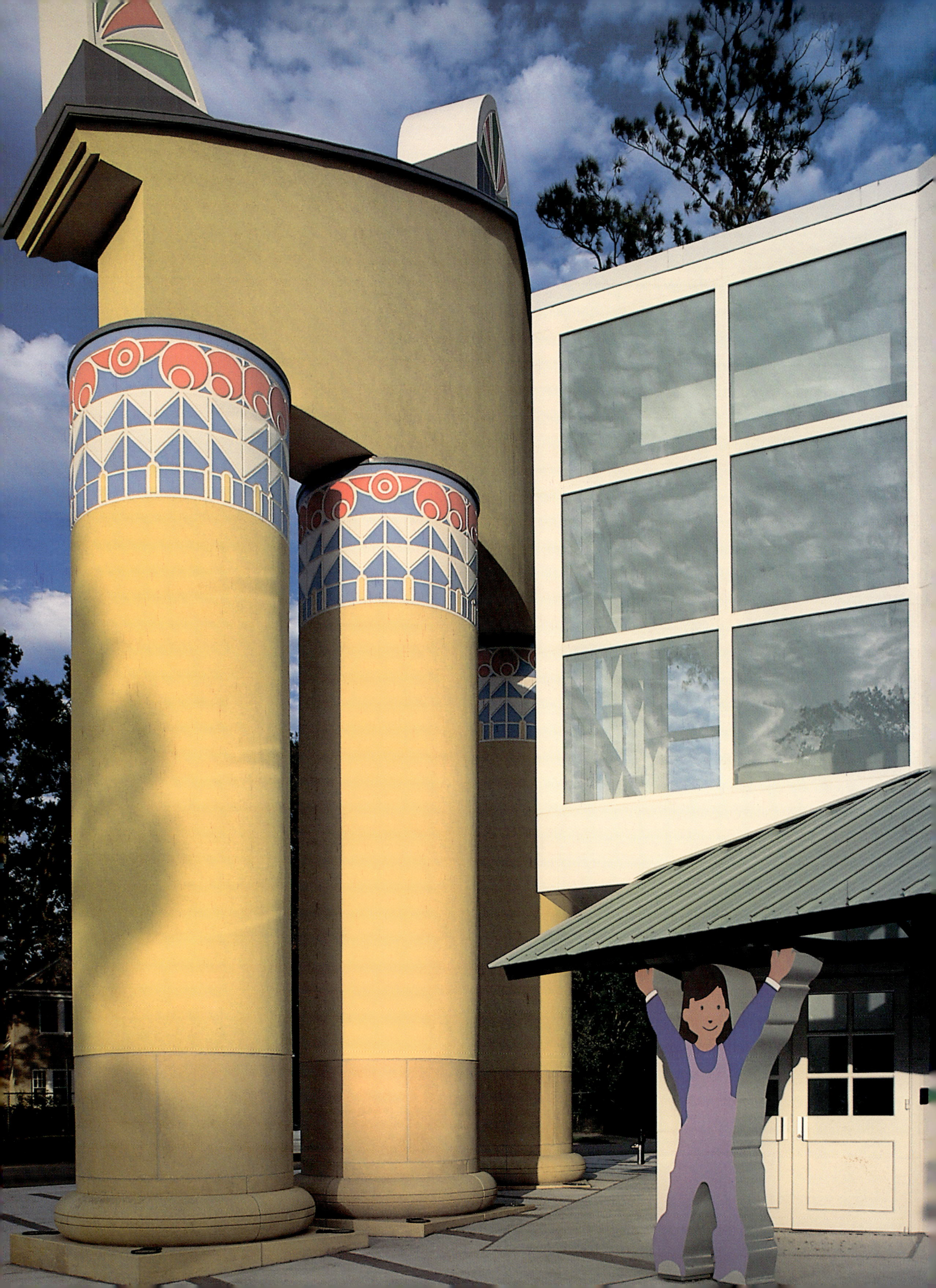

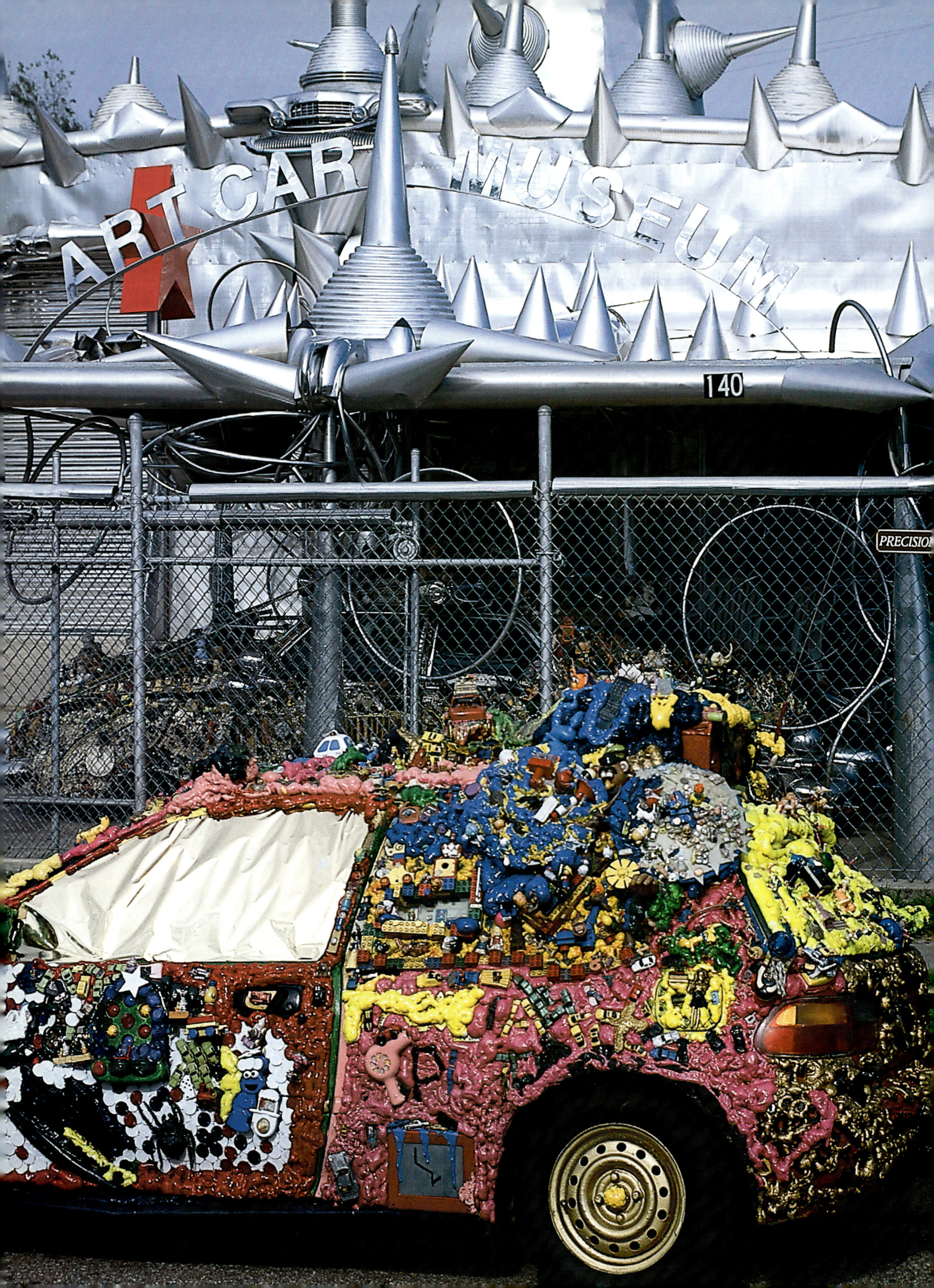
ART CAR MUSEUM
140
PRECISIO

HOUSTON ★ People ★ Opportunity ★ Success

Out of this World Collections. Billed as the closest thing to space on earth, Space Center Houston (above) features the world's largest collection of moon rocks as well as Apollo, Mercury and Gemini capsules, live demonstrations, a space suit collection and special programs and exhibits for children. Opened in 1992, the Disney-designed facility serves as the official visitors center for NASA's Johnson Space Center. ★ One of Houston's newest – and wackiest museums – the Art Car Museum (left) is dedicated to capturing and preserving the imagination and creativity that rolls through Houston each year during the Art Car Parade, the nation's oldest and largest annual gathering of art cars, decorated automobiles, rolling environments and traveling sculptures.

HOUSTON ★ People ★ Opportunity ★ Success

Houston Samplers. The new Houston Visitors Center (above) in downtown Houston features displays and information on a wide range of Houston area sites and visitor attractions — from the Museum District to the Theater District and from NASA's Johnson Space Center to the Texas Medical Center. ★ Each spring, Houston celebrates the city's international heritage by spotlighting a different country or region during the annual Houston International Festival (right). During the 10-day celebration, thousands of attendees sample the arts, music and food of nations and cultures from around the world.

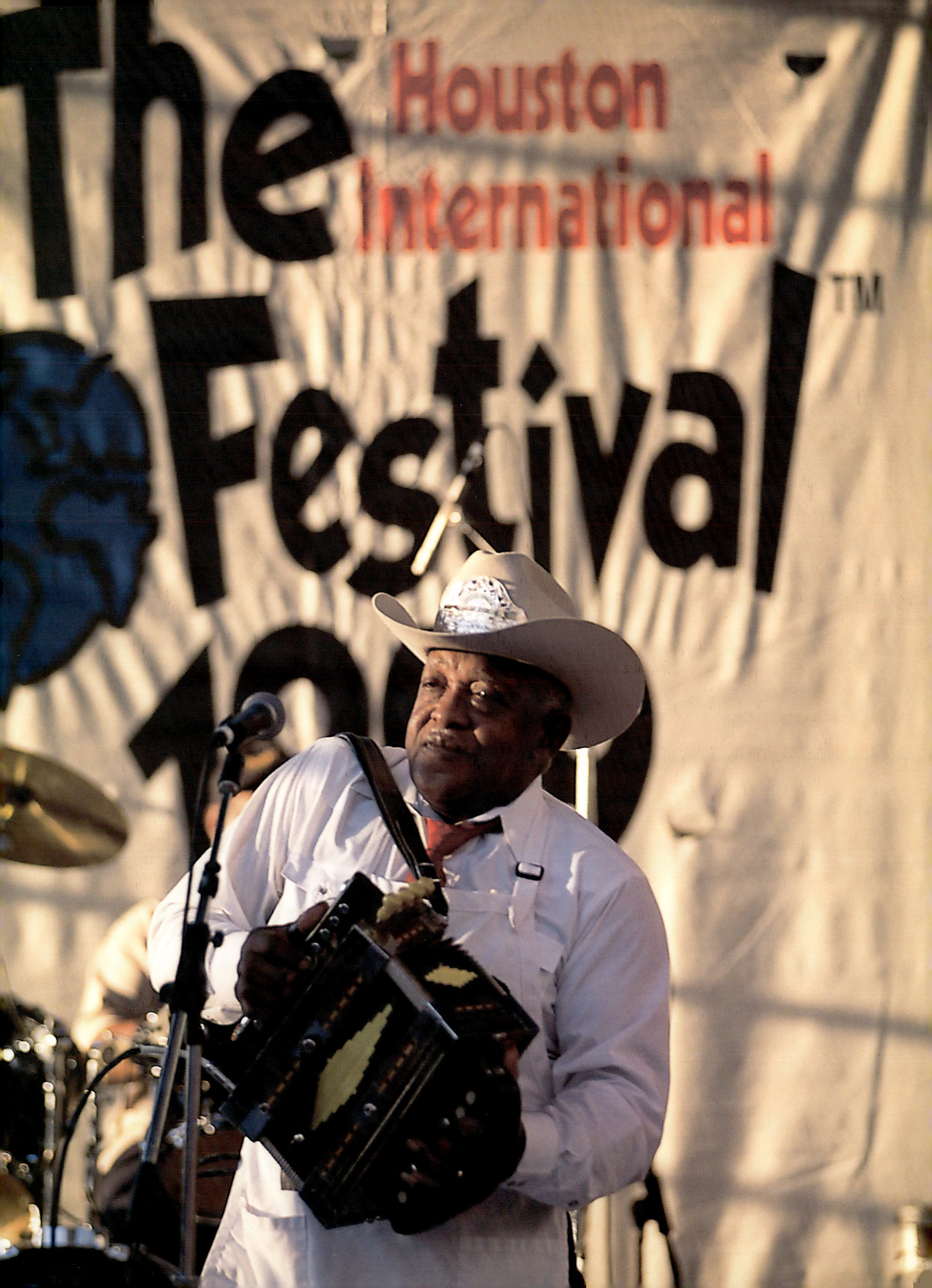
The
Houston
International
Festival
™

HOUSTON ★ People ★ Opportunity ★ Success

Celebrating Emancipation. *Remembering the day that emancipation was declared in Texas, Houston's African-American community each year celebrates Juneteenth with a parade through downtown Houston and other activities. In addition to Martin Luther King Day, the event is one of several events held each year in the Houston region to celebrate the heritage and contributions of African-Americans.*

HOUSTON ★ People ★ Opportunity ★ Success

Recognizing a Growing Community. More than 240,000 Asians now call Houston home, making it one of the largest and fastest-growing Asian communities in the United States. Houston's Asian community includes families and companies from China, Indonesia, Malaysia, the Philippines, Thailand, Taiwan, Vietnam and other parts of the Far East.

HOUSTON ★ People ★ Opportunity ★ Success

Celebrating Heritage in Music, Dance. Houston area artists from the Taiko Kaminari (thunder and lightning drums) perform during the annual Japan Festival sponsored by the Japan Business Association of Houston and other Japanese organizations. ★ Performers from Houston's Mexican-American community (right) provide traditional entertainment during celebrations of Cinco de Mayo. Many other festivals and events are held throughout the year to celebrate the cultures of other countries throughout Central and South America and the Caribbean.

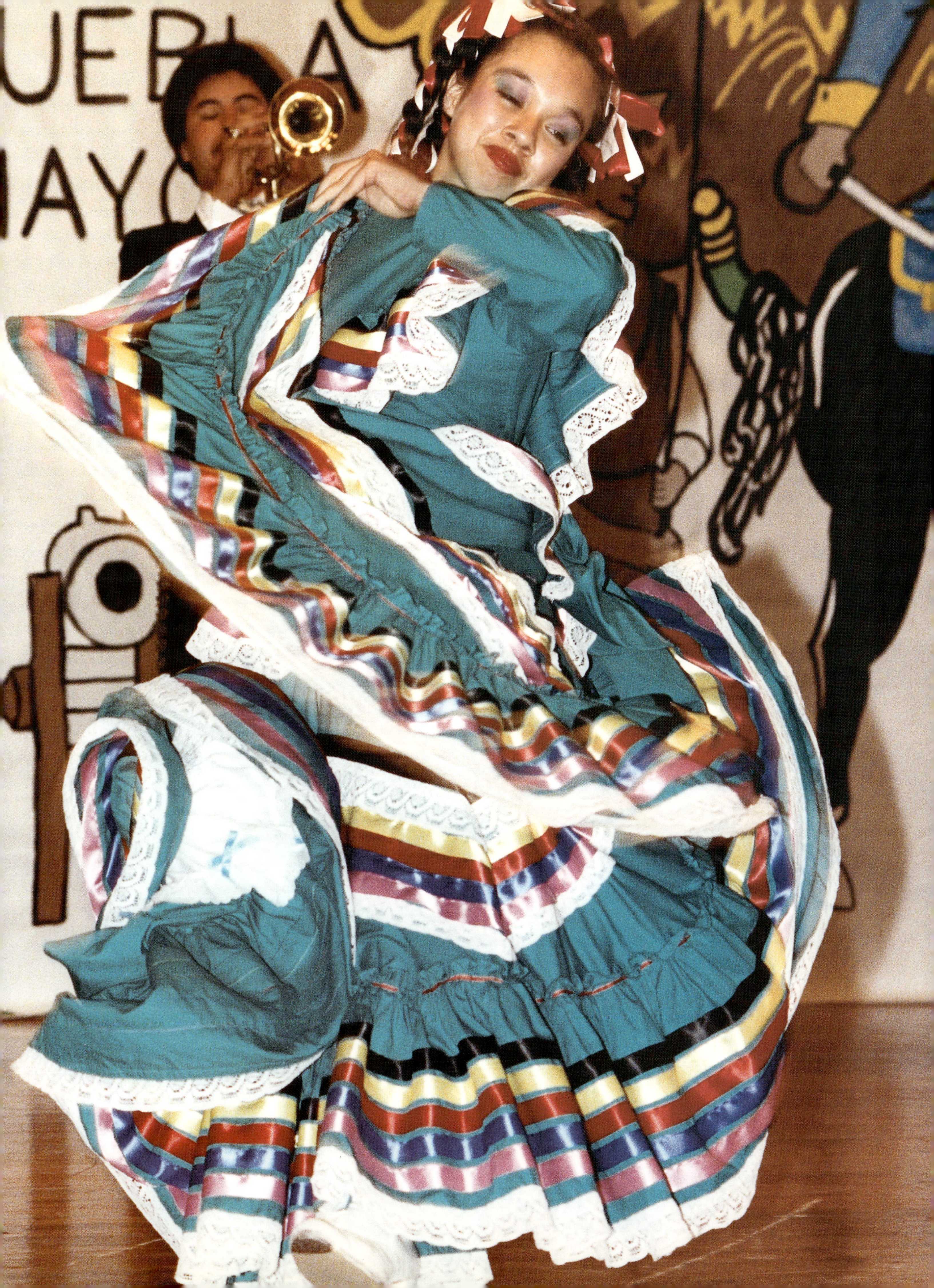
UEBLA
MAY

HOUSTON ★ People ★ Opportunity ★ Success

G*o Texan: Benefiting Youth and Supporting Education. Founded in 1932, the Houston Livestock Show and Rodeo contributed more than $7.7 million to Texas youth and scholarships in 1999. The 18-day annual event draws more than 1.8 million attendees to see rodeo performances, livestock auctions, professional entertainers and an exciting midway of rides and attractions.* ★ *Since 1942, the funds provided by the Houston Livestock Show & Rodeo's calf scramble program (right) have enabled more than 14,605 successful contestants to purchase beef and dairy heifers that they then enter in the next year's livestock judging and auction.* ★ *Sanctioned by the Professional Rodeo Cowboys Association and the Women's Professional Rodeo Association, the Houston Livestock Show & Rodeo only invites the top cowboys (pages 140-141) and cowgirls each year to compete in the seven main rodeo events: bareback bronc riding, saddle bronc riding, bull riding, steer wrestling, calf roping, team roping and barrel racing.*

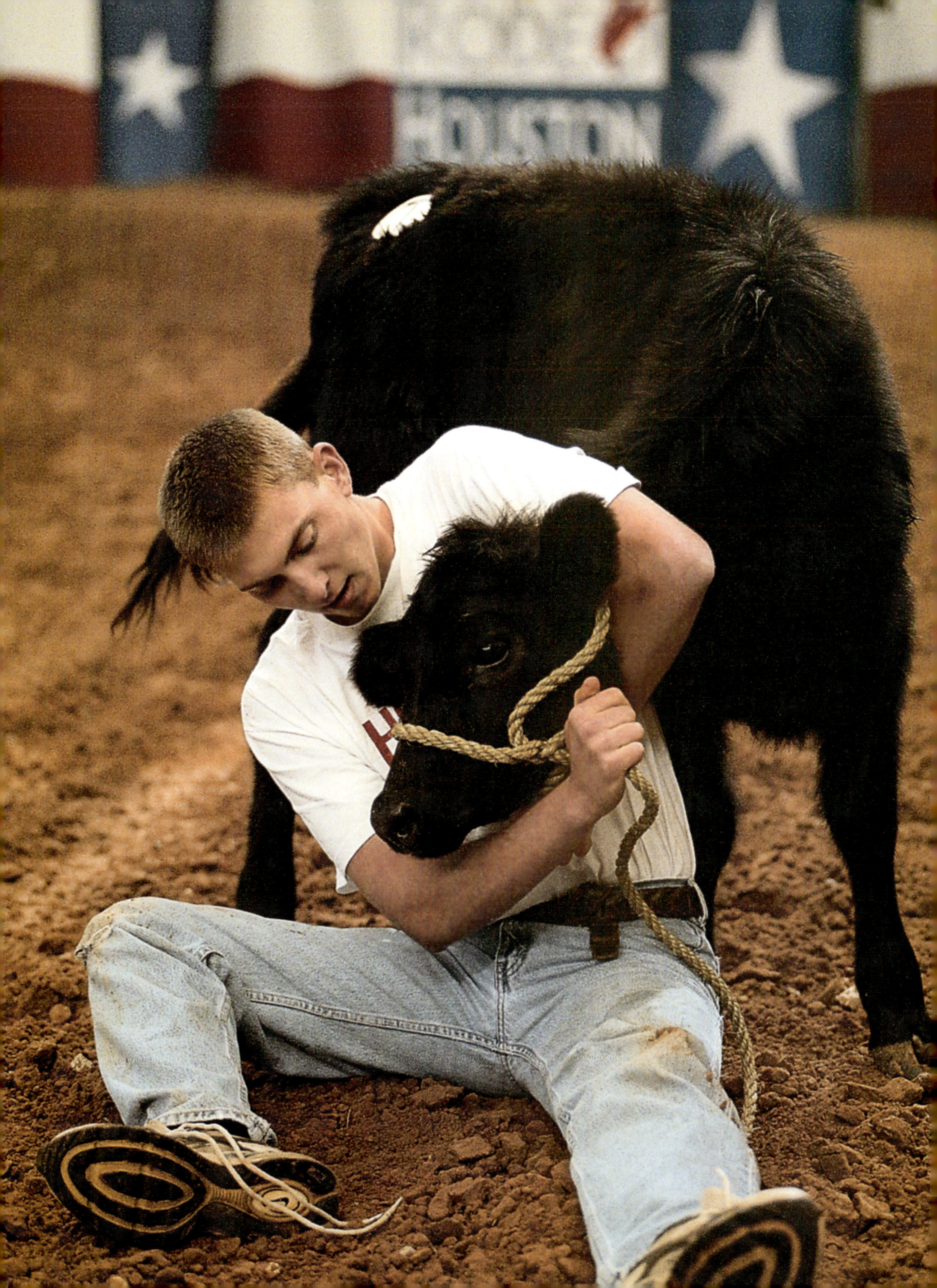
HOUSTON

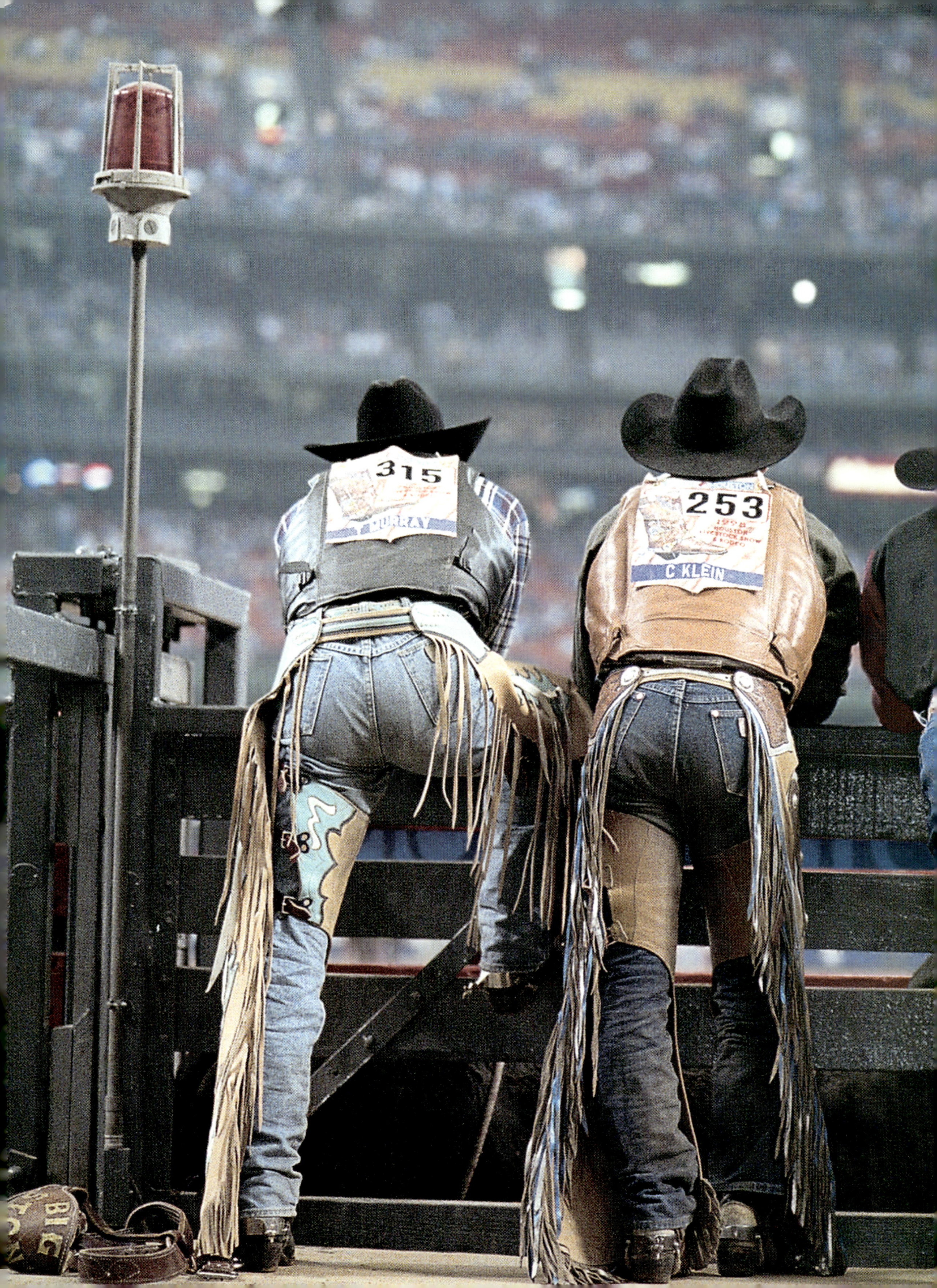
315
MURRAY
253
C KLEIN

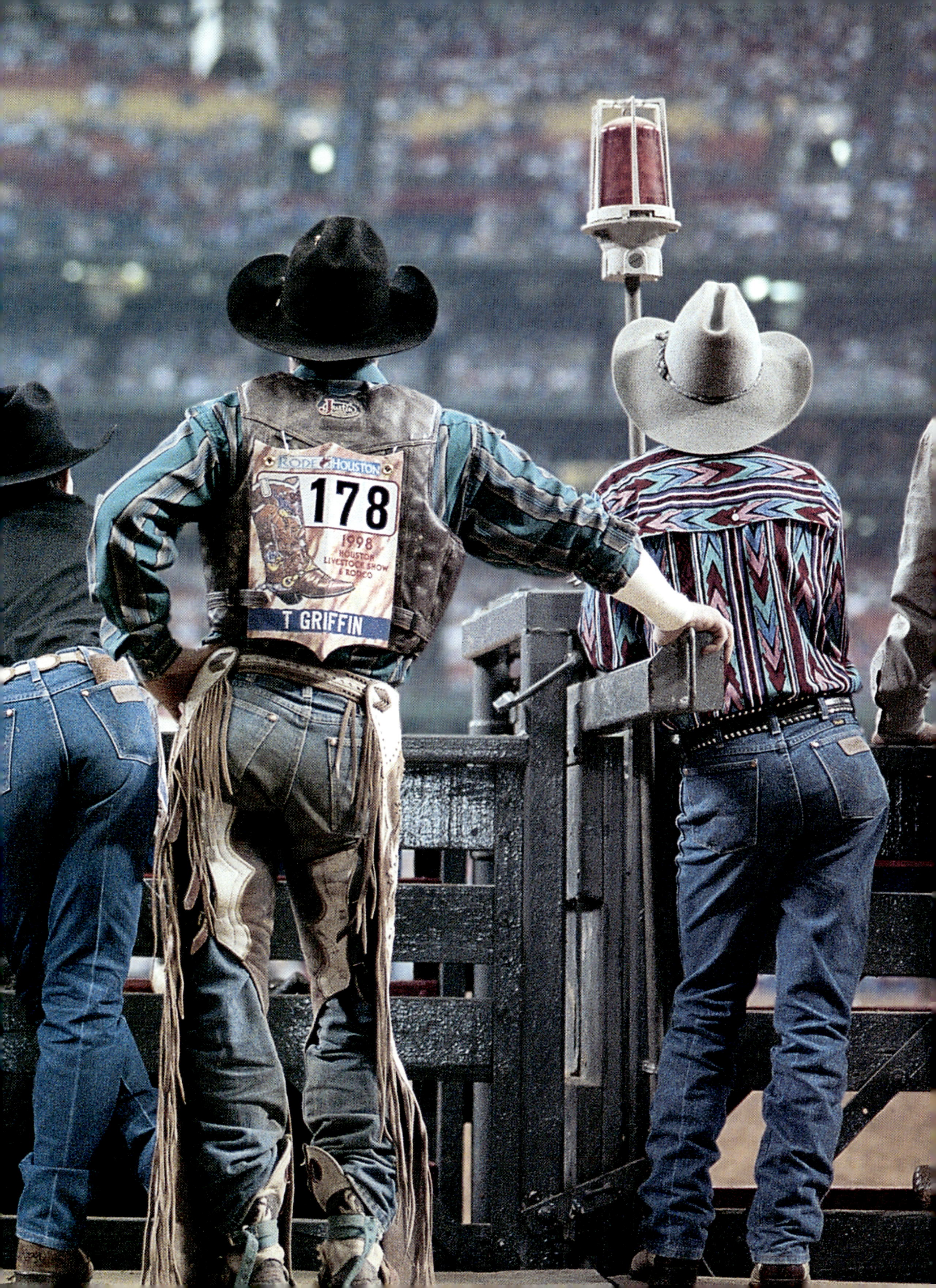
178
1998
HOUSTON LIVESTOCK SHOW & RODEO
T GRIFFIN

HOUSTON ★ People ★ Opportunity ★ Success

Performing Under the Stars. Miller Outdoor Theatre in Hermann Park hosts hundreds of events each year, ranging from the Houston Shakespeare Festival to Broadway musicals produced by Theatre Under the Stars as well as Houston Symphony concerts and Houston Grand Opera productions. The theater is also the site of several cultural and civic festivals throughout the year.

HOUSTON ★ People ★ Opportunity ★ Success

A Home for the Arts in the Woods. Dedicated to providing classical arts events and programs for the people of greater Houston, the Cynthia Woods Mitchell Pavilion in The Woodlands provides a rich assortment of performances, is the summer home of the Houston Symphony and is a major venue for many touring national musicians and groups.

HOUSTON CELLULAR

HOUSTON ★ People ★ Opportunity ★ Success

Modern Wonders and Fields of Dreams. Billed as the "Eighth Wonder of the World" when it opened in 1965, the air-conditioned Houston Astrodome (above) ushered in the era of indoor baseball. Over the years, the Dome also was the site of professional football and other sports events, home of the Houston Livestock Show & Rodeo and site of the 1992 Republican National Convention. ★ Modeled after the Galleria Vittorio Emmanuele in Milan, the Houston Galleria (left) features more than 320 retail stores and restaurants and an indoor ice skating rink. As Houston's most popular shopping center, The Galleria also is one of the region's favorite destinations, drawing shoppers and visitors from throughout the Southwest, Mexico and Latin America as well as other parts of the world.

HOUSTON ★ People ★ Opportunity ★ Success

A New Era for Baseball in Houston. With its retractable roof and a stadium plan designed specifically for modern baseball, the opening of Enron Field (above and right) in 2000 marks the start of a new era in professional sports in Houston and a major boost to the revitalization of downtown Houston.

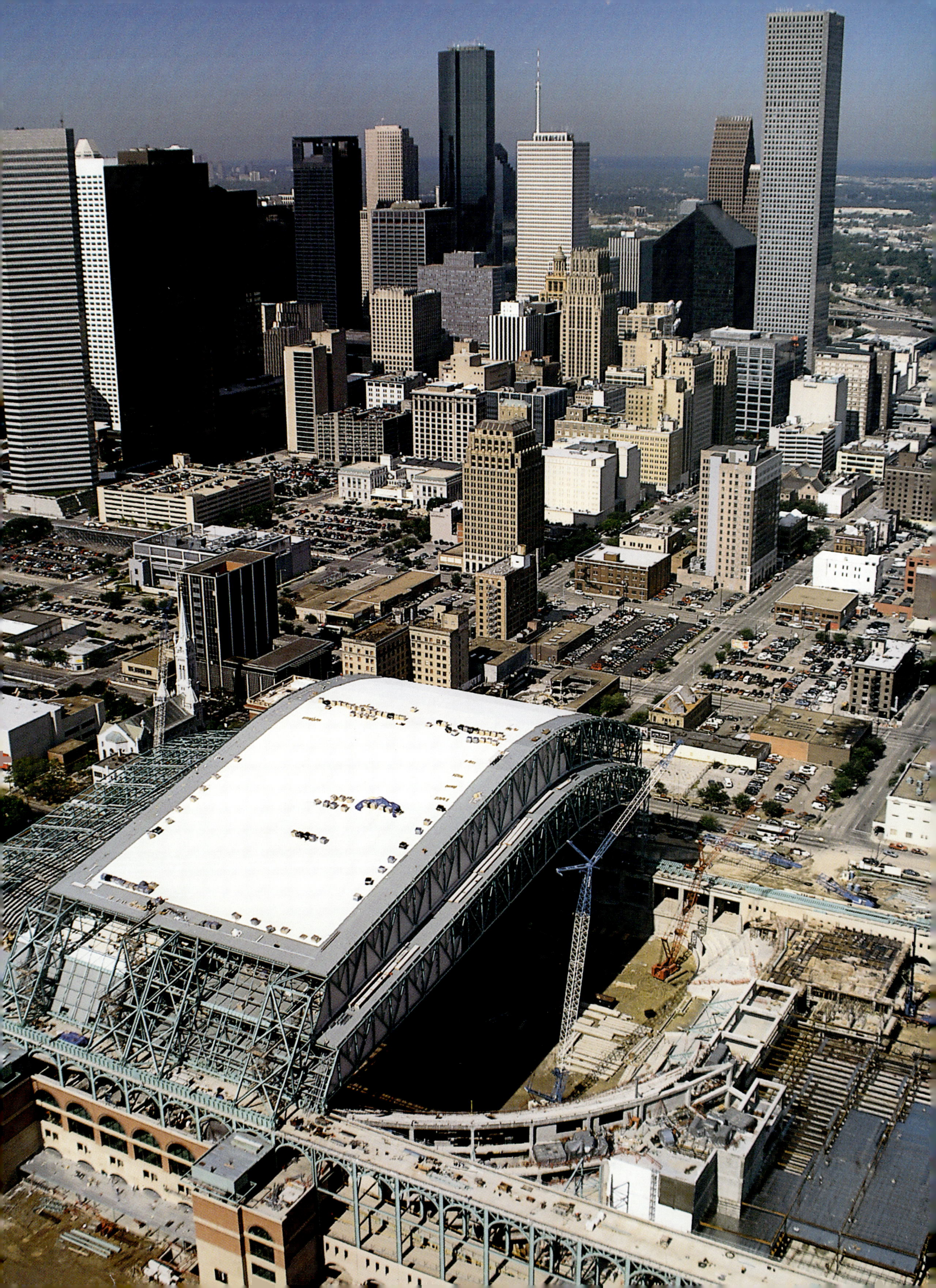

HOUSTON ★ People ★ Opportunity ★ Success

Photo: © 1999 Ellis Vener

A City of World Champions. Led by Tina Thompson, Sheryl Swoopes and Cynthia Cooper, (above, from left) the Houston Comets of the Women's National Basketball Association underscored Houston's position as a city of champions by winning the league's first three world championships. ★ Playing with intensity and desire, Hakeem "The Dream" Olajuwon (right) helped the NBA Houston Rockets secure the city's first world championship trophy. Along the way, he also became the first player to be named NBA MVP, NBA Defensive Player of the Year and NBA Finals MVP in the same season. First recruited to play basketball at the University of Houston, Olajuwon has spent his entire college and professional career in Houston and has been named one of the 50 greatest players in NBA history.

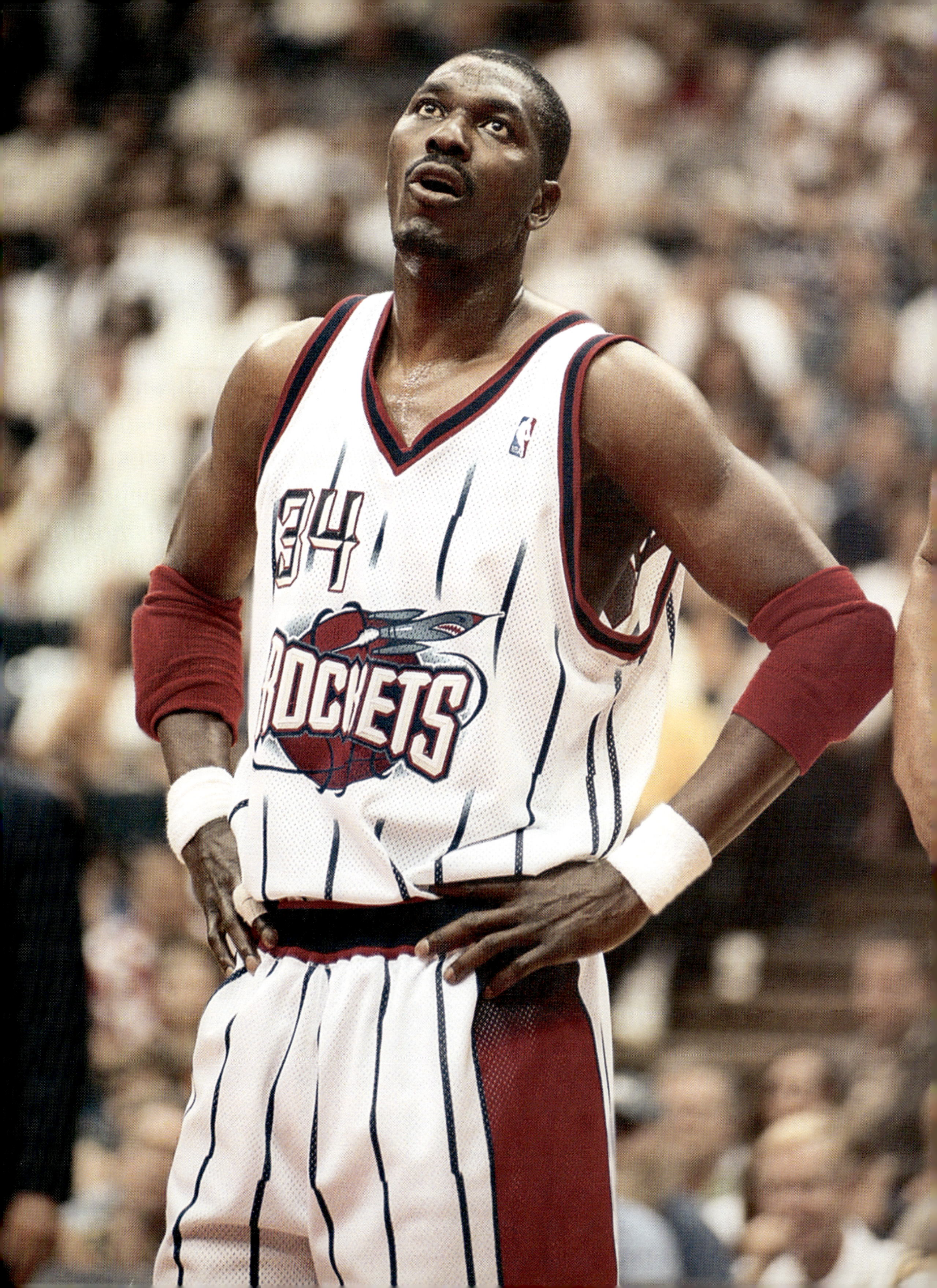
34
ROCKETS

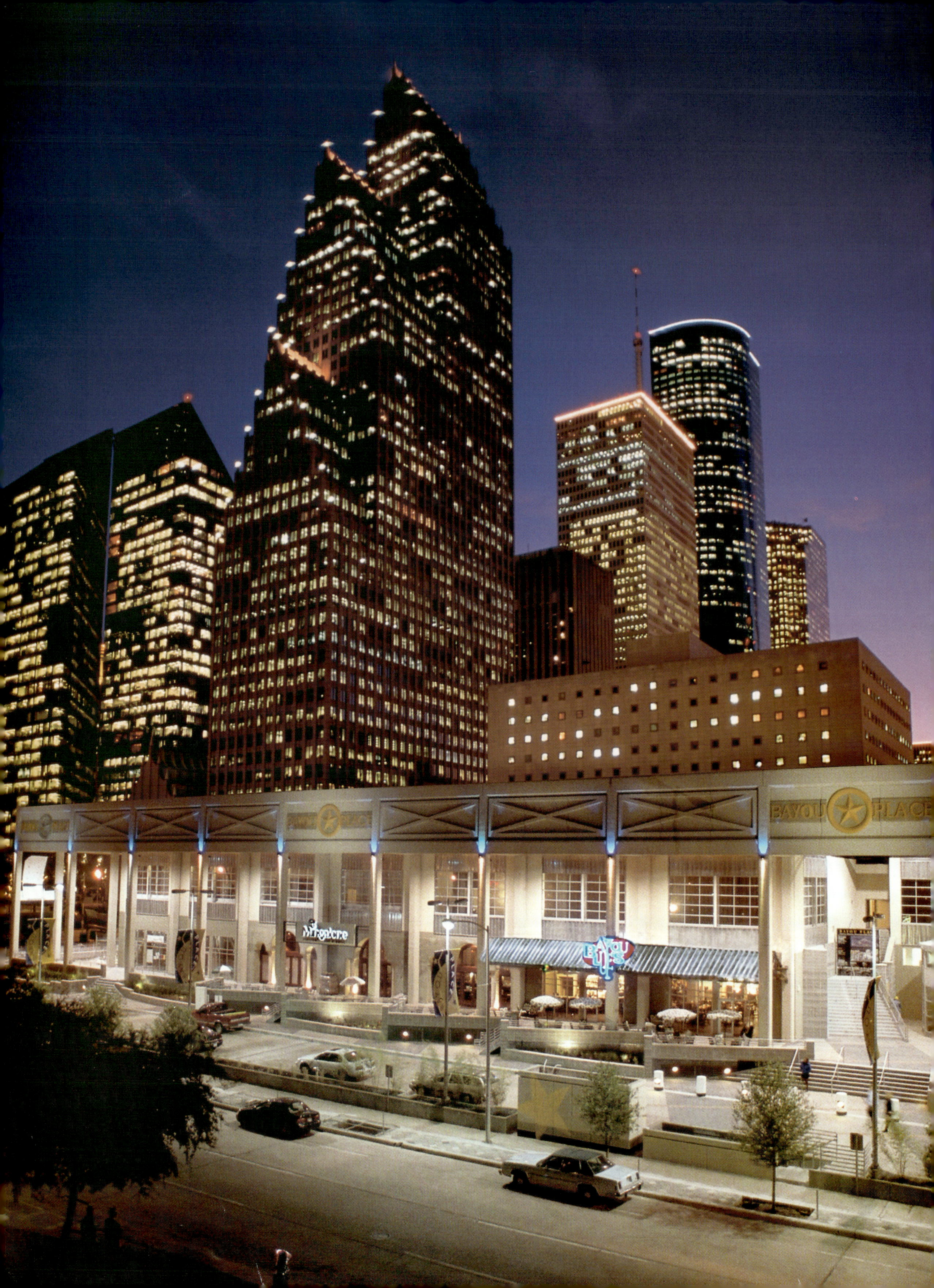
BAYOU PLACE

HOUSTON ★ People ★ Opportunity ★ Success

Life in the Fast Lane. Speeding in front of the George R. Brown Convention Center in downtown Houston, racers in the second annual Texaco/Havoline Grand Prix (above) attracted more than 60,000 race fans in 1999. With its tight corners and lightning-fast straightaways, the race is part of the CART FedEx Championship Series and is broadcast around the world. ★ Featuring restaurants, clubs, live music, billiards and a cinema, Bayou Place (left) has added an extra sparkle to Houston's downtown nightlife.

HOUSTON ★ People ★ Opportunity ★ Success

Enjoying the Nightlife. Houston has been home to many successful regional and national musicians and groups, including La Mafia (above). ★ In the heart of downtown Houston, restaurants such as Cabo (right) have sprung up to cater to a growing number of downtown residents as well as theater-goers and other Houstonians enjoying the resurgence of nightlife.

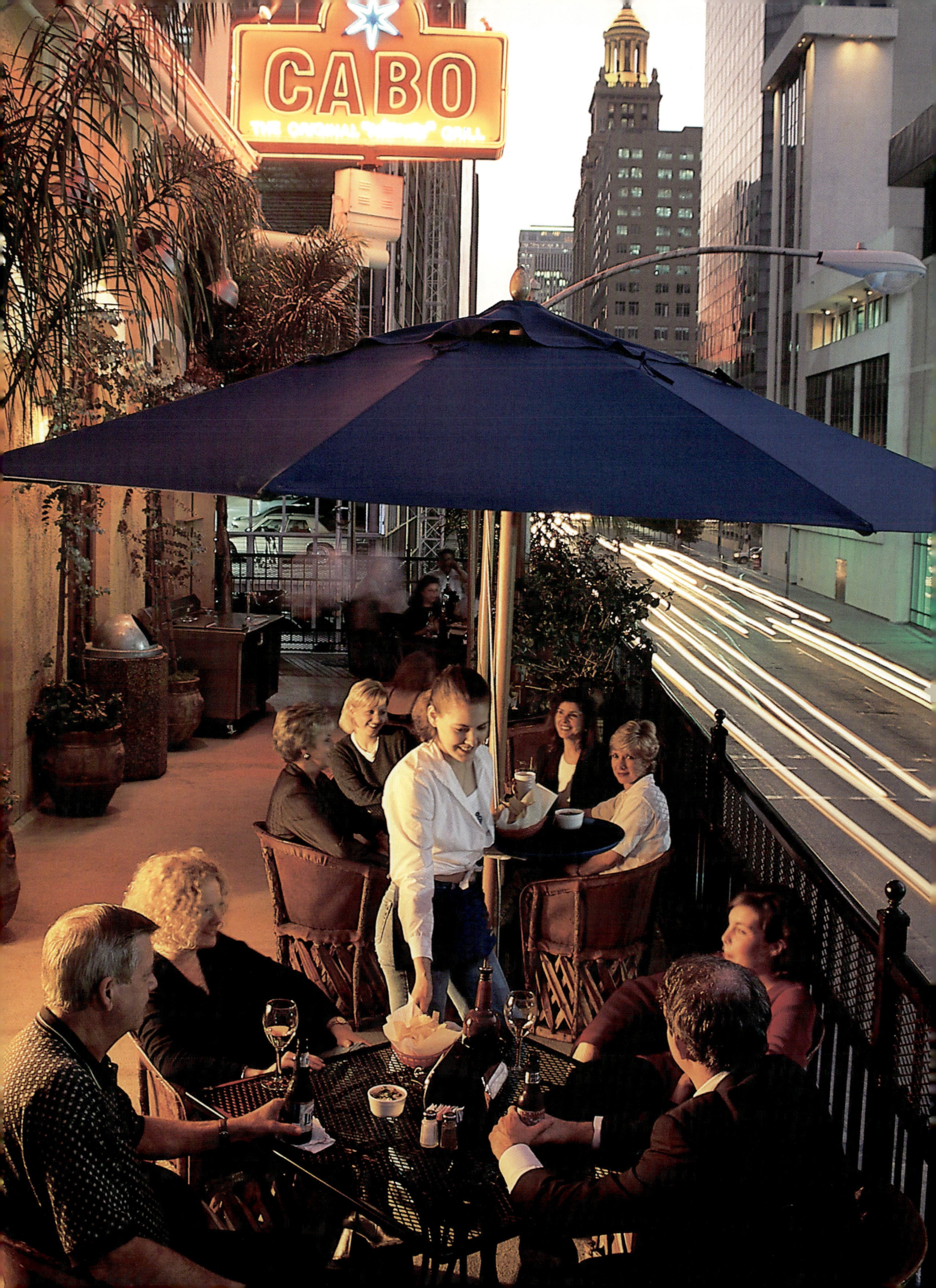
CABO

HOUSTON ★ People ★ Opportunity ★ Success

A Special Time and Place. Each spring brings a blush of color as azaleas come into bloom on the grounds of Bayou Bend and throughout the region. The mansion on the former estate of Houston philanthropist Ima Hogg is also the decorative arts wing of the Museum of Fine Arts, Houston and houses one of the finest collections of American furniture, paintings, glass and textiles from 1620-1870. ★ Located on the banks of Buffalo Bayou, the 14-acre estate of formal and woodland gardens (right) as well as the nearby 155-acre Houston Arboretum provide a quiet sanctuary and woodlands preserve in the heart of Houston. ★ For joggers, walkers and runners, Houston and Harris County offer more than 66 miles of hike and bike and nature trails, including one of the most popular trails through the pines and woods of Memorial Park (pages 156-157). Runners in the annual Houston Marathon pass through the park each January on their way to the finish line in downtown Houston.

Photo: Ray Viator ▶

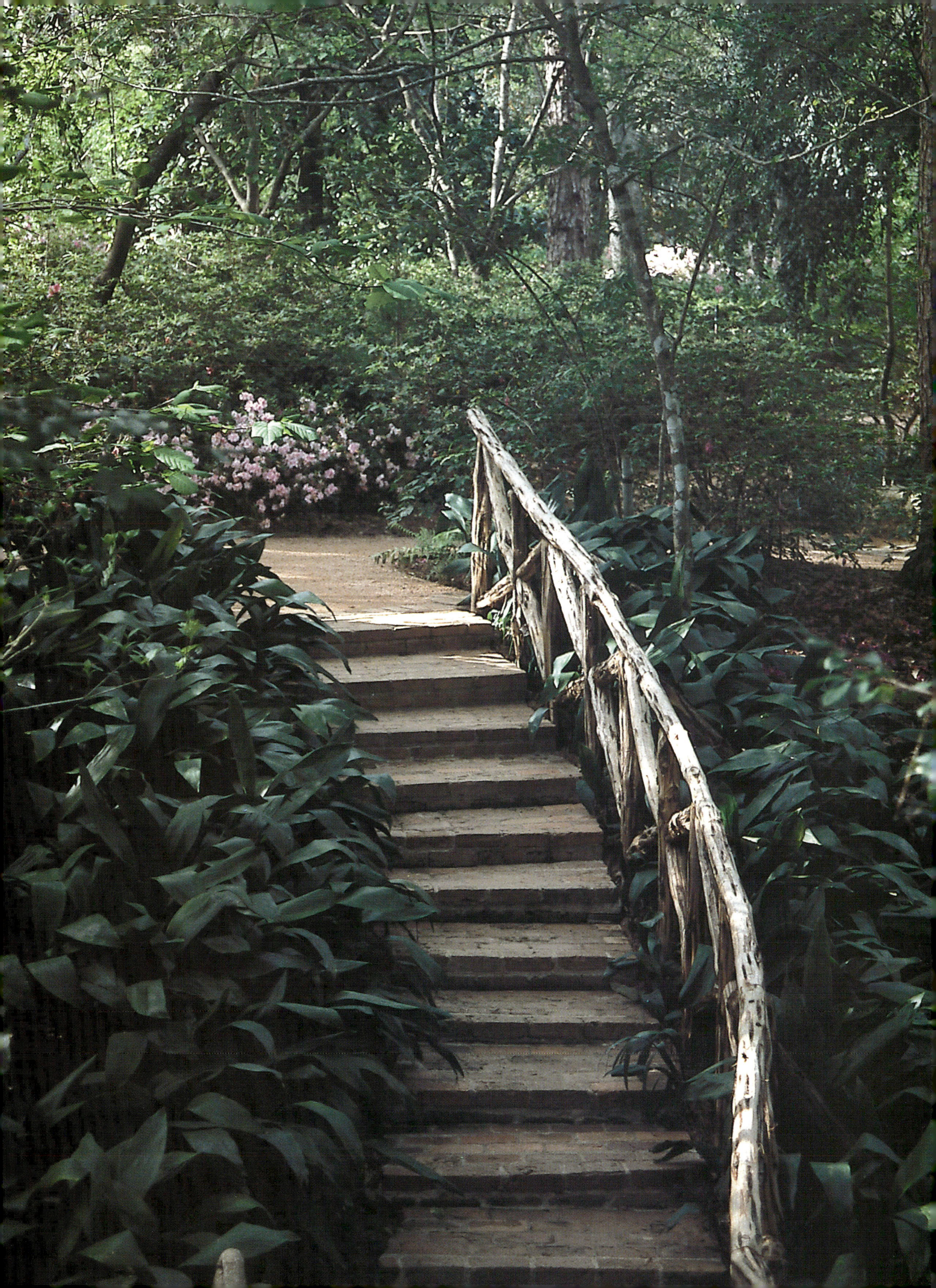

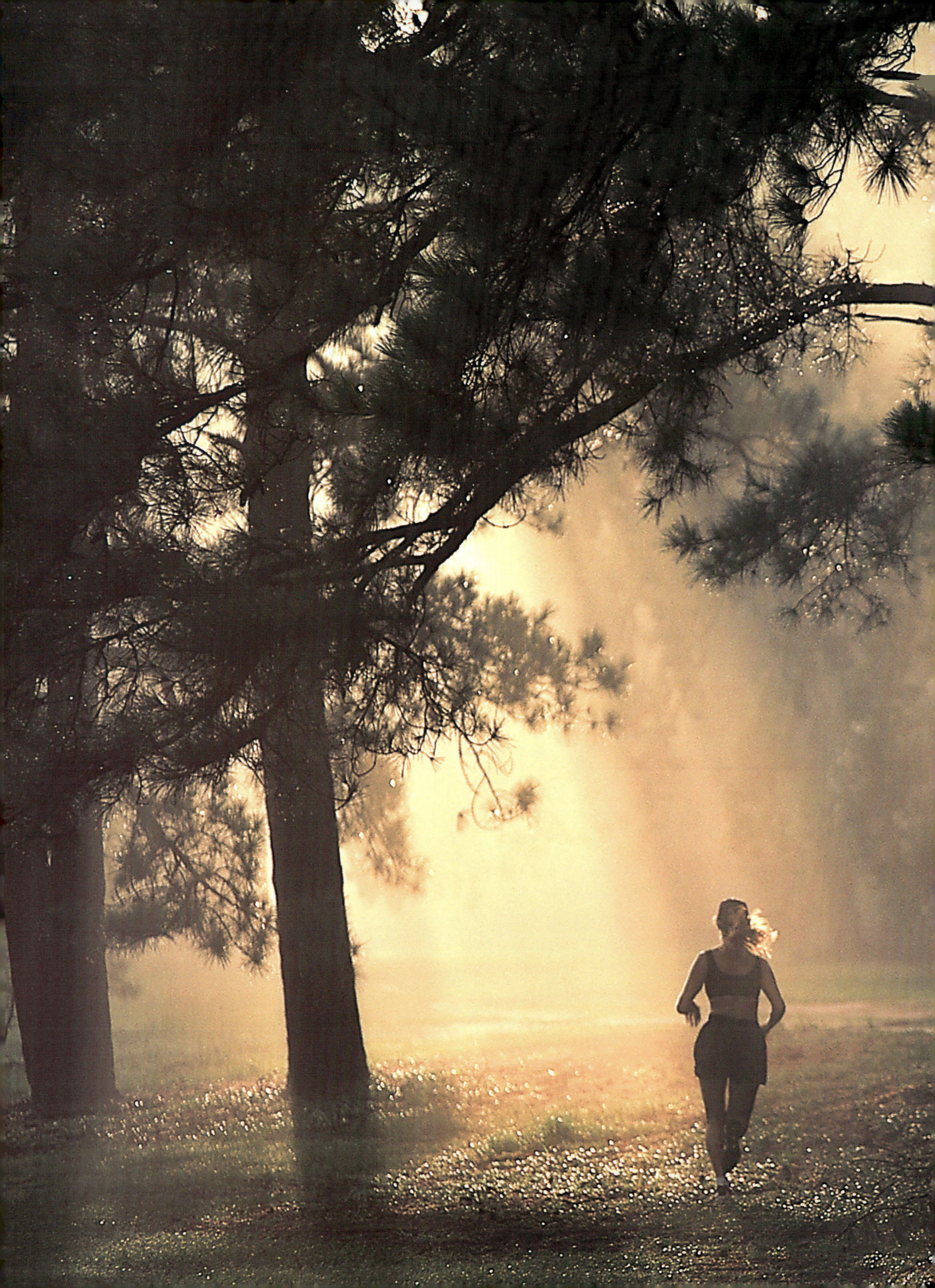

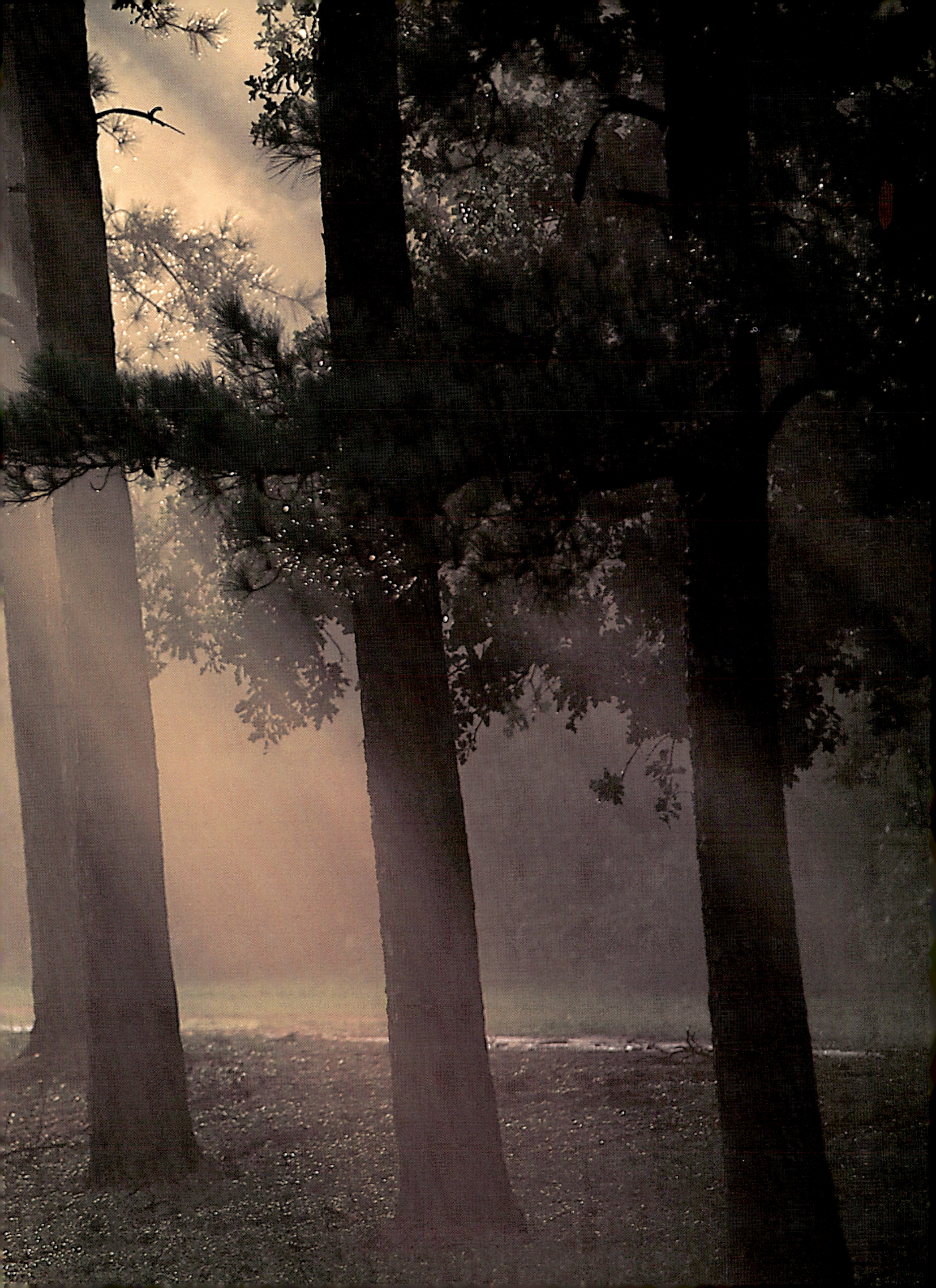

HOUSTON ★ People ★ Opportunity ★ Success

Pushing the Limits. From city streets to dedicated bicycle trails, Houston cyclists roll throughout the region, taking year-round advantage of the area's level terrain. At Cullen Park's Alkek Velodrome, Houston cyclists can try out one of only 19 velodromes in the United States. ★ While the jogging trails of nearby Memorial Park feature special workout stations for joggers and exercise enthusiasts, even the city's public artwork can fill in for an impromptu stretch during a run along Buffalo Bayou's trails.

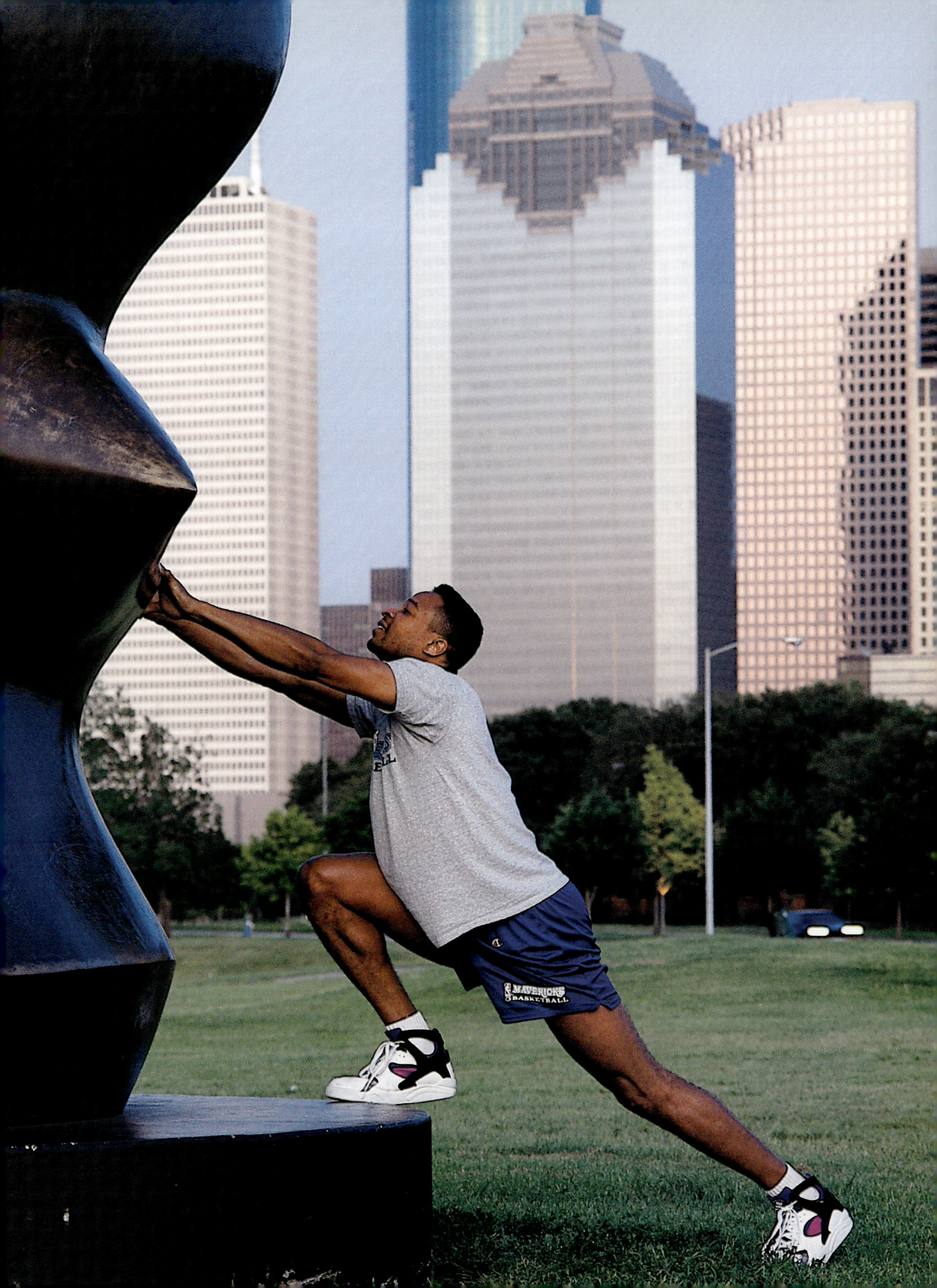
MAVERICKS
BASKETBALL

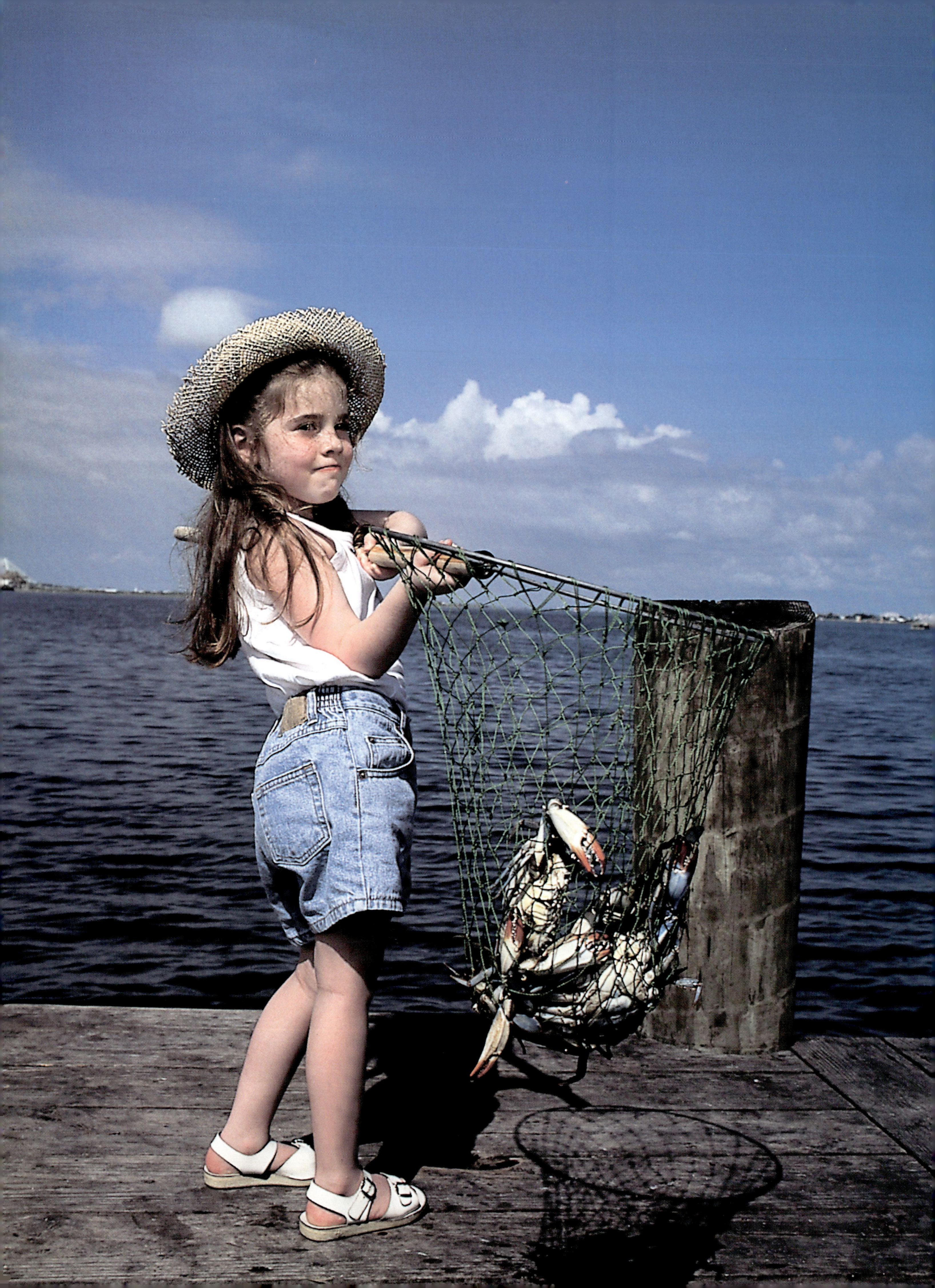

HOUSTON ★ People ★ Opportunity ★ Success

Coastal Harvests of Plenty. Life on the upper Texas Gulf Coast offers a bounty of seafood options that range from blue crabs (left), shrimp and fish harvested from Galveston Bay and along the coast to the lowly crawfish (also known as "mudbugs") that are pulled from coastal marshlands and have become popular favorites at area seafood restaurants and festivals.

HOUSTON ★ People ★ Opportunity ★ Success

On the Water. From the freshwater lakes and rivers north of Houston to saltwater bays, estuaries and the Gulf of Mexico, the Houston area offers boating and fishing options for everyone.

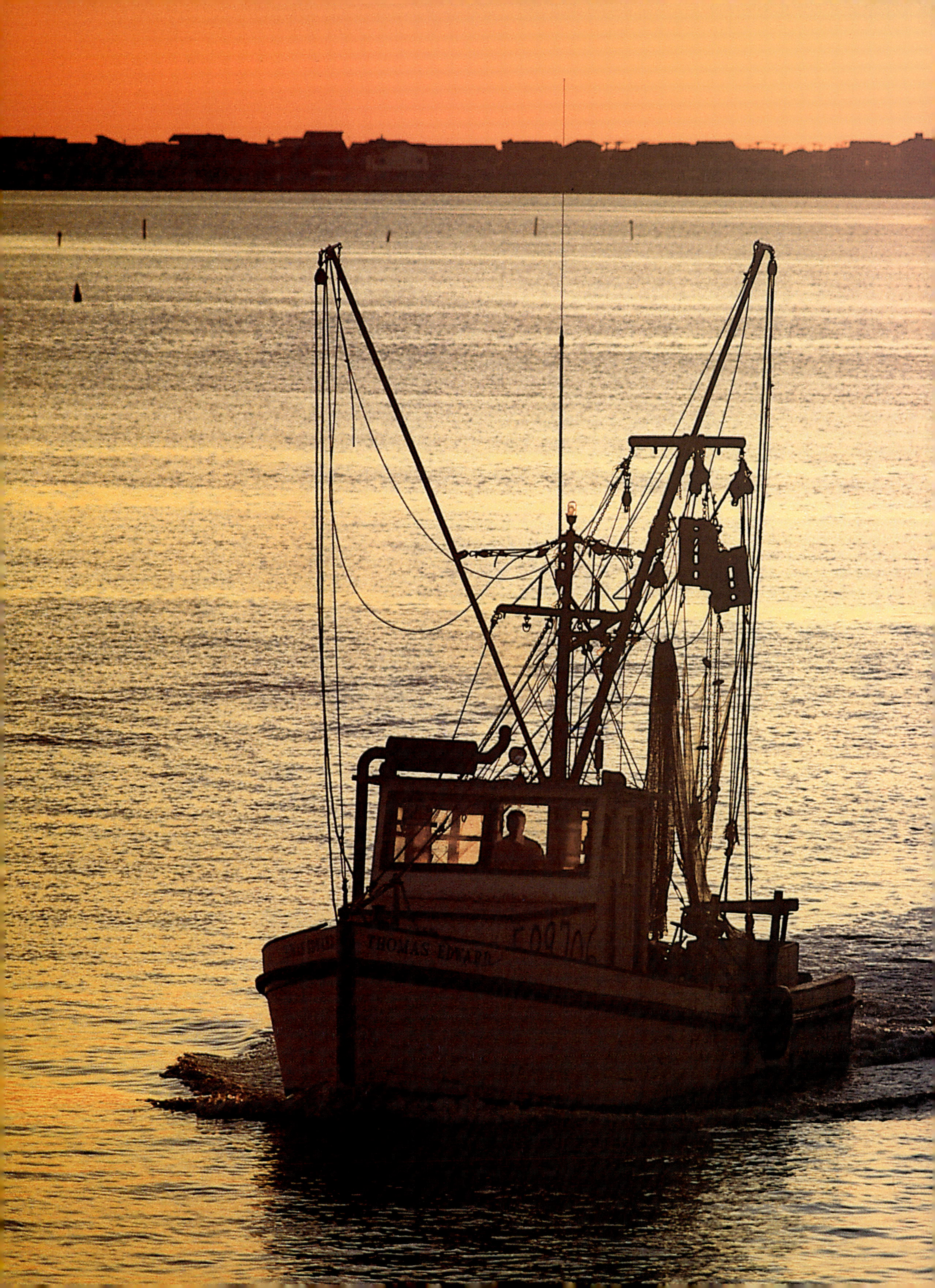
THOMAS EDWARD

HOUSTON ★ People ★ Opportunity ★ Success

Ready to Set Sail. The tiny fishing village of Kemah on Galveston Bay (above) has been transformed into a top visitor destination and a boater's paradise. On the south side of the channel, the Boardwalk at Kemah features shops, rides and attractions and several restaurants, including one with a 50,000-gallon aquarium stocked with 100 species of fish. On the north side of the channel, shrimp boats offer their catch of the day for sale at area fish markets. ★ With more than 7,700 boat slips and seven yacht clubs, the Clear Lake Area (right) on Galveston Bay near NASA's Johnson Space Center is the third largest boating center in the United States.

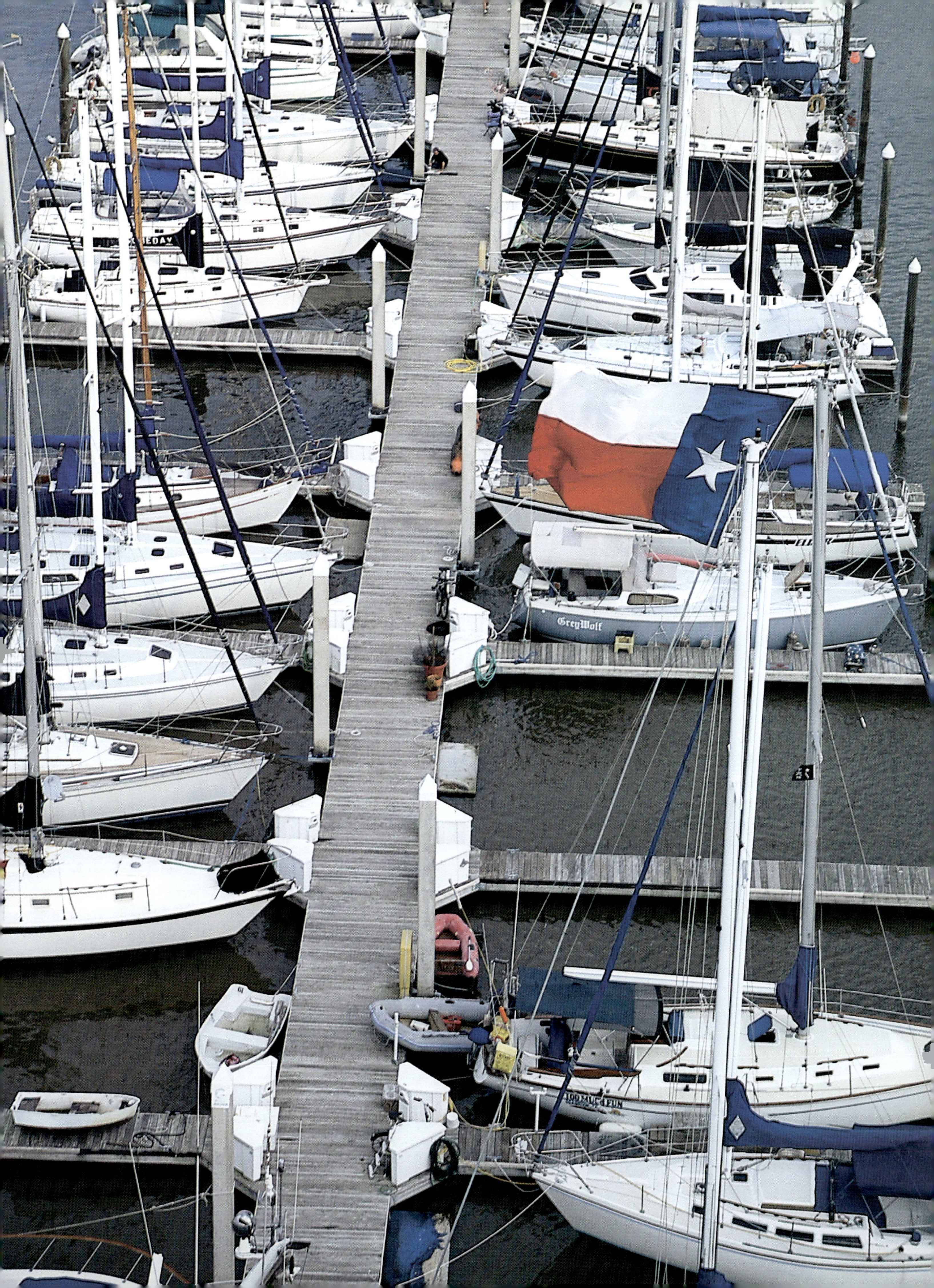
GreyWolf

HOUSTON ★ People ★ Opportunity ★ Success

Houston at the Beginning of the New Millennium

As Houston enters the 21st century and the new millennium, it's important to reflect on the life and times of Houston during the past century. Doing so conjures up many images: portraits of residents who have been drawn to Houston from across the country and around the world; photographs of companies that have helped fuel the world economy and improve the quality of life around the globe; pictures of employees and executives, engineers and architects, teachers and students, scientists and researchers, artists and craftsmen. Each has helped create the ideas and business plans, the tools and technology, the spirit and culture of a city that has grown and matured into a major city for the 21st century and the new millennium.

This once-rural landscape – sliced by bayous and encircled by prairies, forests, lakes and bays – is still home to cattle and cotton and an occasional cowboy. But now it is also a modern, vibrant and cosmopolitan city, resplendent with artists and artisans, museums and theaters, colleges and universities.

Even more important, however, it is a city that welcomes newcomers and new ideas at the start of the new millennium as openly as it did during the start of the 20th century.

What will Houston be like during the next 100 years?

It is a question that is almost impossible to answer or even to comprehend. A century ago, who could have foretold the rise of the energy industry in Houston and its tremendous impact on the region? Who could have predicted the creation of the Texas Medical Center or the myriad medical milestones that have occurred there? At a time before man could fly, who could have forecast that Houston would become the mission control center for flights to the moon and an International Space Station?

It is impossible to predict which research projects taking place today in Houston will have the greatest impact on Houston and the world in the coming century. It could be the discovery of fullerenes at Rice University or the pioneering research in superconductivity at the University of Houston. It could be any of a dozen promising medical and biotechnology research programs at the Texas Medical Center, from cardiac and cancer research to the human genome project and gene therapy programs.

Or, as happened in the 20th century, Houston could become the home to entirely new industries that have yet to begin unfolding.

Regardless of what technology or industries emerge, Houston's role ultimately will be determined by its ability to attract, educate and nurture individuals who embody the commitment, creativity, can-do spirit and entrepreneurial drive of Houston business leaders during the past century. As Houston and the world discovered during the 20th century, it is the people who create opportunities and success – not just for themselves, but for their community, and ultimately their country and the world at large. ■

Reflecting on the Past and the Future. Featuring balustraded terraces, urns, obelisks and a terra-cotta-faced tempietto, the classical architecture of the 1927 Niels Esperson Building stands in contrast to the ultra-modern Reliant Energy Plaza with its 84-foot high open "lantern" or canopy above the top floor. While they mark different eras in Houston's history, both buildings are architectural signatures of their times and representative of Houston's growth, development and progress during the 20th century. ★ Billed as the world's largest celebration in the sky, the fireworks and lasers of "Sky Power & Beyond" (pages 168-169) are the highlight of Reliant Energy's Power of Houston celebration, the city's premiere fall festival. The 10-day event highlights the best of Houston and promotes community volunteerism.

Photo (pages 168-169) Courtesy Reliant Energy HL&P ▶▶

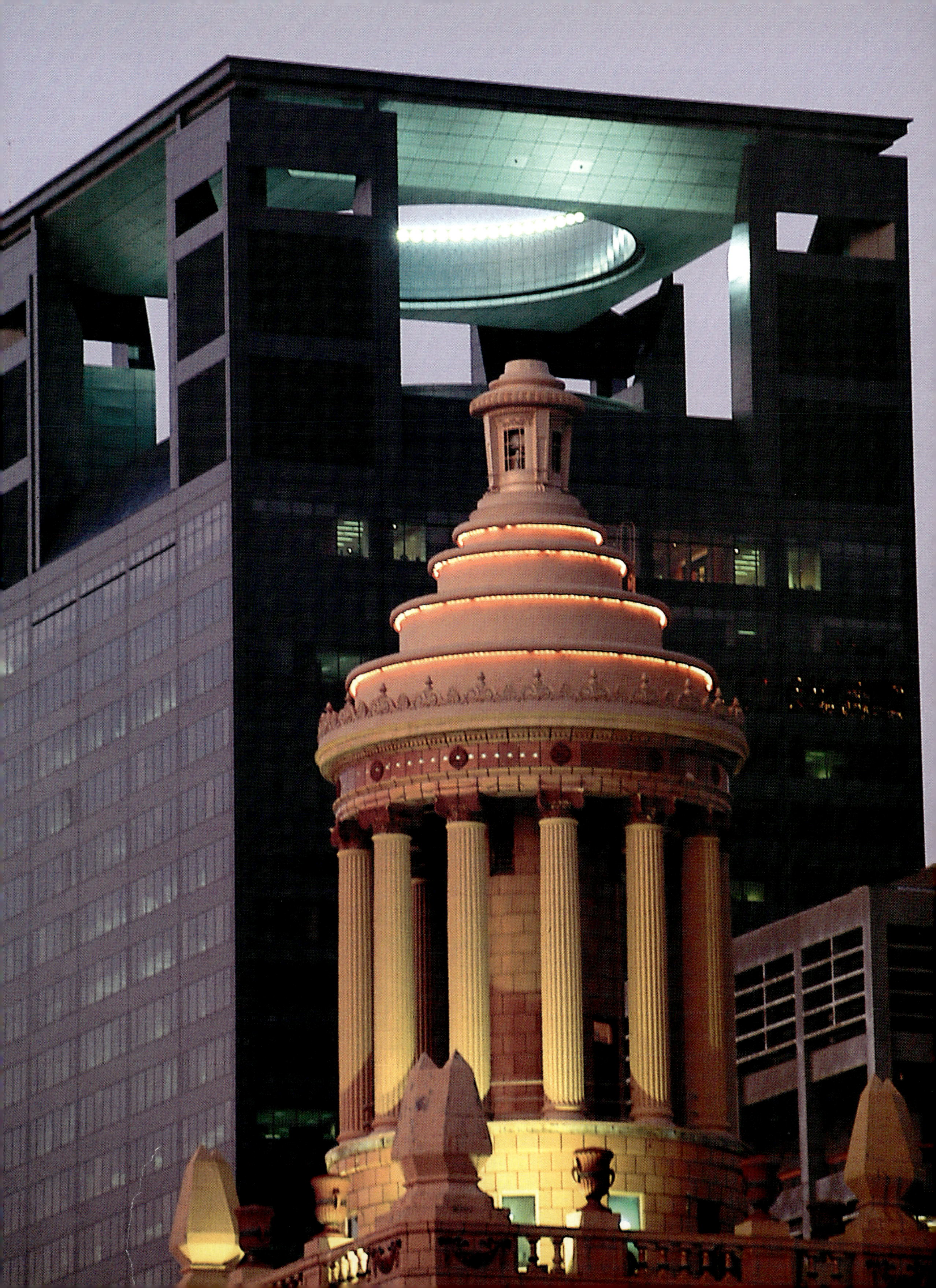

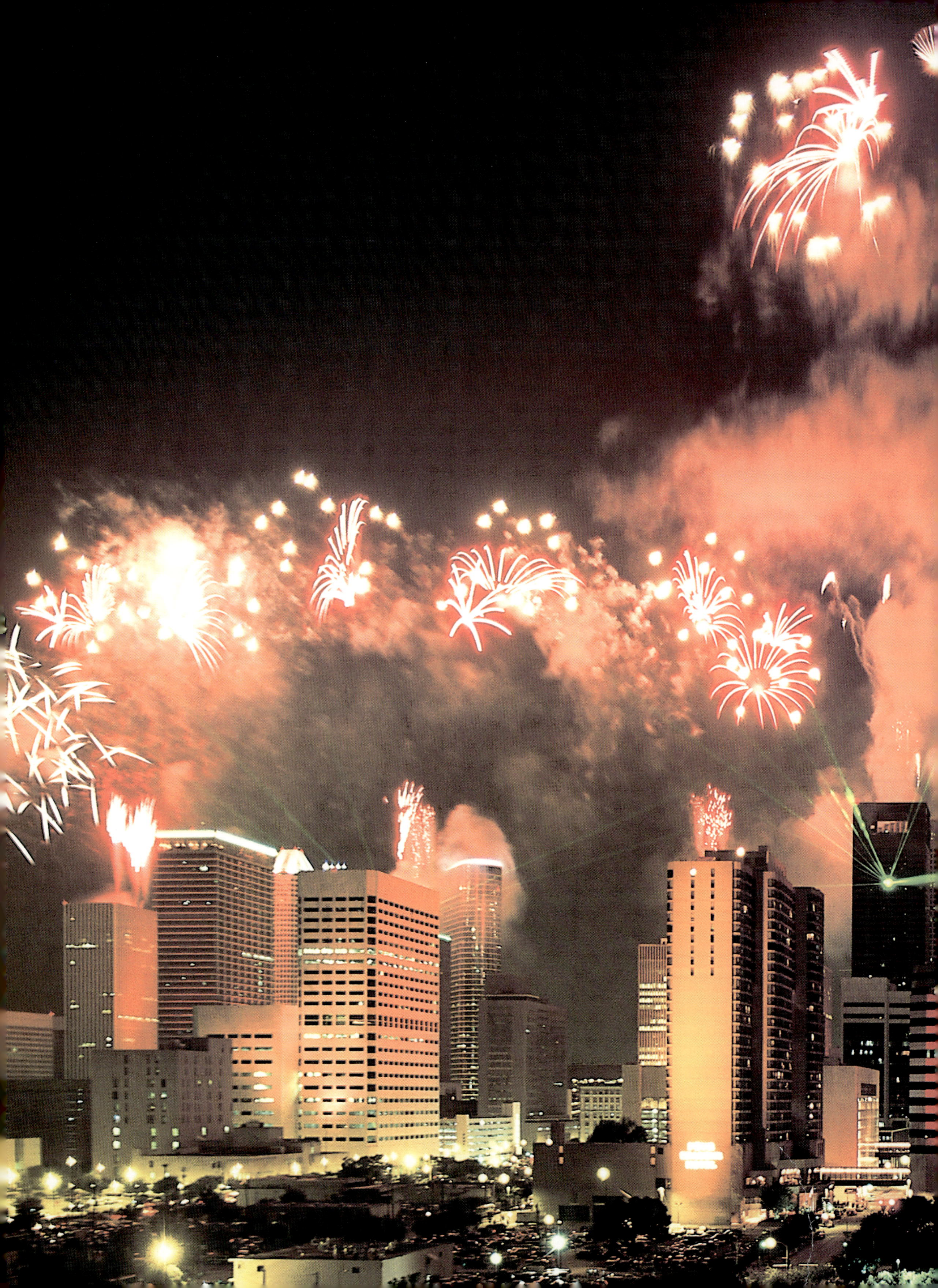

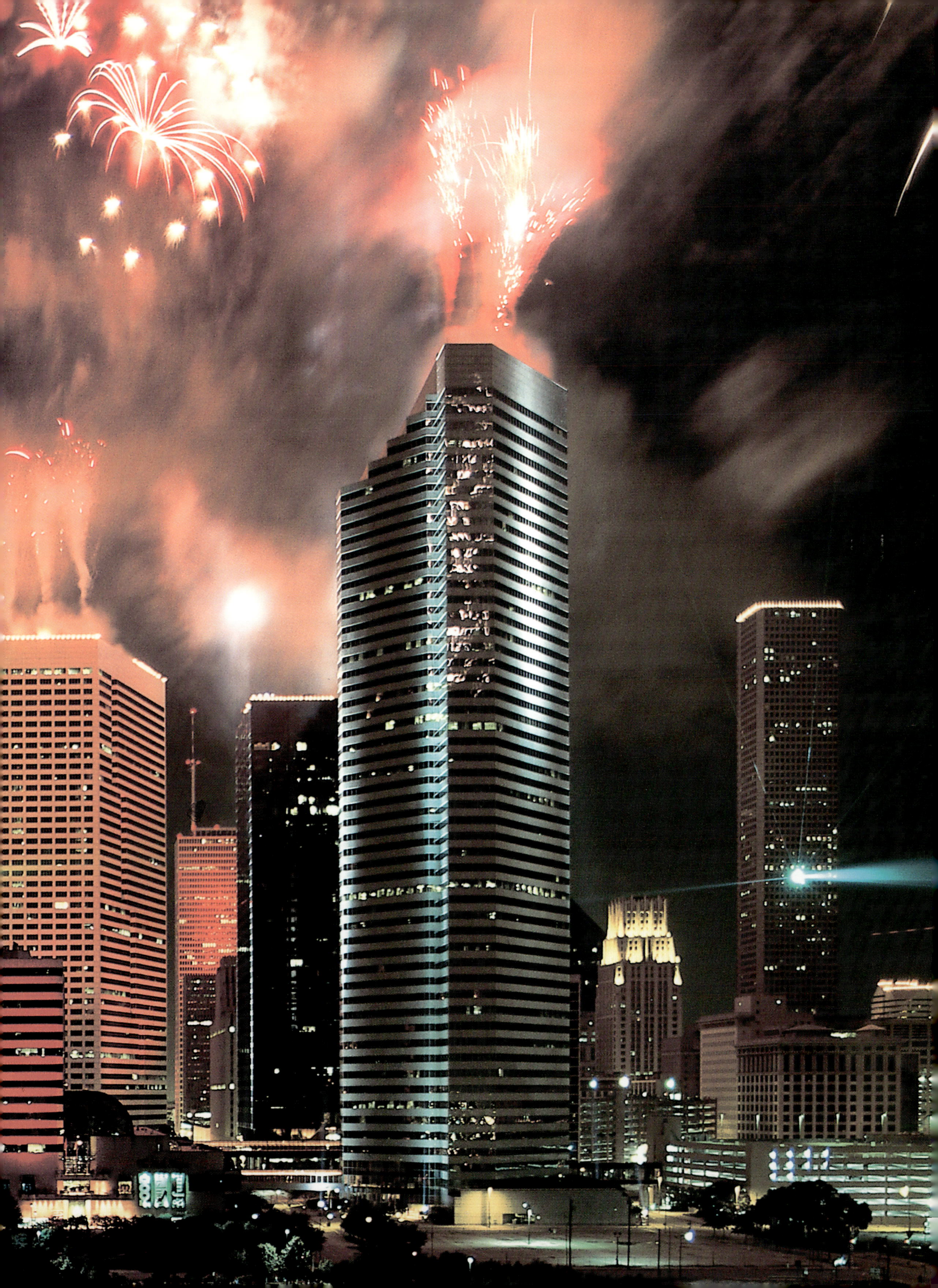

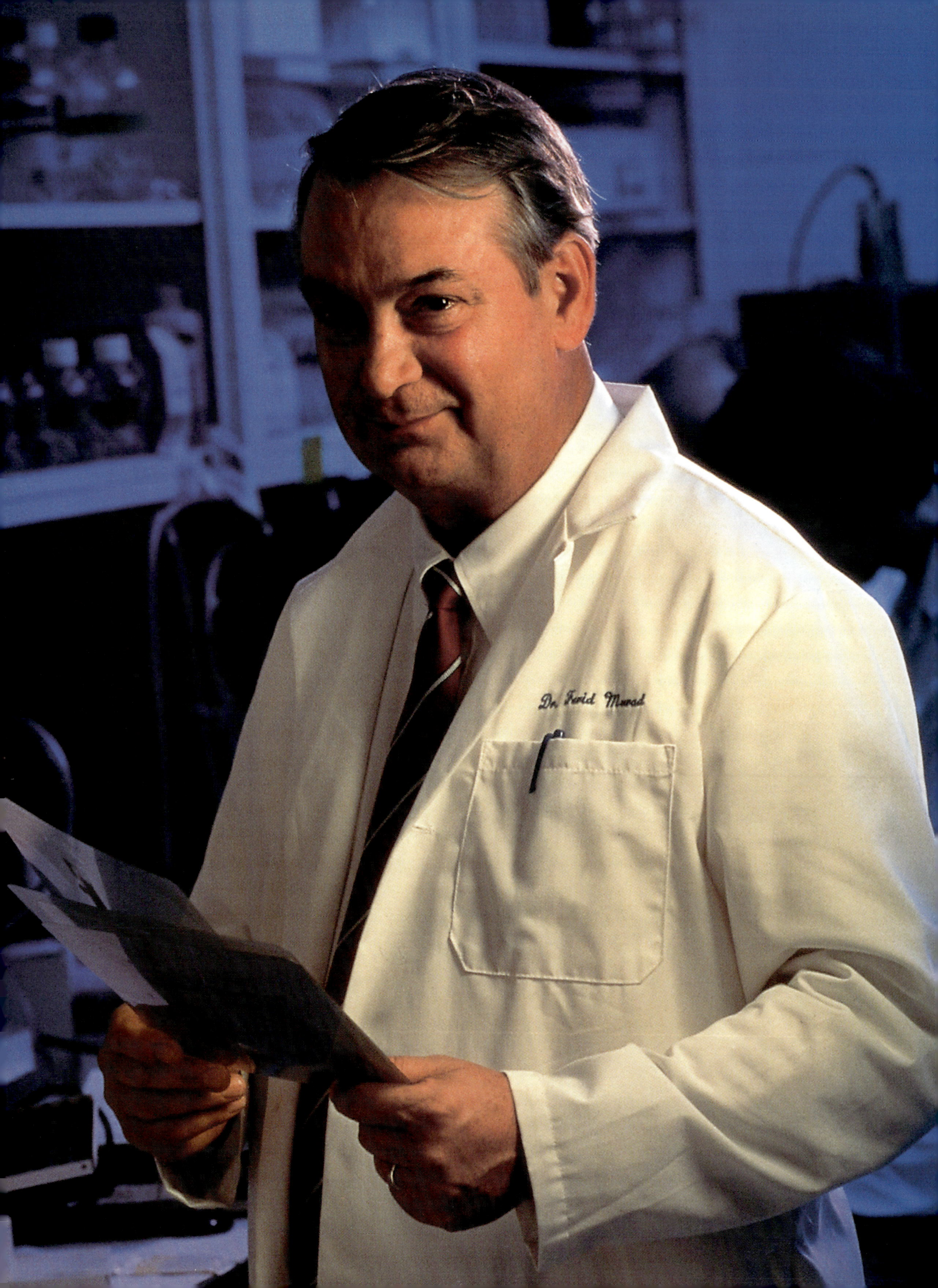
Dr. Ferid Murad

HOUSTON ★ People ★ Opportunity ★ Success

Modern Explorers. *Houston's future is likely to be influenced by the $500+ million in scientific research taking place in the labs and research centers of the Texas Medical Center, the University of Houston, Rice University and other area institutions and companies.* ★ *Rice University chemistry professors Robert Curl (above, right) and Richard Smalley were awarded the 1996 Nobel Prize in Chemistry for their discovery of fullerenes. The molecules may provide the basis for new super strong yet light materials, semiconductors for computers, new drug delivery systems, affordable solar cells and superconductors.* ★ *Ferid Murad, M.D., Ph.D., chairman of the Department of Integrative Biology, Pharmacology and Physiology at The University of Texas-Houston Medical School, (left) received the 1998 Nobel Prize in Physiology or Medicine for his work on nitric oxide, a colorless, odorless gas that signals blood vessels to relax and widen, which in turn lowers blood pressure. His discovery has a wide range of possible applications, including treating heart disease and shock.*

1995 TRILATERAL
BUSINESS
CONFERENCE

HOUSTON, TEXAS

HOUSTON ★ People ★ Opportunity ★ Success

Houston's Role on the World Stage. Houston's future in the new millennium will likely be influenced both by international developments and its commitment to developing a world-class educated workforce. ★ As the state's premier metropolitan research and teaching institution, the University of Houston (above) will have a significant impact on the future of Houston. With more than 30,000 students pursuing undergraduate, graduate and professional degrees, the university is also home to over 40 research centers and institutes, and sponsors more than 300 partnerships with corporate, civic and governmental entities. ★ During the 20th century, Houstonians such as President George Bush (left) represented the city and the country's interests in world affairs and reflected the area's strong interest in international trade and business.

◀ *Photo © Houston Chronicle*

HOUSTON ★ People ★ Opportunity ★ Success

Preparing for the Future. Texas Southern University (above) has served as a cornerstone for developing the potential in leaders from varied socio-economic, cultural, and racial backgrounds. The university is a leader in the preparation of minority health professionals, pharmacists, physicians, lawyers and many other professionals. Like its curriculum, the university's student population is characterized by diversity, representing almost every state in the country and more than 50 nations. ★ Chartered in 1891, Rice University (right) established early on a rich tradition of teaching and research of the highest quality and consistently ranks among the top 15 research universities in the nation. Rice faculty are very well represented in both the National Academy of Sciences and the National Academy of Engineering.

ENSE PETIT PLACIDAM
SUB LIBERTATE QUIETEM

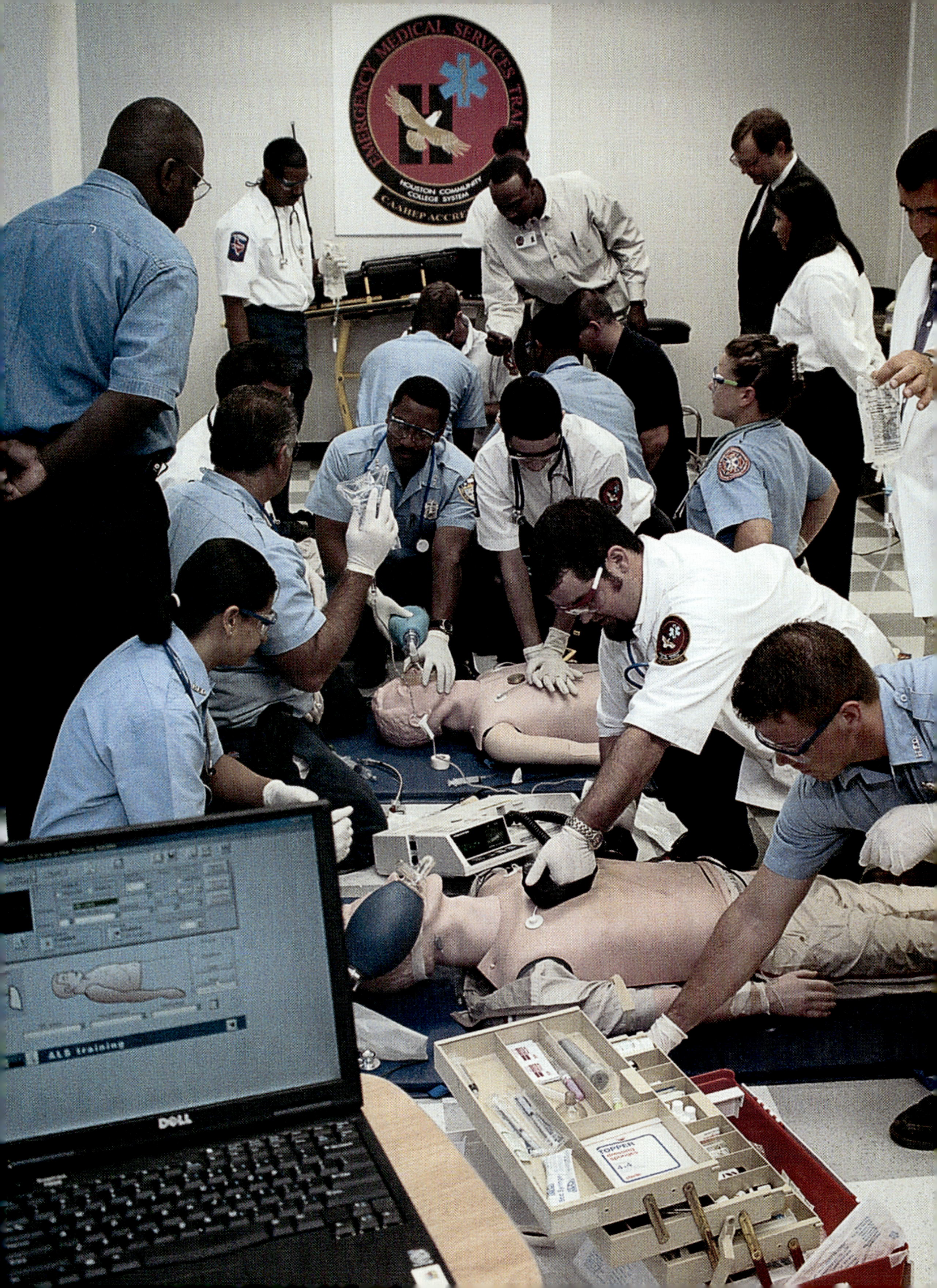
EMERGENCY MEDICAL SERVICES
HOUSTON COMMUNITY COLLEGE SYSTEM
ALS training
DELL

HOUSTON ★ People ★ Opportunity ★ Success

*T*he Future in Their Hands. As the largest public school system in Texas and the seventh largest in the United States, the Houston Independent School District (above) serves a diverse student population in both traditional and alternative classroom settings. Over the past decade, HISD has become a national leader in restructuring public education to meet the present and future needs of a fast-paced, technology-oriented society. ★ Serving more than 55,000 students, the Houston Community College System (left) is the fourth largest community college in the United States. In addition to one of the best-rated courses for emergency medical technicians, the Houston Community College System offers a variety of programs and courses designed to help students keep pace with changing technology and the growing international economy.

177

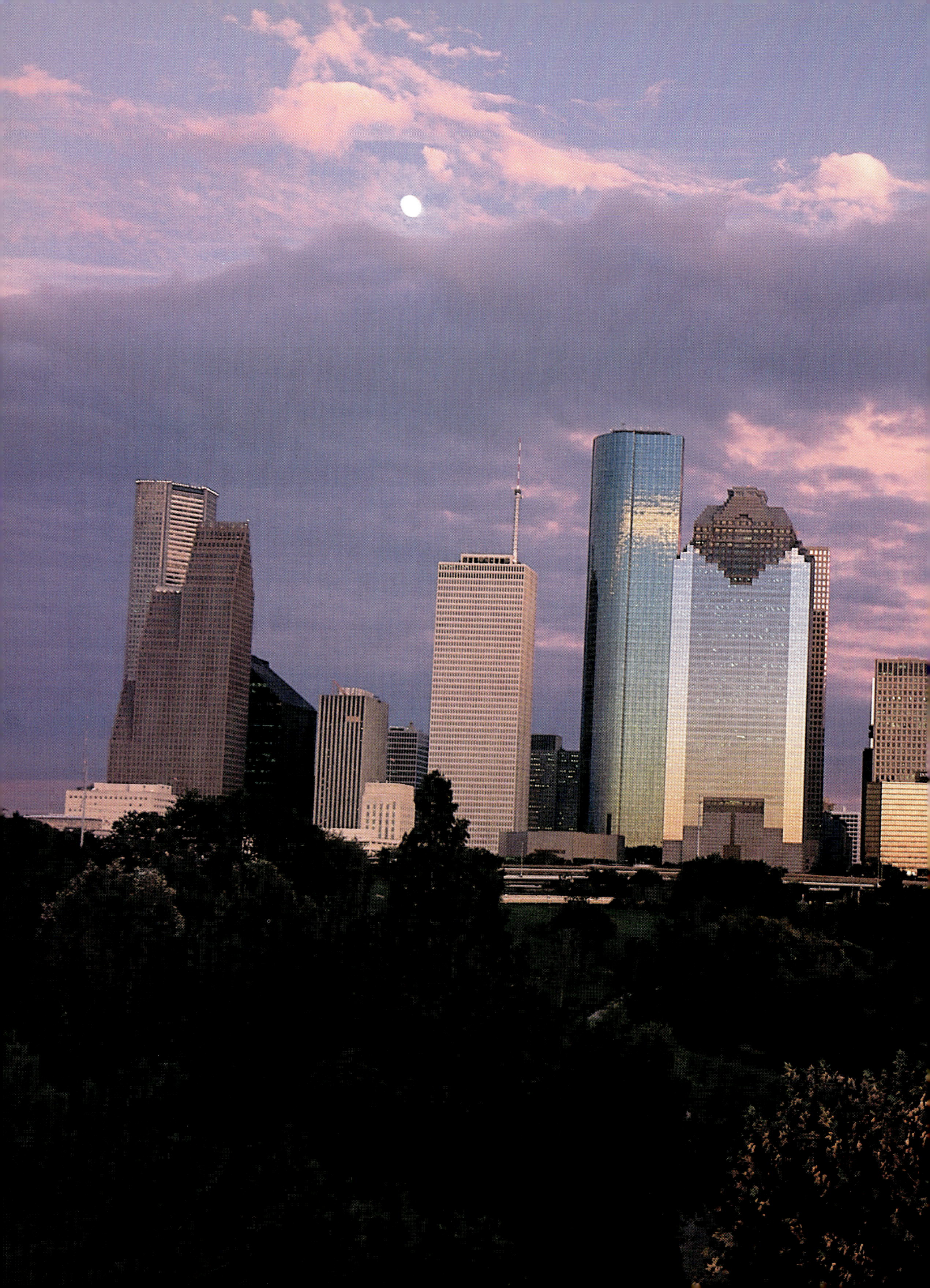

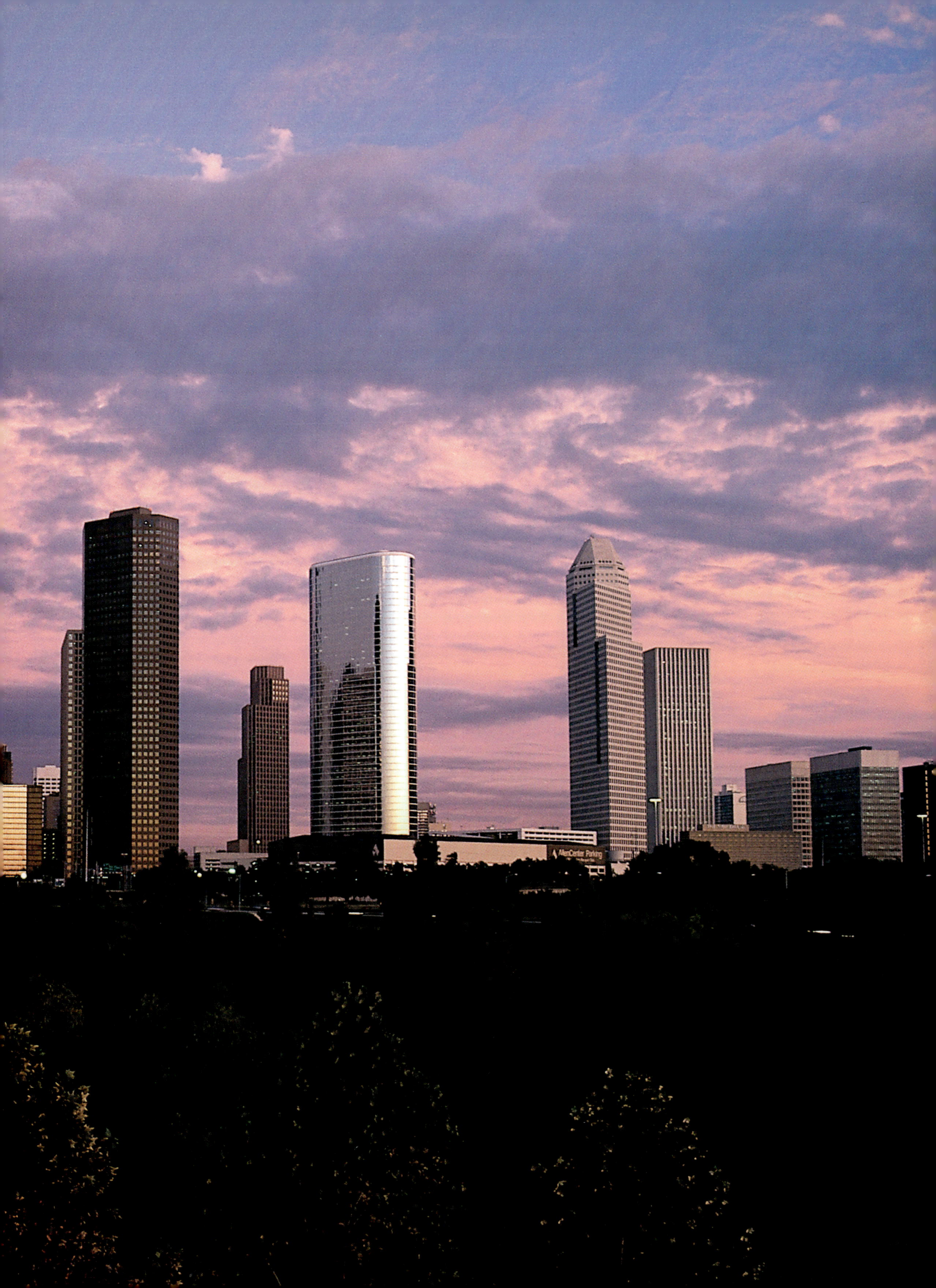
AllenCenter Parking

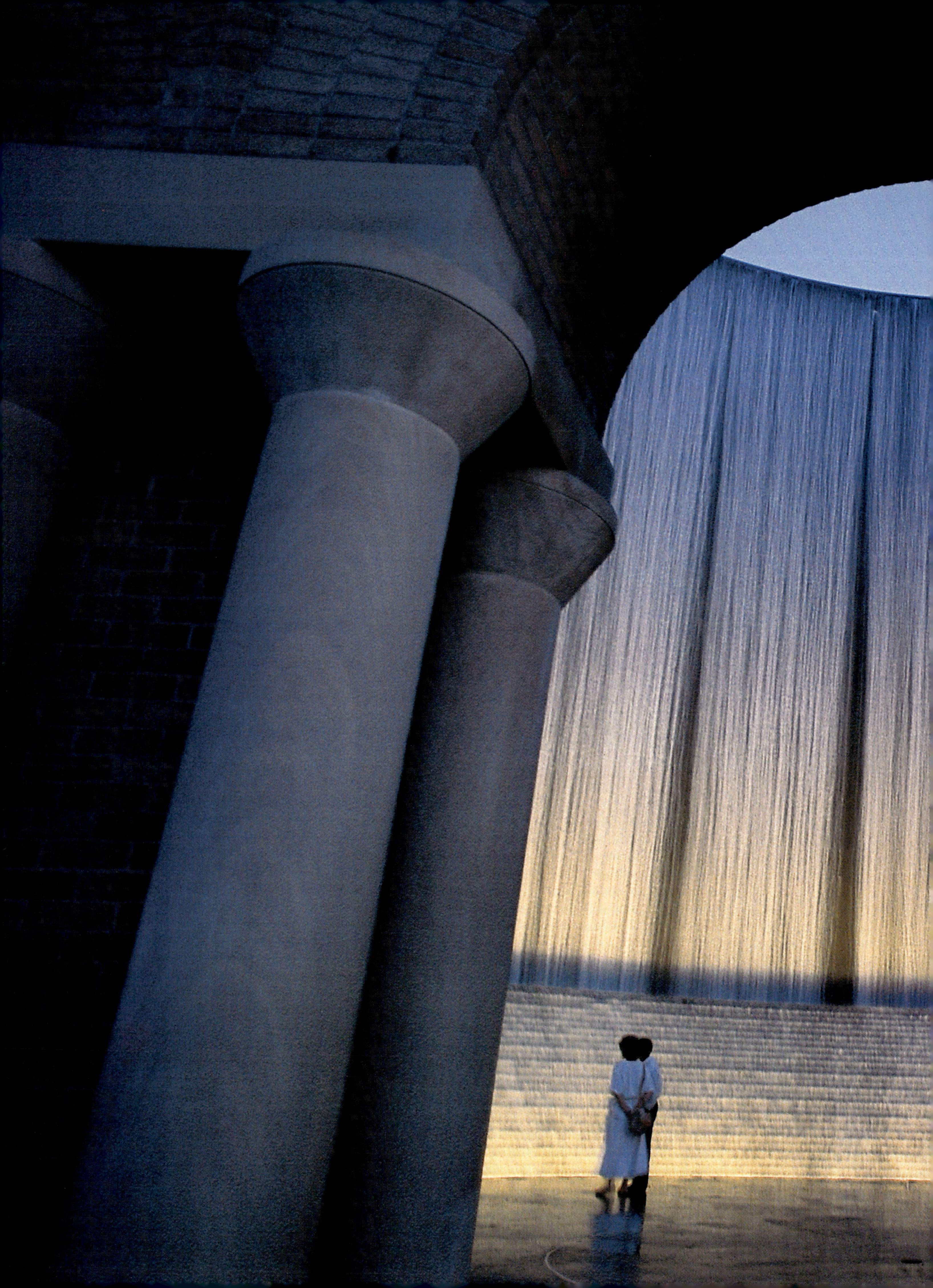

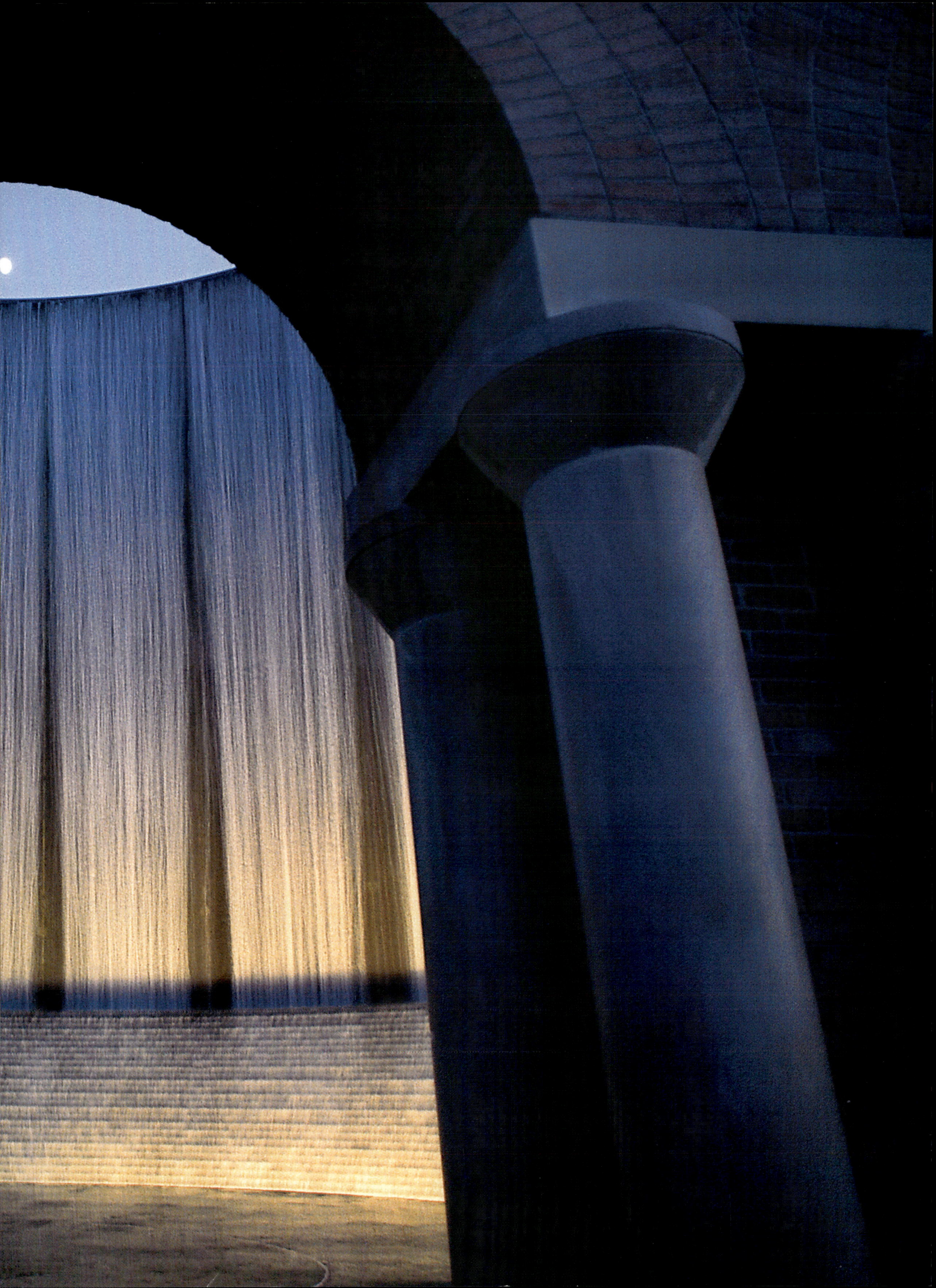

HOUSTON ★ People ★ Opportunity ★ Success

Special Thanks to...

Wendy Adair, B.J. Almond, Carlos Avlarez, Denny Anderson, Denny Angelle, Dionel Aviles, Glenn Avriett, Susan Bandy, Howard Batt, Abby Bowman, John Bremer, Geary Broadnax, John Buck, Caleen Burton-Allen, Ed Campion, Tina Ceppi, Betty Chapman, Mike Chiu, Michael Cinelli, Bob Clickner, Marion Cole, Ximera Copa-Wiggins, Cindy Cordova, Jeffrey Cox, Linda Crays, Patricia Cross, Gary Cullen, Dan D'Armond, Al Davis, Brian Davis, Mark Davis, Lois DeBakey, M.D., Lee DeMontrond, Cuauthemoc Diaz, Joel Draught, Maria Dungler, Andrew Edmundsen, Teresa Ehrman, Don Empie, Don Faught, Murray Fogler, Lynn Foltin, Tim Franks, Lisa Garvin, Jennifer Garza, Pam Griffin, Ernest Hall, Glen Hemperly, John Harvey, Wayne Hill, Eileen Holly, Houston Police Department Helicopter Division, Earlie Hudnall, Richard Huebner, H.R. Hutchins, Claire Johnson, Liz Johnson, Larry Jones, John Jonte, Skip Kasdorf, John Kelley, Carla Klein, Lt. John King, Maureen Kovacik, Stephen Klineberg, Jim Kollaer, Kathleen Koonce, Kia Kriticos, Julie Lambert, Jack Lapinski, T. Scott LaRoche, Patricia LeBlanc, Mary Stark Love, Jamaal Mathews, Rob Matwick, Debra Maurer, Don McAdams, Rita McCoy, Sherry McDonnell, Kathleen McKay, Ivy McLemore, Joan Miller, Marlee Miller, Ray Miller, Rodica Mirea, Vance Muse, Sally Nash, Carolyn Neill, Dan Newman, Susan Newquest, Yoichiro Okazaki, Bill Olive, Chris Orr, Jason Ott, Charlotte Overstreet, Graham Painter, Lorrie Parise, Rick Parker, Lee Pecht, Bill Penkert, Julie Penne, John Ira Petty, Barbara Piagari, Eva Pickens, Larry Pilcik, Keith Pillow, Jessica Johns Pool, Mary Powledge, Joe Pratt, Ben Rediker, Rudy Rey, Rice University Fondren Library, Patricia Riddlebarger, Michelle Rives, Alex Roman, Shana Roper, Charlie Savino, Marilou Schopper, Gail Schwindeman, Lee Scurry, Margarita Simon, Sheldon Smart, Catherine Smith, John Sousa, Frances Carter Stevens, Kristeen Stewart, Stephen Stuyck, Phillip Tree, Heida Thurlow, Bob Tutt, Lia Unrau, Jenny Vaughan, Cynthia, Beth and Angela Viator, Reisha Virata, Brownwyn Wallace, George Wang, Scott Weaver, Laura Westey, John Whaley, Marshall Whinney, Linda Winter, Teresa Wong, Oscar Zertuche.

Houston: A Promising Future. Reflecting one of the greatest accomplishments of the 20th century and the promise of the future, a full moon rises above the lush banks of Buffalo Bayou near downtown Houston (pages 178-179) and inspires a moment of quiet reflection above the Water Wall near The Galleria (pages 180-181). ★ *The oak-lined residential streets of Houston near Hermann Park provide a peaceful setting for an evening stroll.*

Photos (pages 183-184): Ray Viator ▶▶

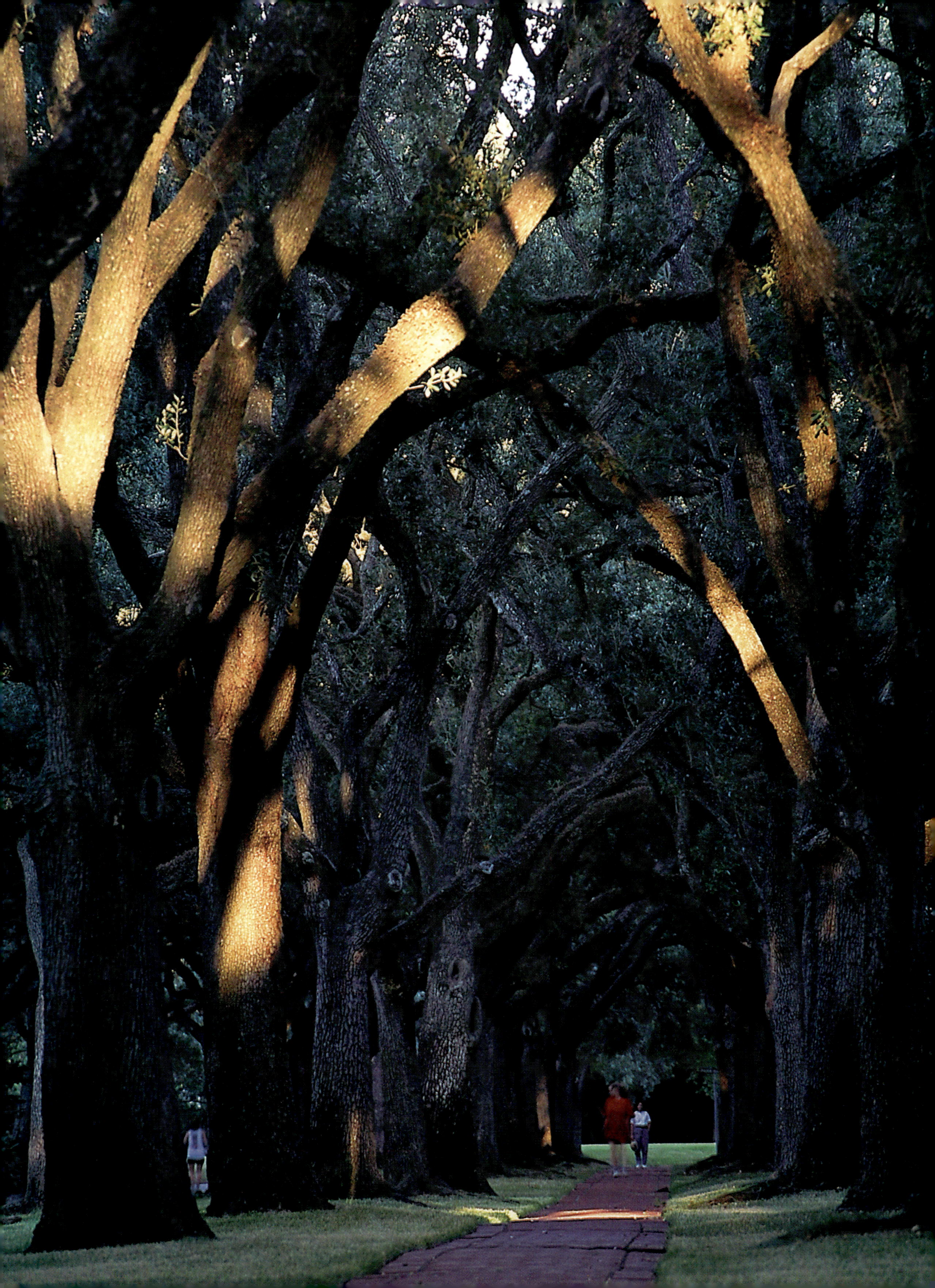

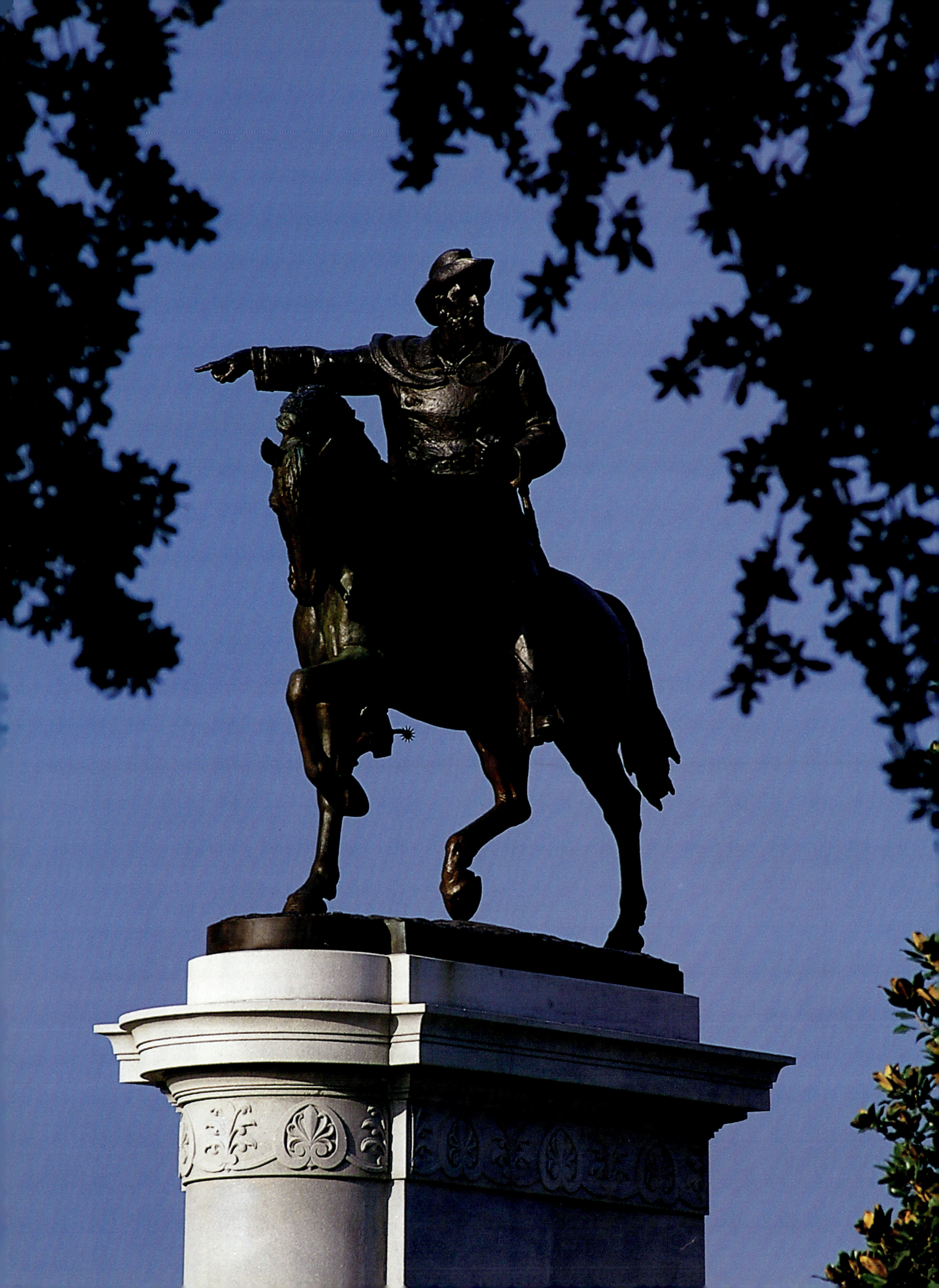

Houston Business Portraits

TECHNOLOGY
BMC Software, Inc. 186
Mind Cellar Consulting 188
BindView 190
Williams Communications Solutions 192
MEDIA, INC. 194
IKON Office Solutions 195
MTI College of Business and Technology 196

QUALITY OF LIFE
The Woodlands® 197
Nino's Restaurant 198
Truluck's 200
Highland Village 202
Gables Residential 204
First United Methodist Church, Houston 206
Momentum Motor Cars Portrait 208
Tour 18 210
Zadok Jewelers 211
The St. Regis 212

ENERGY INDUSTRY
Texaco-Houston 213
Halliburton Company 214
Schlumberger 218
Fluor Daniel, Inc. 221
Duke Energy 222
Lyondell Chemical Company 224
LYONDELL-CITGO Refining LP 225
INTEC Engineering 226
Fugro 228
Vanco Energy Company 230
Altra Energy 231
Weatherford International, Inc. 232
Mustang Engineering 233
Van De Wiele Engineering 234
Air Products 235
Rimkus Consulting Group, Inc. 236

BANKING & FINANCIAL
Ascension Capital Advisors, Inc. 237
Sterling Bank 238
AIM Funds 240
MCG/Dulworth, Inc. 242

MANUFACTURING/INDUSTRIAL
Gull Industries 243
Stewart & Stevenson 244
Cooper Cameron Corporation 246
Suhm Spring Works, Inc. 248
PRIME Service, Inc. 250
Hitachi 252
Madden Bolt 253
Houston Foam Plastics 254
Hydralift, Inc. 255

INTERNATIONAL/TRANSPORTATION
Port of Houston 256
Palletized Trucking Inc. 258
Houston Airport System 260
Circle International 262

PROFESSIONAL SERVICES
PageSoutherlandPage 264
Greater Houston Partnership 266
Jim Olive Photography/Stockyard Photos 268
Andrews & Kurth L.L.P. 269
Fredricks Commercial Brokerage 270
Tindall & Foster, P.C. 271
Chicago Title 272
PricewaterhouseCoopers 273
BDO Seidman, LLP 274
Apollo Paper Company 275
American Bureau of Professional Translators 276
Moss Landscaping, Inc. 277
Robert Huff Landscape Illumination 278
Furniture Marketing Group of Houston, Inc. 279
City Central Courier 280

MEDICAL
The University of Texas Medical Branch 281
Baylor College of Medicine 282
E-Eldercare 283

HOUSTON ★ People ★ Opportunity ★ Success

BMC Software, Inc.

BMC Software enters the 21st century firmly established as a global leader in its industry, fully prepared to build on that leadership. The company established its course for the next hundred years during the 20th century's final year. In perhaps the most significant advance of BMC Software's history, the company realigned into five strategic business units.

The new structure assures BMC Software customers that the global software provider will remain in the forefront of innovation. It also reinforces a commitment to progress that BMC Software has maintained since its founding in 1980.

Today, BMC Software's operations ring the globe, with agents in 50 countries worldwide. Though employment has reached more than 6,000 and the company's revenue surpassed $1.3 billion during the past year, BMC Software enters the new century with Greater Houston continuing to work well as its base of operations. The company also maintains a major facility in Austin.

The recent realignment is already producing tangible results in enhancing customer relationships, raising market presence, developing a more customer-and-market focused field organization and simplifying doing business with the company.

In the new century, the company also moves forward with the backing of an unparalleled senior management team, the industry's best enterprise management experts, a unique corporate/solution focus, new market initiatives, a new corporate identity and global professional services/support organization.

186 TECHNOLOGY

HOUSTON ★ People ★ Opportunity ★ Success

BMC Software's single corporate vision and mission (Assuring Business Availability™) have gained strength following recent acquisitions of Boole & Babbage and New Dimension Software. Integrating the two companies has successfully built upon BMC Software's established industry leadership.

The acquired companies fit neatly into what President and CEO Max Watson describes as "new millennium metrics," which include speed to market, agility, flexibility and relentless pursuit of customer intimacy. Watson explained, "BMC Software can forge powerful alliances with customers that result in strategic integrated solutions that significantly drive business competitiveness and value for our customers and us. To achieve this, we have transformed every element of our company."

Progress continues to emerge in each area of the reorganized BMC Software. For example, management initiatives will demonstrate increased support for e-business, enterprise resource planning, intelligent storage/storage area networks, data warehousing enablement, MQ series, Windows NT, service assurance center implementation and parallel sysplex enablement.

But not everything has changed. The company maintains its earned reputation as the world's leading provider of management solutions that ensure availability, performance and recovery of companies' business-critical applications. For more than 18 years, the world's largest companies have relied on BMC Software.

The company has also stepped forward in a new area of good citizenship, where it has been a leading contributor for years. BMC Software has teamed with USA Cycling, cycling's national governing body, to form the BMC Software Cycling Grand Prix. The series began with two 1999 events—in Houston and Austin.

More agile and sophisticated, BMC Software is fully prepared to better understand customer issues and better prepared to offer the right solutions. ■

BMC Software Chairman, President and CEO Max Watson.

TECHNOLOGY 187

HOUSTON ★ People ★ Opportunity ★ Success

Mind Cellar Consulting

The Alternative Information Technology Staffing Firm

Rebecca Hayward Bergeron, President and CEO of Mind Cellar Consulting

When Rebecca Hayward Bergeron developed the consulting methodology for the staffing firm she would found and lead, two defining characteristics surfaced. First, she would establish an alternative firm to meet Greater Houston's growing staffing needs in Information Technology (IT). Second, she would guide the firm in ways that led Houston businesses, as well as industry peers, to consider this alternative staffing firm a leader.

Mind Cellar Consulting has met and even surpassed these expectations by adhering to an unparalleled personal service commitment when offering contract, contract-to-hire and permanent placement opportunities in the IT field to clients and consultants.

Bergeron explained, "Personal service requires genuine attentiveness to ideas, ideas that are the motive power and birthplace of vision. Taking a personal interest in our consultants and employees generates pride and affords avenues for better ideas and grander vision. Perfectly matching these ideas and visions with the clients' needs produces self-respecting individuals who love what they do, as evident in their reliability, performance and quality of work."

Bergeron also stated, "Building and maintaining satisfied consultants is the cornerstone of productivity and manageability in the workplace."

Mind Cellar Consulting lends its expertise to various software/internet development, hardware manufacturing, energy, petrochemical, financial and commercial development companies. Perhaps the vast industries in which Mind Cellar Consulting serves is outweighed by the dedication which Bergeron's firm offers each client.

Bergeron said, "Mind Cellar's dedication to matching qualified, dependable Information Technology professionals with positive, growth oriented work environments produces endless possibilities for success. Our approach to staffing encompasses technical, personal and corporate standards. We support the theory that isolating candidates with appropriate skill sets is not enough in today's IT market. It is essential to match client and consultant personalities in conjunction with technical requirements to provide the signature component in maintaining a successful and productive working relationship."

As a member of the Greater Houston Partnership, the Better Business Bureau (BBB), the National Association of Computer Consultant Businesses (NACCB) and the National Association of Women Business Owners (NAWBO), Mind Cellar Consulting strives to play an active role in supporting local community activities, as well as national legislative efforts that impact IT and women in business.

In addition to directing the growth of Mind Cellar Consulting, Bergeron is dedicated to fostering women in the field of Information Technology by working closely with the Association for Women in Computing (AWC). During her extensive alliance with the organization, Bergeron has served most recently as President of the AWC Houston Chapter and has completed numerous terms as the AWC Houston Chapter Vice President of Programs and National AWC Corporate Relations Vice President.

As Mind Cellar Consulting enters the new millennium, it concentrates on meeting client and consultant needs in the areas of graphical user interface (GUI), web and database development, hardware, software and quality assurance testing, network operating system/database administration and senior technical/project management support. Consequently, the firm understands the need to remain flexible in responding to and even anticipating the rapid, often dramatic changes that characterize Information Technology. ∎

Bergeron awarding Kim Evans of BMC Software, Inc. at the 1999 AWC Top 20 Houston Women in Technology ceremony.

HOUSTON ★ People ★ Opportunity ★ Success

BindView

BIND VIEW

For BindView, the secret to becoming the premiere developer and leader in the highly competitive world of systems management software products is really very simple: its staff.

Some of the best creative minds in the industry have joined this fast-paced, high-growth company where individual motivation and accomplishment count toward overall company success. The entrepreneurial spirit of the company's employees has enabled BindView to become one of the largest software companies in Houston. It also helped Bind View to achieve a successful initial public offering in July of 1998, and an even more successful secondary offering in December of 1998.

"We take great pride in our work and we take pride in all the great people on staff. Each individual counts, no matter how much this company grows," says President and Chief Executive Officer Eric Pulaski.

Since its founding in 1990 with three employees, BindView has grown to more than 450 employees. In addition to corporate headquarters in Houston, Texas, which is responsible for software development, operations and sales and marketing, BindView also maintains development offices in Boston, Massachusetts and San Jose, California. It also has sales and support offices in Frankfurt, Germany, and Paris, France. Together, BindView's offices support more than 4,000 customers worldwide, including companies like Chase Manhattan Bank, American General Corporation, KPMG Peat Marwick, Comerica and KeyCorp.

BindView's client list includes 23 of the 26 largest banks in the United States and 75 of the Fortune 100 companies. In fact, one Fortune 25 company is managing its network of over 70,000 users on a global basis using BindView products.

190 TECHNOLOGY

HOUSTON ★ People ★ Opportunity ★ Success

"Must-Have" Tools

To understand BindView, Pulaski says, you need to understand the demands placed on a company's systems administrator, the individual who must ensure that a company's computer systems operate smoothly and reliably 24 hours a day, seven days a week.

"Systems administrators of a company needs a product that can be the first thing they turn on in the morning and the last thing they turn off at night, a tool that allows them to get the job done with greater peace of mind. BindView helps organizations achieve this by allowing systems to run more smoothly and securely," Pulaski says.

The BindView suite of systems management software products can manage the security of complex, distributed client/server networks on Microsoft Windows NT and Novell NetWare environments. The company's primary product line, BindView EMS, provides software solutions for systems administration, security management, enterprise industry of LAN assets and Year 2000 assessment of PC hardware and software.

Industry reviews tout BindView's products as "must have" tools for busy systems administrators who are responsible for the security and integrity of their client/server networks.

"One of the key strengths of BindView's premiere product line is security analysis. So companies that are very interested in security on their networks are very interested in our products," Pulaski notes.

For more information about BindView and its software products, call 713-561-4000 or visit the company's web site at www.bindview.com.■

Founded in 1990, BindView's IT risk management solutions have been recognized with the industry's most prestigious awards and are installed in over 4,000 companies worldwide, including over 75 of the Fortune 100 and 23 of the largest 26 U.S. banks.

HOUSTON ★ People ★ Opportunity ★ Success

Williams Communications Solutions

Williams combines state-of-the-art network management facilities and software technology with the expertise of more than 2,400 field engineers and technicians to provide 24 x 7 x 365 network support services to business customers across North America.

In a multi-million dollar, futuristic-looking setting straight out of the U.S. space program, Williams Communications Solutions has created its own "Mission Control" at the Williams Tower in Houston for managing thousands of complex data and voice networks for businesses throughout North America.

The National Technical Resource Center (NTRC) is Williams Communications Solutions' state-of-the-art facility for proactive network management of its customers' data and voice networks. The NTRC is staffed by more than 150 in-house engineers and technicians who remotely monitor and diagnose the performance of networks 24 hours a day, 365 days a year.

In many ways, the NTRC reflects the reality and potential role that telecommunications plays in every aspect of business.

"Clearly, we are entering a new era of communications where a company's success will be greatly affected by its ability to communicate and share a vast amount of information globally among employees, customers and vendors," says Patti Schmigle, president of Williams Communications Solutions. "Williams will play a critical role in providing business communications solutions so that our customers will be successful in this new era."

Because the specific needs—and the resulting solutions—will vary from customer to customer, Williams Communications Solutions sells, installs and services a comprehensive portfolio of communications equipment and network offerings that address the constantly evolving data, voice, video and multimedia needs of businesses. In addition to offering products from the industry's leading manufacturers, the company provides end-to-end network services that include configuration, design, installation, maintenance and management of mission-critical enterprise networks, as well as the design and operation of advanced call centers.

HOUSTON ★ People ★ Opportunity ★ Success

In the Houston area, the company provides single-source communications solutions for a diverse group of companies and institutions, including multinational oil and gas companies, a world-renowned medical research facility, and a champion professional basketball team.

"While our customers range from small businesses to Fortune 500 companies, Williams Communications Solutions plays a critical role in helping each of them develop, integrate and maintain complex communications networks so that they can focus on their core competencies," says Schmigle.

"The complexity and importance of today's communications networks will only accelerate in the new millennium," Schmigle says. The latest trend is in enterprise-wide integration of services, where companies need to combine and manage video network needs as well as voice and data. Williams is already addressing this convergence by offering companies a single-source approach to communications, taking full responsibility for designing, installing and managing the wide range of products and solutions deployed throughout companies' networks.

By offering end-to-end network support services and a vendor-independent portfolio of data, voice and multimedia products, Williams Communications Solutions ensures that the optimal equipment and services are selected for a customer's specific needs and business growth requirements. And, with 4,600 technical, operations and service personnel in 110 sales and service locations, Williams Communications Solutions offers border-to-border and coast-to-coast support for more than 100,000 customer sites throughout North America.

Williams Communications Solutions is a business unit of Tulsa-based Williams Communications Group, Inc., (NYSE:WCG). For more information about Williams Communications Solutions, please visit www.williams.com, or call 1-800-WILLIAMS. ∎

Williams

Communications Solutions

Houston's famed 64-story Williams Tower houses Williams Communications Solutions' National Technical Resource Center, traversing three floors and more than 40,000 square feet of cutting-edge technology.

TECHNOLOGY 193

HOUSTON ★ People ★ Opportunity ★ Success

MEDIA, INC.

MEDIA, INC. is a manufacturer of CD-Rom, CD-Recordable, DVD-Rom, VHS and Cassette. A multitude of *Innovative Packaging* will complement any single media or dual media distribution requirements. Houston's largest *e-Publishing* manufacturer produces thousands of music titles, business applications and multimedia CD-Rom's, in addition to a variety of patented DVD, Multimedia and CD packaging designs.

E-Publishing consists of more than manufacturing CD's and Tape. Our immediate, **Millennium Vision** is to simplify the process for manufacturing digital catalogues through database templates with routine assembly of data files. Imagine reproducing your printed catalogues on $1 Compact Discs rather than $$$ to print. This will revolutionize the printing industry as we depend on it today! Product and Service Catalogs, Technical Specifications and Safety Manuals, Annual Reports, Video Training will all be produced onto CD-Rom in the same time it takes to print–days–and *at a fraction of the cost!*

E-Publishing — MEDIA, Inc. — *a Millennium Vision!*

MEDIA, INC., a recipient of The Houston 100 Fastest Growing Companies 1995-1997, began as a diskette duplicator in 1993, providing for Houston software companies' need to distribute software to their clients. The decade of the 1990's moved from DOS 3.0 to Windows '98, from diskettes holding 360K to DVD-ROM with a capacity of over 7GB. Like Windows, the World Wide Web, SAP, Southwest Airlines, Starbucks and other industry transformers, MEDIA, INC. will move you from *Paper to Plastic!* ■

HOUSTON ★ People ★ Opportunity ★ Success

IKON Office Solutions

Delivering digital office products and Business Communication Technology to greater Houston & the world.

Describing IKON Office Solutions as a company that just sells copiers is a bit like describing Babe Ruth as just a baseball player. IKON Office Solutions creates a comprehensive program that successfully advances a customer from the world of stand-alone copiers and printers to the fully connected, digital office environment.

IKON Office Solutions is uniquely positioned to navigate customers through this digital revolution thanks to strategic alliances with leading manufacturers such as Canon, Ricoh, OCE, IBM and others. Not a manufacturer, IKON offers a best of breed product selection resulting in variety that few competitors can match.

Customers look to IKON Office Solutions to improve the management of their documents and data with enterprise wide solutions from copier and printing systems, computer networking and print on demand services to copy center management, hardware and software product interfaces and electronic file conversion. This solution-based strategy is only possible through the size and diversity of IKON Office Solutions. Previously part of Alco Standard, IKON has quickly flourished into a 5 billion-dollar worldwide corporation with over 1,100 locations and over 400,000 customers.

Above all, IKON recognizes the importance of every customer. IKON Office Solutions maintains a locally based executive management team and service dispatch system empowered to immediately respond to any need or situation. With a commitment to give back to the community where its employees work and live, IKON has intensified its philanthropic initiatives. Through support of Junior Achievement of Southeast Texas, the American Cancer Society and other organizations, IKON is dedicated to help improve the quality of life in Greater Houston. ■

HOUSTON ★ People ★ Opportunity ★ Success

MTI College of Business and Technology

MTI College of Business and Technology— NASA Area Campus. MTI NASA is a branch location of MTI Houston.

MTI College of Business and Technology— Houston Campus.

MTI College of Business and Technology was established in 1980 to provide industry based training programs in electronics technology. From eight students in 1981 to nearly one thousand active students today, MTI has prepared thousands of individuals for gainful employment. As Houston's leading Career College for computer and business technology, MTI keeps pace with the rapidly changing technical and managerial requirements of industry. MTI provides a wide range of comprehensive computer systems technology, business applications, and software programs at the corporate and individual levels.

MTI is an accredited private career school authorized to grant Associate of Occupational Studies degrees in computer systems technology, electronics and business technology. In addition, the institution offers a number of other accredited programs. These include fast-paced certificate programs and English-as-a-Second-Language (ESL).

By taking a proactive, career oriented approach to curricula design and content, MTI is committed to students graduating with specific technical skills and business acumen that employers need. Greater than ninety percent of graduates find employment in the fields in which they were trained.* Today, MTI graduates are found forging careers with many of Houston's most prestigious employers. As a high-profile center for learning MTI is committed to assisting students in reaching their career goals.

*Verified by the Accrediting Commission of Career Schools & Colleges of Technology.
MTI's modern campuses in Southwest Houston and the NASA area serve the complete Houston Metropolitan area. ■

HOUSTON ★ People ★ Opportunity ★ Success

The Woodlands®

America's Hometown™

Acres of forested greenbelts add to The Woodlands' appeal as Texas' number one community.

The Woodlands is a 27,000-acre, forested community where people live, work, play and learn as families and companies. Located 27 miles north of downtown Houston on I-45, it encompasses five residential villages, with a sixth now in development, corporate and commercial centers, a resort and conference center, medical facilities, and a full range of shopping, dining, entertainment, and recreational amenities.

The Woodlands has led the Houston area in new home sales every year since 1990 and ranks No. 1 in Texas and No. 4 in the nation in new home sales. There are more than 17,000 single-family homes and nearly 5,000 apartments and town homes in The Woodlands, homes to more than 55,000 residents.

The Woodlands reached an all-time high of 1,450 new home sales in 1998, and was recognized as the 1999 Developer of the Year by the Greater Houston Builders Association.

Nearly 850 businesses and corporations have a home in The Woodlands, providing jobs for more than 21,000 people in more than 13 million square feet of commercial, industrial, and institutional development.

The 1,000-acre Town Center is the destination for shopping, dining, and entertainment, with attractions including The Woodlands Mall, and performing arts at The Cynthia Woods Mitchell Pavilion. Construction has begun on The Woodlands Waterway, a 1.25-mile-long landscaped water feature that will link the shopping, business, dining and entertainment venues in Town Center.

"In the new millennium, we will continue our mission to create quality environments where people can live, work, play and learn," said Michael H. Richmond, president and CEO of The Woodlands Operating Company, L.P. ■

QUALITY OF LIFE 197

HOUSTON ★ People ★ Opportunity ★ Success

Nino's Restaurant

The Mandola family has been treating Houston to outstanding Italian food for more than 20 years. In Nino's, Mary and Vincent are standing behind their daughters, Mary Dana (left) and Vinceanne (right).

When Vincent and Mary Mandola opened Nino's Restaurant in 1977, they knew that preparing fine Italian food would be only part of their challenge.

Near downtown, their 2817 West Dallas location was well-placed for business people in search of a tasty lunch. But to attract evening diners, the Mandolas would need to develop a consistently superior level of food and service that invited repeat diners.

They did.

Their personal commitment to service has made Nino's and two subsequent establishments on the same grounds—Vincent's and Grappino di Nino—one of Greater Houston's extraordinary dining successes. It's a success that demanded, in addition to inviting menus and memorable service, an everybody-roll-up-your-sleeves family commitment.

Vincent and Mary Mandola established Nino's in what had been a combination grocery store and home since the 1930s. Vincent worked six long days each week. Mary put in nearly as many hours, keeping books and balancing her restaurant duties with caring for their two young girls.

The four native Houstonians resourcefully crafted each of their three restaurants out of structures that had served as homes, apartments and businesses. Each dining

198 QUALITY OF LIFE

HOUSTON ★ People ★ Opportunity ★ Success

The house specialty, Vincent's is known for, is the spit-roasted lemon and garlic chicken. The wood-fired rotisserie & pizza oven set a warm and relaxing atmosphere.

setting—whether traditional or strikingly new—generates a warmth that matches service.

Resourcefulness also helped their planning. Back in 1977, Vincent bought most of their cooking equipment used.

The Mandola daughters, Mary Dana and Vinceanne, grew up with—and in—the family business. They began by making desserts after their days in elementary school. Each took off for four years to attend college. Today, they are married, back in the business and among 140 employees. Mary Dana manages beverage services and inventory. Vinceanne is general manager and banquets/party coordinator.

Continuing success still prompts careful growth and ongoing improvements. Next door to Nino's, the Mandolas opened Vincent's in 1984. They travel to other cities to observe customer trends and how to anticipate them. For example, the wood-fired rotisserie in atmospheric Vincent's was the first of its kind in Greater Houston. Chicken orders for the rotisserie now account for about one-third of Vincent's business.

As Mary Dana and Vinceanne urged their parents to meet demand for more banquet and party facilities, they expanded south from their two West Dallas establishments in 1996. They opened Grappino di Nino, an Italian grappa bar. The full-service bar features antipasto, cappuccino and desserts. Grappino's also offers an elegant private banquet setting, a wine room and a charming courtyard.

Density of businesses around their location boosts lunch traffic. But the Mandolas know that those who come for supper—"destination diners"—continue to relish the dining experience. They choose either Nino's, Vincent's or Grappino di Nino because it's the place they choose to be. The Mandolas want to keep earning that business. They respect loyalty as a two-way street.

They're also grateful to businesses that supported them in the beginning. After produce and import companies helped open the doors in 1977, the Mandolas bought only from the two companies for years. The Mandolas still do business with the bank that got them started.

At the Mandola restaurants, change is always a careful step. In Vincent Mandola's words, "We started out hands-on, and we're still hands-on." ■

Grappino di Nino's bar serves Grappa, wine, cocktails, cappuccino, antipasto and dessert. The courtyard is used for cocktail gatherings. The banquet and wine rooms are available for private events.

QUALITY OF LIFE 199

HOUSTON ★ People ★ Opportunity ★ Success

Truluck's

Seafood, Steak and Stone Crab

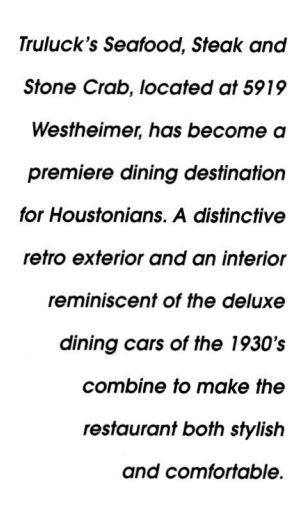

Truluck's Seafood, Steak and Stone Crab, located at 5919 Westheimer, has become a premiere dining destination for Houstonians. A distinctive retro exterior and an interior reminiscent of the deluxe dining cars of the 1930's combine to make the restaurant both stylish and comfortable.

DAVID DIETRICH PHOTOGRAPHY

When restauranteurs Stuart Sargent and Pattie Mooney opened Truluck's in 1992, they envisioned a restaurant that would "break the mold".

"We certainly did that," they laugh. "We broke it so well that for a year or so, nobody could quite figure out exactly what we were".

Not so today. After receiving various awards and citations for its food and service (as well as being named by Food & Wine Magazine as one of Houston's Top 10 Restaurants in both 1993 and 1997), Truluck's Seafood, Steak and Stone Crab has become one of the city's premiere dining destinations.

"Breaking the mold, to us, means a lot of different things," says Managing Partner Mike Armstrong. "For instance, we believe that you can have a beautiful restaurant that's still comfortable. And that you can have superior service without being pretentious."

Most of all, breaking the mold begins with an imaginative mix of both steaks and seafood. So often, a steakhouse pays only lip service to seafood, while seafood restaurants seem to offer only a token steak or two. Truluck's on the other hand, offers a variety of Select Angus steaks hand-rubbed with Truluck's proprietary seasonings. Adding to the menu's strengths are over a dozen seafood entrees, ranging from a seared, sesame crusted tuna to snapper stuffed with crabmeat, mushrooms and tomatoes. A large selection of vintage wines and classic cocktails are also integral to the Truluck's mix.

And then there's the stone crab.

HOUSTON ★ People ★ Opportunity ★ Success

"That's where we truly set ourselves apart," said Sargent. "Stone crab claws are our signature item and we're one of the few restaurants in the country that really specializes in fresh stone crab. In fact, in 1999 alone, we served over 60,000 pounds of stone crab to our Houston customers."

To meet that demand (and that of two Truluck's in Dallas and one set to open in Austin), Truluck's operates a fleet of 16 fishing boats in Naples, Florida. The highly regulated industry requires that stone crabs be harvested individually. One claw is removed, the stone crab tagged and then returned to the sea. Within 18 months, the stone crab's claw is fully regenerated.

Truluck's intention to break the mold has gone beyond even food and service. The partnership behind the restaurant is committed to being an active member of the Houston community. And that means donating their food and services to many of the city's charitable organizations.

"Houston has been very kind to Truluck's. We feel an obligation to be an active and reciprocal part of the community—we're especially close to the Texas Children's Hospital, the Covenant House and the Susan G. Komen Foundation. The work they do is so important to our community," says Armstrong. "We're glad we can help".

It makes sense that a restaurant that has succeeded in breaking the mold has found such a receptive audience in a city that has always done the same.

"And that," according to Mooney and Sargent, "is why it works." ■

TRULUCK'S SEAFOOD, STEAK AND STONE CRAB
5919 WESTHEIMER
(713) 783-7270

Although fresh stone crab is Truluck's signature item, their flawlessly tender, intensely flavored steaks have developed a devoted following. Hand-rubbed, with a special, proprietary blend of seasonings, these steaks are considered by many to be the best in Houston.

QUALITY OF LIFE

HOUSTON ★ People ★ Opportunity ★ Success

Highland Village

Stroll leisurely amid the sculpture gardens. Sip espresso on the walled patio surrounded by swaying palms. Examine the intriguing windows of Houston's most elegant storefronts. Savor the unhurried luxury and genteel ambiance of Houston's premiere shopping and dining destination. Shopping or dining at Highland Village is the ultimate in sophistication, a feast for the senses.

Housing some of the most upscale and exclusive stores and services in Houston, Highland Village offers the highest standards in architectural design, landscaping, decor, merchandise quality and personalized customer care.

Locale Extraordinare

Nestled just inside-the-loop in the 4000 block of Westheimer, in the midst of Houston's most exclusive residential neighborhoods such as River Oaks, Memorial and the Rice University area, Highland Village caters to the customer looking for merchants and dining establishments of distinction.

When it opened in 1952, Highland Village was a smart neighborhood center serving a developing residential area. Over the years, upscale housing came to the area and Highland Village was transformed into a cohesive, specialty environment, becoming the most distinguished shopping and dining address in the heart of Houston. Today, pristine stucco-clad buildings framed by tailored awnings are home to some of the most recognizable names in retail in addition to exclusive, one-of-a-kind establishments. For personalized service in an upscale shopping environment, there is no more inviting destination than Highland Village.

Merchants of the Highest Standard

Prestigious retailers such as Banana Republic, Williams-Sonoma, Pottery Barn, The Gap, Cole Haan, Ethan Allen, Fitigues, James Avery Craftsman, Harold Powell and Victoria's Secret are easily accessible in Highland Village's pedestrian-friendly environment. They are joined by names well known to Houstonians like Tootsies,

HOUSTON ★ People ★ Opportunity ★ Success

Norton Ditto, Surprises, Michael Kemper Salon and Day Spa, Joseph, Max Lang, Top Drawer Lingerie, Deustch & Deutsch, and Gayle's. Distinctive eateries include Anthony's, Grotto Ristorante, P.F. Chang's China Bistro, La Madeleine and Starbucks Coffee. Every luxury one could possibly desire is available at Highland Village, warm and inviting, attentive and accommodating, easy to access with ample free parking.

Since taking over the property in 1990, Highland Village Holding, Inc., has repositioned Highland Village as the most exclusive outdoor retail center in Houston, creating a truly civilized shopping and dining experience especially tailored to the needs of the discerning upscale customer. As we enter the new Millennium, the center will continue to evolve and seek new levels of exclusivity and refinement, always dedicated to satisfying the needs of both the valued customer and the distinguished retailer or restaurateur.

For more information about Highland Village, telephone (713) 850-3100 or visit our website at www.highlandvillage.net. ∎

HOUSTON ★ People ★ Opportunity ★ Success

Gables Residential

"Our service-oriented philosophy drives us to be first to market innovative services that benefit our residents."

Gables Residential has relied on more than elegant interiors, beautiful landscaping, sparkling pools and other visible qualities to build its exemplary reputation. Gables has paid attention to how people live in crafting itself as an innovative force in the development, construction, management, and acquisition of quality multifamily communities.

Gables' motto, "Taking Care of the Way People Live," may understate the company's position. According to Senior Vice President Cathy Cabell, "Our service-oriented philosophy drives us to be first to market innovative services and features that benefit our residents. We don't just rent apartments. We provide homes where people enjoy living."

The company has a very high standard when it comes to taking care of residents. It's a standard that manifests itself in a high quality community, an immaculate home and a guarantee that all appliances and systems will be in good working order at move-in. Gables' 24-hour maintenance guarantee will allow a new resident to terminate their lease within 30 days if they are not satisfied with their home.

Public service is an integral part of Gables' corporate character, especially in Houston. This means a serious commitment to good citizenship, exemplified by the 1999 Race For the Cure®, a major event in funding breast cancer research. Twenty Gables' associates participated in the race. For the third consecutive year, Gables has been the major sponsor of the Gables Residential 20K Championship. Beneficiaries have included New Hope Housing, and Hope for ALS (also known as Lou Gehrig's disease).

HOUSTON ★ People ★ Opportunity ★ Success

Two years ago, Channel 2's Akins Army introduced Gables to a widow living in her garage because her house had collapsed. Gables associates, along with their subcontractors and vendors, tore down the old house and built a new one on the same spot in less than a month.

Last year, Gables added a handicapped-equipped room and bathroom to a home for a girl with multiple sclerosis. Gables has also been involved in projects for Sheltering Arms, the Lutheran Church, Houston Voice Mail, and Habitat for Humanity. Every year during the Christmas season, each Gables community adopts a needy family from the Texas Medical Center Volunteer Center.

Founded in 1982, Gables Residential became a public Real Estate Investment Trust in 1994, and is listed on the New York Stock Exchange (symbol GBP). With corporate headquarters in Atlanta and regional offices in Houston, Dallas, and Boca, Gables has become an ongoing success story across the Sunbelt, winning awards for design and development of apartment communities. This reputation led the National Association of Homebuilders to award the firm unprecedented recognition as 1997 winners of its two most prestigious awards, Best Management Company and Best Development Firm. Gables Residential enters the new century intending to build on its many distinctions.

For more information on Gables, visit their web site at www.gables.com. ■

QUALITY OF LIFE 205

HOUSTON ★ People ★ Opportunity ★ Success

First United Methodist Church, Houston

The historic Downtown sanctuary with its spectacular stained glass windows provides a magnificent setting for Sunday worship.

If only the walls of First United Methodist Church could talk, what beautiful glimpses of life they could reveal. Weddings and christenings of generations of Houstonians, helping hands outstretched to the homeless and spiritless, a vibrant congregation spreading the Gospel to others.

Nestled in the heart of downtown Houston, First United Methodist Church is a magnificent Gothic building adorned with stained glass windows and a historic pipe organ, all designed to give glory to God. But more than bricks and mortar, the 12,300 members who make up the church are involved in more than 100 ministries, forming a dynamic church community that is expanding beyond the boundaries of downtown.

The church's Westchase Campus, which opened on the west side of Houston in 1993, offers worship opportunities outside of downtown, in addition to a school and a recreation center complete with swimming pools and softball fields.

"First United Methodist is where history and modern times intersect," said Dr. William Hinson, senior pastor. "We're adapting to the changing needs of people, but we always keep a central and unchanging Gospel close to our hearts. We're a warm and caring congregation where people instantly feel at home."

A Rich Legacy

The church's history dates back 160 years when the first church was built on Texas Avenue on the site of the current Houston Chronicle building. When the land was sold and church trustees decided to build a new church "all the way out" at Main and Clay streets, some members complained that the site was too far from downtown. The building was completed in 1910, and today stands amid Houston

HOUSTON ★ People ★ Opportunity ★ Success

skyscrapers as a monument to the vision and rich legacy the Methodist community has created in Houston.

Methodist Hospital, one of the largest private, non-profit, acute care hospitals in the United States, was founded in 1919 through a member of First United Methodist, a physician who made property available at a very low cost for the hospital. Methodist Hospital moved to the Texas Medical Center in 1951. The Bluebird Circle, a long-time hospital volunteer group which has raised millions of dollars for medical needs, also was founded at First United Methodist.

A Vibrant Community

The church also founded Wesley Community Center, one of the city's largest children and youth centers; Clarewood House, an intermediate and nursing care facility; and a summer camp for 300 children each year at Quillian Memorial Center.

Methodist church members also operate a downtown Life Line Ministry for those who are homeless or in distress. "We try to give them a hand up," Hinson said. "We counsel, talk with them, pray with them. It's very important."

First United Methodist Sunday morning services have been broadcast on television since 1956 on Channel 13. Services also are broadcast live at 11 a.m. Sunday on Channel 55. "We were among the very first in America to televise our services," Hinson said. "There are many people who have never been inside our sanctuary who have bonded with us. Our televised services are a powerful ministry to all those people who are homebound."

The Downtown campus is located at 1320 Main Street and the Westchase Campus is at Westpark and Beltway 8. For more information about getting involved in the legacy of care, love and service at First Methodist, call 713-652-2999 or visit the church's website at www.firstmethodist-houston.org. ■

First United Methodist Church Westchase opened its doors on June 27, 1999 and over 2,768 persons participated in the service of worship. Bishop Woodrow Hearn consecrated the building on September 12, 1999.

QUALITY OF LIFE 207

HOUSTON ★ People ★ Opportunity ★ Success

Momentum Motor Cars Portrait

Momentum Motor Cars effectively conveys the prestige of seven distinguished European autos that it sells and services.

"We take pride in the quality of our services and amenities that enhance the quality of our products," said Ricardo Weitz, Momentum's president and founder.

Said Walter Weibel, Momentum's vice president of sales, "Someone can buy, for example, a BMW anywhere. The important difference at Momentum is that because of our dedication to customers, 85 percent of them continue to return to have us service their automobiles."

Those customers rely on Momentum for Audi, BMW, Jaguar, Porsche, Saab, Volkswagen and Volvo sales, service and parts. Momentum is Jaguar's No. 1 dealer and the exclusive dealer in Greater Houston. Momentum has ranked among BMW's top three national dealers for seven consecutive years. Momentum continues to conclude each year among the top ten Porsche dealers.

Obviously, Momentum's leadership and staff fully understand that to sell elegant vehicles, customers must be treated elegantly.

According to Weibel, "We don't believe we can stay in business just by selling a car to a customer. Momentum tries to build value that exceeds the worth of the car, which results in doing what's best for the customer." The dealership's steady rise to prominence indicates that the plan continues to improve the dealership.

A tour of the strikingly attractive facility near the Southwest Freeway-Sam Houston Tollway intersection should persuade anyone to purchase an auto or have one serviced there. No amenity seems absent. Those coming to purchase a Jaguar or have one serviced enjoy the quaint experience of waiting in a genuine Irish pub.

HOUSTON ★ People ★ Opportunity ★ Success

Anyone who comes to Momentum might choose to wait in a comfortable cappuccino bar, enjoy lunch or watch stock-market developments. Momentum also maintains 80 BMWs for customer use during servicing.

And where else but Momentum can someone test drive a vehicle on a three-quarter mile performance track? Momentum developed the track on an unused 13-acre tract behind the dealership. Believed to be the only dealership "extra" of its kind, the track offers several driving challenges, including operating on both smooth and cobblestone surfaces. A water-soaked "skid pad" demonstrates how a Momentum product will perform under adverse conditions.

An experienced test driver will operate the car for a customer to assure the highest level of safety during the drive — and to demonstrate the car's safety features and performance expectations when it goes on the road.

"The track represents only one of our many commitments," Weitz said. "We endeavor to keep the experience of coming to Momentum like no other in our business."

How did this remarkably successful dealership develop? One of the city's most prominent business owners and philanthropists, Weitz entered the luxury automobile business and rapidly succeeded by focusing on the three points of sales, service and parts.

Weibel attended the University of Arkansas on a baseball scholarship and played one year in the Kansas City Royals' organization. Today, Weibel and his wife, Valinda, are involved in Starlight Gala, Houston Grand Opera, American Heart Association, Museum of Fine Arts and the Houston Livestock Show and Rodeo.

For additional information about Momentum Motor Cars, phone 713-981-7300. ■

QUALITY OF LIFE 209

HOUSTON ★ People ★ Opportunity ★ Success

Tour 18

Imagine yourself playing golf on carefully simulated holes from some of the greatest holes of America. This collaboration of incredible replicas offers one fantastic challenge after another, creating a memorable golf experience.

Opened in autumn, 1992, Tour 18 stands among the most memorable sites for individuals and corporate tournaments or other business events. The short drive from George Bush Intercontinental Airport means that an event need not limit itself to participants who live in Greater Houston. And the opportunity to golf 12 months a year here means that businesses with staff in snow-bound regions can bring employees and guests to Tour 18 for a successful event.

Tour 18 is a daily-fee facility that specializes in corporate entertainment comfortably accommodating groups of 20 to 200, or almost any other size.

A newly remodeled clubhouse featuring one of the finest golf shops in the country (The Tour Shop) and a new restaurant and bar (Tour Cafe') have added to Tour 18's appeal. Tour Cafe's chef can customize a menu for any size golf outing—from a "classic" Texas BBQ buffet to fine dining.

Come play "America's Greatest 18 Holes™" and if you're looking for a unique setting for your next corporate event, or if you would like to play the Tour yourself, contact us today at 281-540-1818 or visit us at our website at www.tour18.com. ■

HOUSTON ★ People ★ Opportunity ★ Success

Zadok Jewelers

Our reputation is our trademark

Family owned and operated in Houston for 24 years, sons Jonathan (far left) and Segev (far right) pictured with their parents, Dror and Helene Zadok, represent the seventh generation of Zadok's in the jewelry business.

Specialties of Zadok's include designer jewelry, pearls, custom design and personally selected diamonds from the gem capitals of the world.

Zadok Jewelers is the official agent of over twenty fine Swiss watch companies.

Six generations ago, the Zadok family was the royal court jewelers to the Yemen royal family. Every generation since has proudly carried on that master craftsman tradition.

When Helene and Dror Zadok emigrated from Israel to Houston in 1975, Dror brought his family's legacy with him, founding Houston's Zadok Jewelers at Post Oak Blvd. and San Felipe. The store was just 1,200 square feet, with two employees and a small collection of jewelry.

Today the store has seen four expansions and boasts more than 7,000 square feet, 25 employees and an unsurpassed collection of luxury jewelry, timepieces and gift items. The seventh generation of Zadok's has joined the business; son Jonathan is a certified gemologist, and Segev pursues that distinction this spring.

Zadok's is *the* place in Houston for the finest, including Baccarat crystal, Bvlgari jewelry and watches and Franck Muller watches. The store is a direct importer of diamonds and offers jewelry in the most au courant styles as well as traditional time-tested designs. There are jewelry and watch workshops on the premises.

But what distinguishes Zadok's is their commitment to excellence, along with uncompromising quality, lasting value and professional, courteous service. "Our reputation is our trademark," is our motto, Helene says.

In 1998, Zadok Jewelers received the Award for Excellence from the Houston Business Journal, Better Business Bureau and University of Houston College of Business Administration.

"You're only a stranger once at Zadok Jewelers," Dror states. "We look forward to serving our customers into the next millennium." ■

QUALITY OF LIFE 211

HOUSTON ★ People ★ Opportunity ★ Success

The St. Regis

Renovated guest rooms

Maitre D'etage Butler Service on Astor guest floors

Hotel lobby

Travelers from around the world recognize when their itineraries include Houston, they will be made to feel as if they had never left home. In a city known for its fine hospitality, The St. Regis, Houston creates a unique residential experience with personal attention to every detail.

Located at 1919 Briar Oaks Lane, less than one mile from The Galleria shopping/entertainment center and 10 minutes from Houston's theater and central business districts, The St. Regis imbues one with a sense of relaxed comfort amid old-world opulence.

Spacious guestrooms at The St. Regis, Houston are handsomely appointed with plush furnishings, rich fabrics and the celebrated "Heavenly Bed" experience. On upgraded Astor floors, professionally-trained Butlers unobtrusively accommodate every guest's need for the ultimate in comfort.

More than 11,000 square feet of meeting and social space create a diverse choice of environments for business and entertainment. An addition to these venues is the recently unveiled Astor Court. The room pays tribute to John Jacob Astor, the visionary who built the legendary St. Regis, New York in 1904.

The property's culinary approach is equally world-class. The Remington Grill serves the finest bone-in chops, dry-aged beef, wild game and fresh, regionally-selected seafood. In the hotel's Lobby Lounge, guests can enjoy the time-honored tradition of afternoon tea while The St. Regis Sunday Brunch Buffet, served in Astor Court, offers an astonishing array of culinary delicacies and free-flowing champagne amidst spectacular, award-winning ice sculptures.

The St. Regis, Houston re-defines personal attention and service on every level. It is this commitment that allows the property to maintain its standing as Houston's signature hotel. ■

HOUSTON ★ People ★ Opportunity ★ Success

Texaco - Houston

In 1903, vision, opportunity and a little luck came together for Joe "Buckskin" Cullinan, an oilpatch veteran from Corsicana, Texas, and Arnold Schlaet, a New York investor. Their fledgling oil firm, The Texas Company, formed in Beaumont, Texas, just a year earlier, hit "black gold" in the nearby Sour Lake field. What started on a $3 million investment grew to become Texaco Inc., a perennial Fortune 50 performer, which today has more than 18,000 employees and operations in more than 150 countries.

For nearly 100 years, Texaco and its affiliates have been finding and producing crude oil and natural gas; manufacturing and marketing high-quality fuel and lubricant products; operating transportation, trading and distribution facilities; and, more recently, producing alternate forms of energy for power and manufacturing.

In Houston, Texaco has had a significant presence since it opened its corporate offices downtown in 1908 at the corner of Rusk and San Jacinto. Today, that same building is being renovated into a major hotel as part of the extensive revitalization taking place in downtown Houston.

With more than 3,200 Texaco employees in the area, Houston is home to the single largest concentration of Texaco employees anywhere in the world and to several of the company's key business units, including Worldwide Exploration & New Ventures and Commercial Development. Several hundred more Houstonians are part of the company's refining and marketing joint ventures, Equilon Enterprises LLC and Motiva Enterprises LLC, which is the largest retail gasoline marketer in the United States.

Texaco possesses a solid asset base, a talented and diverse workforce and leading edge technologies. In a changing industry landscape, speed, flexibility and decisiveness will be the hallmarks of a great corporation. The people of Texaco are working hard every day to achieve that greatness for the 21st century. ■

ENERGY INDUSTRY 213

HOUSTON

Halliburton Company

The future of Halliburton Company is inextricably linked to the fortunes of the Houston region and its energy-based economy. Over the past 90 years, Houston was the genesis for many of the products and services that enabled Halliburton to become a $17 billion global company. And many of the business leaders that helped build Halliburton into a leading international business also played key roles in building Houston into a world-class city.

In the 20th Century, Halliburton employees literally helped build Houston. Many of Houston's highways and roadways were designed and built by the company's engineering and construction division, Brown & Root. In addition, Halliburton employees contributed to many of Houston's landmarks, such as Rice Stadium and the Ship Channel bridge. And, as the century comes to a close, Halliburton employees are still at work building Houston with projects like the new Enron Field baseball stadium and NASA's Johnson Space Center where Halliburton employees are helping maintain America's leadership in space by providing engineering support for both the Space Shuttle and International Space Station programs.

Houston Roots

In Houston, Halliburton traces its roots back to 1919 when brothers George and Herman Brown and their brother-in-law Dan Root formed an engineering and construction company and landed several road construction projects across Texas. Today, Halliburton has grown to become one of Houston's largest private-sector employers, with more than 17,500 Houstonians and another 17,000 area sub-contractor employees working on a variety of energy, engineering and construction projects for customers around the world. In fact, with 750 offices in 130 countries, Halliburton is one of the few companies that can boast having operations on each of the seven continents.

Halliburton Today

In addition to its global reach, Halliburton is dedicated to developing new technology to help its customers in the energy industry reduce costs and be more competitive. In the 1990s alone, for example, Halliburton received more than 4000 patents and industry awards for its engineering and technical contributions to the energy and engineering industries.

Organized into six key business units to prepare for the 21st Century, Halliburton offers quality, integrated solutions. In the energy business, Halliburton's integrated products and services are designed to extend from initial exploration and production through downstream transportation and processing. For engineering and procurement projects, Halliburton is often involved through all phases of fabrication, construction, management, maintenance and even decommissioning for some projects.

Headquartered in Houston, Halliburton's Landmark Graphics Corporation is the leading supplier of open, integrated information systems and professional services to the upstream exploration and production industry.

214 ENERGY INDUSTRY

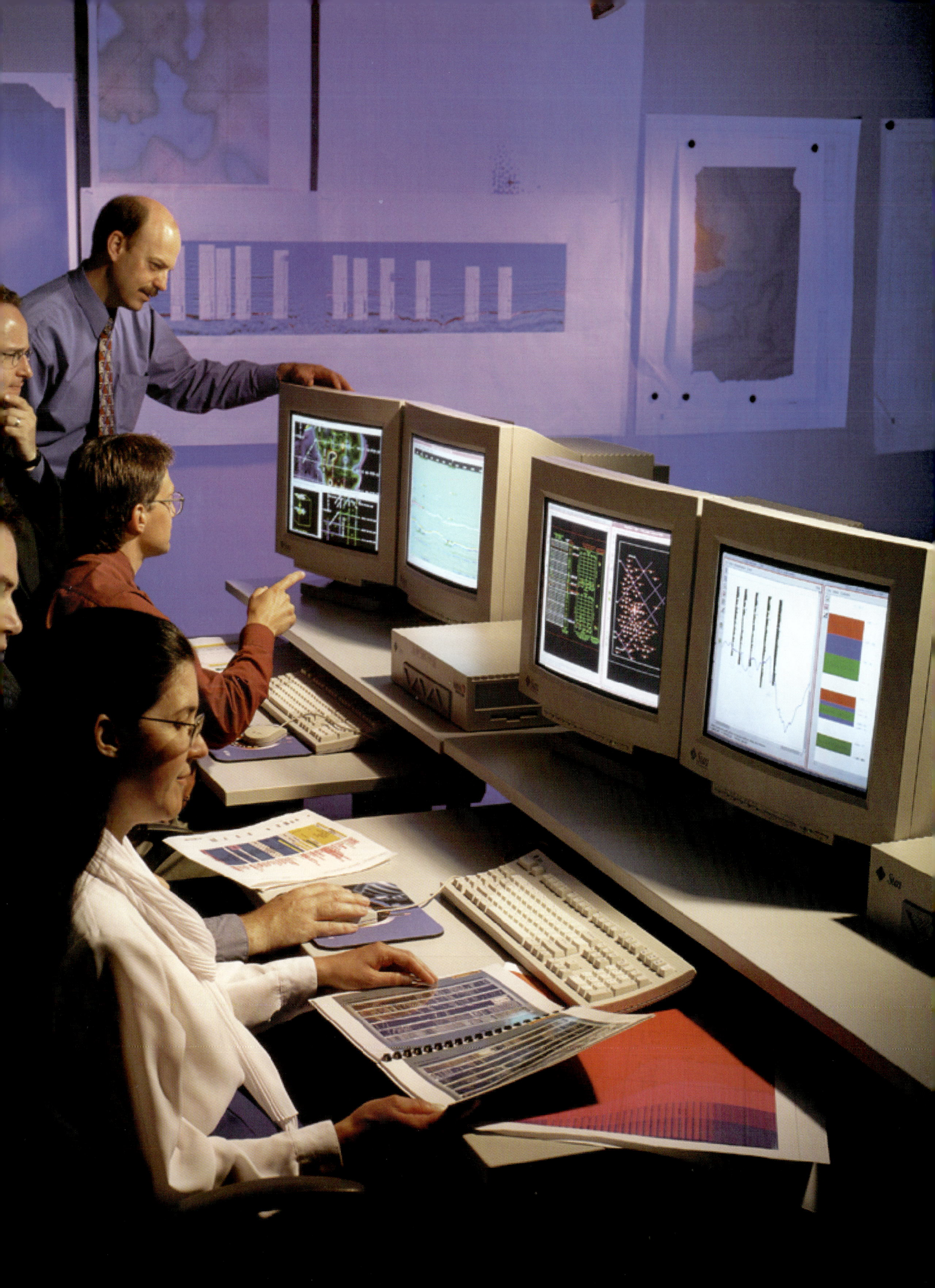

HOUSTON ★ People ★ Opportunity ★ Success

Halliburton Company

Houston's new ballpark and home to the Houston Astros, Enron Field, was constructed by Halliburton's Brown & Root Services.

Halliburton Energy Services, for example, provides products, services and integrated solutions for oil and gas exploration, development and production. Its services—including initial evaluation of producing formations to drilling, completion, production and well maintenance—can be specially tailored for a single well or an entire field.

Finding oil and gas today requires greater use of information and technology than at any time in the past. Landmark Graphics Corporation's integrated technology and data management capabilities help energy companies find, produce and manage oil and gas reservoirs. In fact, over the past decade Landmark has fundamentally changed the economics of exploration and production by enabling multidisciplinary teams to find and bring on-line oil and gas reserves that were previously impossible to detect or were considered uneconomical to produce.

After oil and gas is discovered, the next challenge is getting those valuable resources to market. Over the century, many of the world's largest energy companies have turned to Brown & Root Energy Services to design, build and operate oil and gas production and transportation facilities. BRES has designed and built production and transportation facilities in every corner of the world, from distant and demanding fields in the North Sea, Europe, Africa, Asia and Australia to the equally challenging deep waters of the Gulf of Mexico.

Two companies combined in Halliburton's 1998 merger with Dresser Industries—M.W. Kellogg and Brown & Root—pioneered many engineering advances and developed the technologies used to turn hydrocarbons into more commercial products such as petrochemicals. Today, Kellogg Brown & Root is the world's leading provider of technology-based engineering and construction services for the hydrocarbon, chemical, forest products, mining and minerals, and manufacturing industries. With 20,000 employees in more than 70 countries, Kellogg Brown & Root is involved in some of the most challenging engineering, procurement, and construction projects in the world.

To complete the process of finding, extracting, processing and delivering petroleum products to global markets, Halliburton's Dresser Equipment Group designs and manufactures equipment such as compressors, pumps, measurement instrumentation, flow control devices and power systems. Dresser Equipment Group also participates in a wide range of other industries such as food processing, aerospace, paper and utilities.

216 ENERGY INDUSTRY

HOUSTON ★ People ★ Opportunity ★ Success

Halliburton Company

*The Exxon Chemical Plant in Baytown Texas, engineered and constructed by Halliburton's **Kellogg Brown & Root**.*

In addition to its experience in the energy industry, Halliburton is drawing upon and expanding its expertise in designing, constructing and managing large, complex projects. As the world's largest services company, Brown & Root Services provides Lifecycle Management for global government and private clients. The company's services address comprehensive infrastructure needs, facilities, construction, modification, maintenance and/or operations. Lifecycle Management includes master planning, design, construction, operation, maintenance, investment management and decommissioning of facilities.

While Halliburton today is very different from its early years, some things have remained the same, such as an emphasis on developing new technology, a commitment to the communities in which it operates and a vision for the future.

Technological Leadership

If there is a single thread that can be found in Halliburton's founding companies it is an overriding interest in developing new products, equipment, technology and services. Today, new technology is a hallmark of Halliburton. Each of its divisions is charged with identifying and developing new products and services that capitalize on new technologies and ensuring that the company achieves and maintains technological leadership in the industries that they serve.

Commitment to the Community

Complementing the company's physical legacy of major buildings and roadways in Houston, Halliburton leaders and employees continue to create a legacy of improving the quality of life in the Houston area and around the world. Each year, thousands of Halliburton employees volunteer and support a variety of programs in Houston, including the March of Dimes, Juvenile Diabetes Foundation, Houston International Festival, Junior Achievement and others, as well as contributing to many programs related to education, health/welfare, civic and arts and culture.

A Vision for the Future

Halliburton's founders probably never dreamed that their company would one day become the world's largest oilfield services company and one of the world's largest engineering and construction companies. But they did have a vision to create a company dedicated to quality. Today that vision can still be found throughout their company as Halliburton continues its efforts to be the premier global solutions provider for energy services, engineering, construction and maintenance services, and energy equipment. ■

*Halliburton's **Brown & Root Services** is involved in a joint venture contract to provide comprehensive base operating support services at the Johnson Space Center. RSP crane/bailer system mechanic Ross Rubio makes an adjustment on one of the huge overhead hoists at the JSC's astronaut training pool.*

ENERGY INDUSTRY 217

HOUSTON ★ People ★ Opportunity ★ Success

Schlumberger

The new Schlumberger Reservoir Completions Center, located just south of Houston, is home to a cross-section of engineers focused on products and services that will ultimately enhance recovery from hydrocarbon reservoirs.

If asked to pick a company that best illustrated the symbiotic relationship between Houston and the energy industry during the 20th century, you would be hard-pressed to find a better example than Schlumberger. And the story that could be told would reflect the goals, values and visions shared by both Houston and the company: newcomers in the energy field with innovative ideas welcomed by a city and an industry that value hard work and creativity; a family business that grew to become one of the top three international oilfield companies; a love of the arts and a willingness to nurture and share it openly with the entire community.

Pioneering Oilfield Research

The Schlumberger story began simply enough when the Schlumberger brothers, Conrad and Marcel, developed the theory that various kinds of rock—sandstone, shale and limestone—would react differently to electrical charges. By recording the differences, they discovered that much could be learned about what lay hidden under the surface of the earth. While the technology has dramatically changed, the original Schlumberger theory is still the basis for much of the multi-billion dollar oil and gas exploration industry.

In 1927, Schlumberger ran the first electric log down an oil well, enabling geologists to accurately correlate the strata of one well with those of other wells nearby and gain a clear picture of the location of faults and other structural information. After several years of conducting tests in area oil fields, Conrad Schlumberger incorporated the company in Houston in 1934 and began marketing the company's wireline logging services.

Growing with Houston

Since then, the company has grown in tandem with the energy industry around the world, but especially in Houston. From its original offices in the Esperson Building in downtown Houston, Schlumberger expanded to a 241,000-square-foot complex on the Gulf Freeway that was heralded as "a major factor in Houston's industrial growth" when it opened in 1953.

HOUSTON ★ People ★ Opportunity ★ Success

Schlumberger

On location, a field crew rigs up cost-effective coil tubing equipment to perform operations targeted at boosting production.

A Schlumberger technician runs quality checks on materials used in the production of shaped charges destined for the completion of oil and gas wells.

In 1993, Schlumberger expanded again in the Houston area, this time moving to a 200-acre complex in Sugar Land with 17 buildings and 650,000 square feet of office space and research and development laboratories. Today, Schlumberger Oilfield Services has 2,500 employees in the Houston area.

Through the years, the Schlumberger family also has enriched the cultural life of Houston—and the world—through the vision and generosity of Jean and Dominique de Menil, the daughter of Conrad Schlumberger. Considered one of the most important privately assembled collections of the 20th century, The Menil Collection opened in Houston in 1987 to preserve and exhibit the couple's art collection that includes approximately 15,000 paintings, sculptures, prints, drawings, photographs, and rare books. Exhibits include the tribal cultures of Africa, Oceania, and the American Pacific Northwest as well as masterpieces from antiquity, the Byzantine and medieval worlds, and the 20th century.

From Wirelines to Integrated Reservoir Optimization

From its humble beginnings in providing wireline services, Schlumberger has emerged as a leader in developing a complete life-of-the-reservoir portfolio of products and services. For an existing field, this approach means focusing on strategies and remedial actions to extend longevity, improve financial performance and increase recovery potential. For new fields, it represents a cradle-to-grave approach to reservoir understanding, from discovery through to abandonment.

At Schlumberger, this concept is referred to as Integrated Reservoir Optimization and focuses on four key, interrelated elements: reservoir characterization, development planning, field implementation, and reservoir monitoring and control. The goal of this approach is to create a closed-loop process that optimizes the performance of oil and gas fields while maximizing return and asset value for oil and gas companies.

To complement its vision for Integrated Reservoir Optimization, Schlumberger technology development is now organized around three product groups: Reservoir Evaluation, which includes land and marine seismic together with open-hole and cased-hole logging; Reservoir Development, which includes drilling bits, drilling and measurements, cementing and stimulation, completions and productivity and well intervention; and Reservoir Management, which includes data processing and consulting services, integrated project management and production operations.

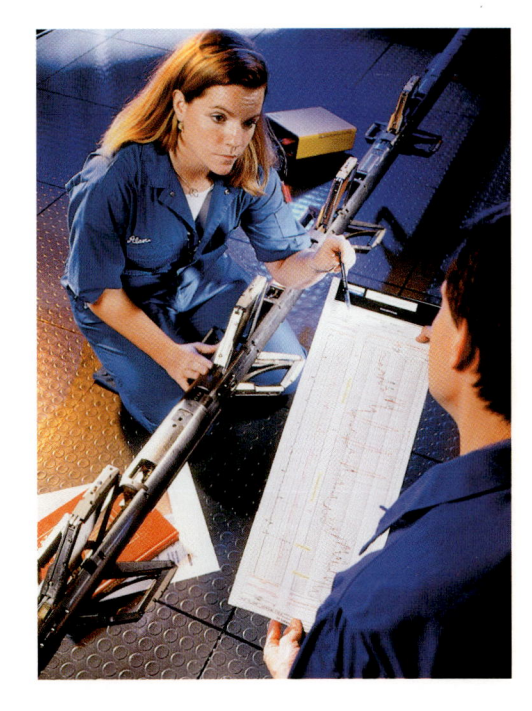

Conscious of the company's beginnings in wireline logging, engineering staff check data recorded by the latest generation of resistivity measurement devices.

HOUSTON ★ People ★ Opportunity ★ Success

Schlumberger

The Schlumberger campus in Sugar Land is home to 1,700 staff who develop and produce a range of products, from marine seismic cables to reservoir fracturing fluids.

Combined, these three Schlumberger product groups exploit synergies and develop innovative techniques to provide virtually every type of exploration and production service required during the life of an oil and gas reservoir. Delivery of Schlumberger services and products worldwide is the responsibility of a connected network of GeoMarkets that bring together geographically focused teams to meet local needs and to provide customized solutions. Houston plays a key role in this network not only through product development, but also through coordination of GeoMarkets in North and South America.

Recognizing that technology has been and will continue to be the key to the future of the global oil and gas industry, Schlumberger is investing more than one million dollars a day in research and development programs focused on delivering the greatest value for its oilfield clients.

It's that kind of dedication to innovation, research and development that has enabled Schlumberger during the 20th century to become one of the leading oilfield companies serving the energy industry in Houston and throughout the world.

For more information about Schlumberger, please visit our web site at www.slb.com. ■

HOUSTON ★ People ★ Opportunity ★ Success

Fluor Daniel, Inc.

FLUOR DANIEL
A *FLUOR* Company

For more than 85 years Fluor Corporation has been a frontrunner in addressing the engineering and construction needs of the energy industry. Today, Fluor Daniel, the company's engineering, procurement, and construction services subsidiary, provides a broad range of technical services to hundreds of clients on over 1,350 projects in more than 50 countries. In the process, Fluor Daniel has grown during the past decade to be consistently ranked as the number-one engineering and construction company in the U.S. according to Engineering News-Record magazine.

In many respects, the company grew up with the oil and gas industry. Since it received its first oil and gas industry contract in 1915, the company has been involved in some of the oil and gas industry's largest projects in the United States and around the world: from the mainline pumping stations and Valdez terminal facilities of the trans-Alaska crude oil pipeline to one of the largest gas-gathering, treatment and transmission projects in Saudi Arabia.

The company's involvement in the oil and gas and chemicals industry initially brought it to Houston in 1948. Today, with more than 2,500 employees and 250 project management and process engineering specialists, the Houston area office is one of the largest among Fluor Daniel's 50 worldwide networked offices located on six continents. Two strategic business units—Oil, Gas and Power, and Chemicals and Life Sciences—are based in the Houston office, focusing primarily on designing, constructing and maintaining facilities that process and refine petroleum, petrochemicals, specialty chemicals and complex biotechnology chemicals.

Houston also is home to Duke/Fluor Daniel, a joint venture formed in 1989 with Duke Energy Corporation. This partnership provides comprehensive engineering, procurement, construction and plant operating services for fossil-fueled electric power generation facilities worldwide.

More than just a traditional engineering and construction firm, Fluor Daniel offers clients total business solutions. Fluor Daniel offers a competitive advantage by providing project management expertise, design and construction to the highest standards of quality and safety, global procurement capability, and extensive experience across a wide range of services and technologies.

For more information about Fluor Daniel, please visit our web site at www.fluordaniel.com. ∎

ENERGY INDUSTRY

HOUSTON ★ People ★ Opportunity ★ Success

Duke Energy

Duke Energy employees volunteer their time and talents to hundreds of worthy causes — from home repair to mentoring students — as a way to improve life in Houston.

The story of Duke Energy is the story of a company that was created by men of vision who wanted to serve the needs of the country and their communities. Today, as Duke Energy enters the 21st Century, the only thing that has changed is the scale of the vision as Duke Energy has expanded to become a global energy provider.

Serving the Country, Communities

In Houston, Duke Energy traces its roots back to the dark days of World War II when enemy submarines sank U.S. oil tankers and the country needed a pipeline to safely transport oil from the Gulf Coast to the East Coast. Those critical pipelines, now listed on the National Register, were later bought by the Houston brothers, George and Herman Brown, and formed the basis of Texas Eastern Transmission Co. These pipelines run from the energy rich supplies of the South to markets in the Northeast.

In the 1980s, Texas Eastern created Houston Center, a dynamic new office and shopping development on 30+ square blocks in downtown Houston, and donated land for the City of Houston's George R. Brown Convention Center, one of the largest convention centers in the country.

222 ENERGY INDUSTRY

HOUSTON ★ People ★ Opportunity ★ Success

Duke Energy

Duke Energy's legacy of serving the community goes even further back in time. In 1904, James Buchanan Duke realized that the future economic health of North and South Carolina was dependent upon developing a reliable source of electricity. Duke's vision was to harness the power of the Catawba River to bring hydroelectric power to the growing textile industry in the Carolinas. Today, Duke Energy employees give back to Houston and the other communities they serve through extensive volunteer activities.

Industry Leadership

Today, Duke Energy is an acknowledged leader in the energy industry. Fortune magazine, for example, has ranked Duke Energy as one of America's Most Admired Companies while a survey by the Financial Times of London of CEOs from around the world has ranked the company as the world's most respected utility company.

Despite being one of the largest global energy companies—with 22,000 employees around the world, $17 billion in revenues and $29 billion in assets—Duke Energy has a comprehensive yet simple and clear corporate strategy: Duke Energy makes energy, moves energy, manages energy and markets energy. Duke Energy companies, for example, make energy at nuclear, fossil-fueled, hydroelectric and other renewable power generation facilities. The company also is the largest U.S. producer of natural gas liquids.

Through its natural gas transmission system headquartered in Houston, Duke Energy moves 7 percent of the natural gas consumed in the United States. In addition, the company moves electricity over 12,000 miles of lines in the Carolinas.

Duke Energy also helps its customers better manage their energy needs through energy audits, equipment retrofits, performance contracts and other services.

Finally, Duke Energy markets multiple forms of energy. In Houston, the company's bustling trading floors market natural gas and electricity. By serving the entire energy value chain by making, moving, managing and marketing energy, Duke Energy is also well positioned to continue to expand on a global scale. The company, which already operates on six continents, put together a package of energy assets and services targeted to address the needs and growth opportunities in Asia Pacific, Latin America and Europe.

For more information on Duke Energy, please visit the web site at www.duke-energy.com. ■

Relying on market experience and a proven business strategy in price and risk management, Duke Energy employees trade and market multiple forms of energy by the hour, the day or the month.

Duke Energy℠

ENERGY INDUSTRY 223

HOUSTON ★ People ★ Opportunity ★ Success

Lyondell Chemical Company

Lyondell creates the basic elements for life, through manufacture of quality chemicals and polymers that are the basic elements of thousands of consumer and industrial goods, such as home remodeling products.

Lyondell Chemical Company's predecessors have roots in Houston that go back to 1917. The company maintains world headquarters in Houston, and the nearby Channelview area is home to two major manufacturing facilities for Lyondell and its Equistar Chemicals, LP, joint venture.

In 1998, Lyondell expanded globally with the acquisition of ARCO Chemical Company. Today, Lyondell is one of the world's largest chemical companies, positioned for chemical industry leadership in the 21st Century.

Positioned for the Future

Lyondell was formed in 1985 from selected petrochemical and refining assets of Atlantic Richfield Company. Through aggressive change management to create and add value, Lyondell has become a global leader in numerous industry segments. The company has approximately $17 billion in combined assets, operations in 15 countries and some 10,000 employees.

Lyondell manufactures the basic elements of thousands of consumer and industrial products that are part of everyday work and family life. Products made from Lyondell's chemicals fill supermarket shelves and are integral components of automobiles, housing, clothing and other necessities.

"We have built Lyondell into an integrated global chemical company, incorporating advanced technologies, with leading market positions in our major businesses," says Lyondell President & CEO Dan F. Smith. "We have accomplished this by driving change within the industry and creating value-enhancing opportunities, including alliances and joint ventures."

For more information about Lyondell Chemical Company, please visit its web site at www.lyondell.com. ∎

HOUSTON ★ People ★ Opportunity ★ Success

LYONDELL-CITGO Refining LP

LCR's future success lies in employees like Janell McClelland and Dave Jenkins, shown here at the 230 Gas Plant, which was built during the 1997 upgrade of the refinery.

While LYONDELL-CITGO is a relatively new name in Houston, the company's roots go back to the very early days of the energy industry in Houston during the 20th century.

The company got its start in 1917 when the former Sinclair Refining Company purchased 710 acres of land along the Houston Ship Channel from members of Houston's founding Allen family. The land included the point at which General Sam Houston and the Texas Army crossed Buffalo Bayou as they marched to victory at the Battle of San Jacinto.

Today, that site is the headquarters of LYONDELL-CITGO Refining LP, a partnership created in 1993 between Lyondell Chemical Co. and CITGO Petroleum Corp., an indirect wholly-owned subsidiary of Venezuela's national oil company, Petroleos de Venezuela. In 1997, the partnership completed a $1.1 billion upgrade of the refinery to process increasing volumes of very heavy Venezuelan crude oil. While the original refinery at the site had a capacity of 500 barrels a day when it opened in 1920, today LYONDELL-CITGO is able to process 265,000 barrels of oil per day to produce high-value products such as gasoline and jet fuel.

"For nearly 80 years, our refinery has successfully risen to the challenges of the petroleum industry, developing new technology, new products and new processes to meet the changing demands of the market," says Charlie Rampacek, president and CEO of LYONDELL-CITGO Refining. ■

ENERGY INDUSTRY 225

HOUSTON ★ People ★ Opportunity ★ Success

INTEC Engineering

Offshore pipeline installation support structure being lowered into position.

INTEC Engineering enters the 21st century with a worldwide reputation as the industry leader in Deepwater Pipelines and Subsea Production, as well as specializing in the Engineering and Construction Management for Long Distance Marine and Onshore Pipelines, and FSO/FPSO systems. This hard-earned reputation has been gained though INTEC's constant involvement in leading edge studies, projects, and full field development within the oil and gas industry.

Strong, Consistent Leadership

INTEC was founded in Houston in March 1984 by four colleagues, who later became the heart of this multi-national firm. Willem Timmermans, Jim Gillespie, David McKeehan, and Bert Schultz started the company with limited staff and funding and nurtured it into a highly successful enterprise. Having recently celebrated its 15th anniversary, INTEC has the added benefit of continued guidance by the same top management team since its inception, and is fortified by a unique and talented group of managers and specialist engineers.

HOUSTON ★ People ★ Opportunity ★ Success

Global Success

With approximately 200 employees worldwide, INTEC has 26 different nationalities representing a global workforce, which gives the company a broad international perspective. INTEC applies a proactive approach to challenges, which has distinguished our efforts during both up and down oil price cycles in the oil and gas industry. In addition to its headquarters in Houston, INTEC has regional offices in Kuala Lumpur, Malaysia; Delft, The Netherlands; and Buenos Aires, Argentina.

Among INTEC's international assignments is the Blue Stream Project, which is a gas transportation system for delivery of processed gas across the 2000-meter deep Black Sea. INTEC was responsible for the Feasibility Study and the Detailed Engineering for two 24-inch submarine pipelines that traverse an exacting route from Djubga, Russia to a landfall just east of Samsun, Turkey. Gas delivery via the Blue Stream Pipeline System is planned for the year 2001.

INTEC assisted Mobil in Equatorial Guinea with the Zafiro Field Development Project offshore West Africa. In Phase I of the project, INTEC was responsible for the routing of all flowlines and umbilicals; design review of the flowlines and risers; fabrication inspection; installation supervision of flowlines, umbilicals, and well jumpers; and general coordination of offshore installation activities and logistics. In Phase II, INTEC is responsible for the coordination of a multiple subsea template system.

Closer to Houston, INTEC was involved in the Texaco Gemini Project located in the deepwater Mississippi Canyon area of the Gulf of Mexico. The project consists of three subsea wells tied back to a subsea manifold in a 3,400 ft. water depth. INTEC's responsibility included Front End Engineering Design, Systems Engineering and Technical Support during offshore installation and commissioning. First gas was produced in June 1999, with the remaining two wells completed in September 1999.

Today, INTEC's list of successful projects covers nearly every ocean and energy producing area of the world. Looking towards a bright and rewarding 21st century, INTEC continues to break new ground and explore innovative horizons.

For more information on INTEC Engineering, and how INTEC can assist you on your next project, contact any one of INTEC's four worldwide offices: Houston (281) 987-0800; Kuala Lumpur 60 (3) 202-2488; Delft 31 (15) 25 65 675; Buenos Aires 54 (1) 14 327 4120. ■

Pipeline end termination for connecting flowlines to subsea production wells.

HOUSTON ★ People ★ Opportunity ★ Success

Fugro

Enron Field will be the new home of the Houston Astros Baseball Team. Joe Kasparek, President of Fugro USA, and Astros second baseman Craig Biggio visit the ballpark construction site. Fugro geotechnical engineers outlined likely foundation problems with the unique retractable roof during construction of the ballpark at Union Station.

From high above the planet to the ocean depths and the earth below, Fugro's services cover the globe. Fugro is a Netherlands-based multi-national group of consulting engineers with more than 200 offices in over 45 countries. Houston serves as regional headquarters for Fugro's North and South American operations and several of its operating companies.

Fugro offers a unique combination of technologically advanced services comprising the collecting, processing and interpreting of data about the ground, air, and water, advising on soil conditions, foundation design, and providing precise positioning services. Onshore and offshore geotechnical engineering and surveying are Fugro's core businesses.

Fugro-McClelland Marine Geosciences, Inc. (FMMG)

Fugro merged with McClelland Engineers in 1987, forming the world's largest offshore geotechnical engineering firm. McClelland drilled the first marine boring for an offshore petroleum structure from a fixed platform in 1947. FMMG has since operated worldwide and drilled over 70 deepwater borings in water depths up to 1,900 meters.

John E. Chance & Associates, Inc. (Fugro-Chance)

One of the world's most trusted and innovative survey service companies, Chance joined Fugro in 1991. In business since 1947, Fugro-Chance provides a wide range of surveying and positioning services and positions more offshore drilling rigs, production platforms and pipeline barges than any other survey company.

Recognized for pioneering new technology, in 1986 Fugro-Chance introduced STARFIX, the world's first continuous 24-hour satellite-based positioning system.

Fugro GeoServices, Inc. (FGSI)

FGSI was formed in 1999 from the Geophysical Services division of Fugro-Chance and the Geosciences division of FMMG. FGSI specializes in marine geohazards data acquisition, pipeline route surveys, and related geohazard consulting and permitting services.

Omnistar, Inc.

Omnistar, Inc., the world leader in precise positioning via satellites, provides signals for land use in North and South America, which are used to correct errors in Global Positioning System (GPS) signals. Omnistar is the number one provider of corrected GPS signals for agricultural users involved in precise farming, for surveyors and other users involved in populating Geographic Information Systems (GIS).

Fugro South, Inc.

Fugro South is engaged in providing onshore and near shore geotechnical engineering and construction materials testing, specialized laboratory testing, and drilling/exploration services. It's Houston based soils laboratory is considered one of the premier facilities in the world, offering conventional as well as specialized soils testing to clients around the globe.

Fugro Geosciences, Inc. (FGI)

Through its drilling and Cone Penetrometer operations (In-Situ testing), FGI supports the larger engineering community in its efforts to collect and analyze soil samples for infrastructure design purposes.

Fugro Global Environmental & Ocean Sciences, Inc. (Fugro GEOS)

Fugro GEOS is a specialist consultancy in oceanographic and meteorological (metocean) data collection, analysis, interpretation and forecasting services for offshore and coastal engineering applications.

Fugro-LCT, Inc.

Fugro-LCT leads the world in marine gravity and magnetic data acquisition, processing and interpretation. Acquired in 1998, Fugro-LCT currently owns and maintains the world's largest inventory of marine gravity meters, which are used to collect a complimentary data set on seismic surveys.

For more information visit the Fugro web site at www.fugro.com. ∎

Fugro Geosciences, Inc. has provided Cone Penetration Testing (CPT) throughout North and South America since the 1970's. CPT testing determines the composition and properties of subsurface soil; geotechnical analysis is conducted on these samples for foundation design and environmental analysis.

HOUSTON ★ People ★ Opportunity ★ Success

Vanco Energy Company

"The time for an independent could not be better," says Vanco Founder and President Gene Van Dyke.

In the new millennium, the future of the offshore oil and gas industry will be in the deepwater regions of the world. And Vanco Energy Company is there. With foresight, imagination and a creative approach to exploration, Vanco is exploring frontier deepwater regions that can produce world-class reserves.

"The future of the oil industry is in deepwater exploration, and the time for an independent could not be better," says Gene Van Dyke, Founder and President of Vanco Energy Company.

For nearly 50 years, Van Dyke has provided the vision and leadership necessary for the company to grow from the oilfields of North Texas to become one of the most promising international independent exploration and production companies headquartered in Houston today.

Since 1973, the company has specialized in international offshore exploration, first in the Dutch North Sea where it was responsible for many of the most significant oil discoveries, and now in Africa where it is focused exclusively on deepwater opportunities. Since 1996, Vanco has obtained exploration licenses in Gabon, Morocco, Côte d'Ivoire and Senegal, and is ranked as the largest deepwater license holder in West Africa with over 20 million gross acres.

"Vanco's success is a direct result of our company's experience, our highly qualified staff, our extensive exploration database and the relationships that we have built within the industry and host governments," says Van Dyke.

For more information about Vanco Energy Company, please call 713-877-8544, or E-mail: info@vancoenergy.com. ■

HOUSTON ★ People ★ Opportunity ★ Success

Altra Energy

Electrifying the 21st Century

Altra Energy Technologies Inc. is the model of 21st century Houston, with its roots grounded firmly in the energy industry and its branches reaching into the Internet Age.

Altra is a leading provider of business-to-business electronic markets and software solutions to the energy industry. The company operates a real-time, Internet-based electronic marketplace where energy buyers and sellers meet on-line to trade natural gas, electricity, crude and natural gas liquids. Altra's electronic trading platforms are linked to the company's suite of software products and services used around the world for scheduling, transportation management and accounting for energy transactions.

Chairman Rusty Braziel founded Altra in 1996 by combining information technology businesses started by The Williams Companies and PanEnergy Corp. (now Duke Energy) to form an independent company dedicated to the integration of energy electronic commerce and transaction management solutions.

Deregulation has been a key driver in Altra's formation and subsequent rapid growth. Altra stands at the nexus of two extraordinary developments: an energy industry being reshaped by deregulation, and business-to-business commerce being redefined by the Internet. Today, the energy marketplace has truly become an information business.

As a Houston-based company, Altra supports groups ranging from the United Way and the Houston Livestock Show and Rodeo to citywide book drives for literacy and the Toys for Tots campaign. The company employs 300 energy professionals in Houston, and in regional offices in Atlanta, Calgary and Portland, with distributors in Europe, Latin America and Australia. ■

ENERGY INDUSTRY 231

HOUSTON ★ People ★ Opportunity ★ Success

Weatherford International, Inc.

Weatherford International, Inc. (NYSE:WFT) is one of the world's largest oilfield service companies. Weatherford offers its customers leading-edge products and responsive, specialized services that focus on the well installation, well completion and production enhancement sectors of the global oil and gas industry.

Weatherford sells its products and services through four business divisions that operate in more than 300 locations worldwide: Weatherford Drilling & Intervention Services, Weatherford Completion Systems, Weatherford Artificial Lift Services, Weatherford Global Compression Services, and drilling products manufacturer Grand Prideco.

Employing more than 10,000 people worldwide in every major oil producing region of the world, Weatherford's global headquarters are in Houston, along with the company's advanced technology and training center.

The 1998 merger of EVI and Weatherford Enterra enabled the company to aggressively streamline, refocus, reorganize and position the new Weatherford to retain its historical strengths as it grows to meet its customers' demands into the new millennium. Today's Weatherford offers more innovative technologies, greater capabilities and increased products and services to meet the industry's growing need for production enhancement and reservoir revitalization. ■

Weatherford®

232 ENERGY INDUSTRY

HOUSTON ★ People ★ Opportunity ★ Success

Mustang Engineering

MUSTANG ENGINEERING

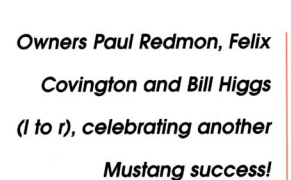

Owners Paul Redmon, Felix Covington and Bill Higgs (l to r), celebrating another Mustang success!

*Usari Development Project
Mobil Nigeria Unlimited
Bight of Benin, Nigeria*

*Coastal Aruba Refining Company N.V.
San Nicolas, Aruba*

*World's Highest Known Gas Transmission Pipeline
17,783 feet above sea level
Andes Mountains between Argentina and Chile*

Some four-letter words are always inappropriate, but at Mustang Engineering, the forbidden word has 12 letters. It's "conventional."

Founded in 1987 by "three scared engineers," Mustang has demonstrated anything but conventional growth and conventional style. From three employees on its first day (founders Felix Covington, Paul Redmon and Bill Higgs), the company now surpasses 1,000. Employees own about one-third of the private company.

Hardly stiff, programmed business people, Mustang's founders have lived out the notion that a happy workplace is a more productive workplace. In the early days of festive events, Higgs' home became the Christmas party site. The growing firm enjoyed shrimp boils, small golf tournaments and Friday lunches in the conference room. Now sheer size causes Mustang to choose larger venues for its frequent gatherings.

"People told us that we would not be able to keep our spirit due to business pressures," Higgs said. "Our experience has been just the opposite. We're doing more of it now than we ever did. Operating Mustang Engineering is an excuse to take care of our people, to keep giving them steady employment. We work with Christian principles. We treat our people with respect. We include customers and vendors among our people."

The firm first specialized in offshore projects. In Higgs' words, "About 60 percent of oil and gas projects either happen in or are greatly influenced by Houston." Mustang then expanded smoothly to pipelines and process plants to meet global customer and market demand.

In its early days, Higgs said, the firm "kept completing projects under budget and ahead of schedule. When that happens, can you guess where the client will take its next project?"

The projects keep coming. And the parties, too. ∎

ENERGY INDUSTRY 233

HOUSTON ★ People ★ Opportunity ★ Success

Van De Wiele Engineering

President & C.E.O., John Van De Wiele

The lake system engineered by VEI at Falcon Point subdivision and golf course provides a source of water for irrigation, detention of storm water and aesthetic beauty and contributes to area ecology.

The year and the century are changing for Van De Wiele Engineering, Inc. (VEI), but the firm's reputation will remain the same.

Dedication to quality since its 1978 founding has helped make VEI a proven leader in civil engineering consultation.

"Throughout Houston and the counties that surround us, our firm is recognized for combining the newest technologies with a true talent for understanding client needs," said President John Van De Wiele, P.E. "Our approach has consistently delivered effective solutions under budget and on time. Punctuality is important to us."

VEI's expertise includes civil engineering consulting services that relate to land development-drainage, storm water, wastewater, water supply, transportation, planning and special studies. The firm also provides construction management services.

VEI traditionally works with Greater Houston Municipal Utility Districts (MUDs), the City of Houston, Harris County, counties adjacent to Harris, Harris County Toll Road Authority and the Texas Department of Transportation. VEI is the engineering consultant of choice for more than 21 MUDs.

Van De Wiele explained, "With MUDs go residential and commercial land development projects. A substantial part of our engineering service is provided to some of Houston's premier land development firms."

In recent years, VEI has also engineered the rebuilding of Fannin Street downtown, a METRO project that exceeded $11 million in value. Montgomery County engaged the firm to design Walden Road, a contract worth more than $4 million. VEI also served as construction inspector for a $40-million segment of Sam Houston Tollway.

"Our firm specializes in infrastructure improvements for residential and commercial areas," Van De Wiele said. "I believe we have the capabilities and experience required to keep our clients' projects on schedule and in compliance with rules and regulations." ■

HOUSTON ★ People ★ Opportunity ★ Success

Air Products

With increased global competition, manufacturers in the chemical process industries (CPI) are being challenged to produce better quality products with fewer resources at lower cost. Air Products' technological innovations, both production and applications-based, have been helping CPI customers do just that—reduce costs, increase their production and obtain greater operating flexibility. Supplying customers via a complete range of industrial gas options—including pipeline hydrogen, oxygen and nitrogen, on-site hydrogen and syngas plants, cryogenic and non-cryogenic oxygen and nitrogen plants, merchant supplied liquid, cylinders; industrial nitrogen services, and more—Air Products consistently provides value to more than 200 customers along the Gulf Coast.

In the Houston Ship Channel area, Air Products operates or has under construction several facilities for the production of carbon monoxide, syngas and/or hydrogen, supplying the demanding reliability requirements of the CPI. The company's hydrogen/CO/syngas supply network, the largest in the world, consists of over 200 miles of pipeline, connecting more than 40 customer locations from the Houston Ship Channel to the Texas/Louisiana border. Air Products' oxygen and nitrogen pipeline also provides multi-source, highly reliable, economic industrial gas supply for chemical and refining customers. Already the leading domestic industrial gas supplier in the Ship Channel area, Air Products is continually working to enhance production processes to provide economical gaseous and liquid oxygen and nitrogen capacities.

Utilities Integration Services

In some cases, combining supply of industrial gases and other utilities can provide a cost-effective overall supply package. Integrating world-class engineering and operating expertise with a focus on the customer-specific situation, Air Products has comprehensive capabilities and experience in design, procurement, construction and reliable operation of process plants supplying industrial gases, power, steam, water and air optimized for the individual customer requirement.

As an active participant in Responsible Care® initiatives, Air Products is an industry leader in industrial gas safety. ∎

HOUSTON ★ People ★ Opportunity ★ Success

Rimkus Consulting Group, Inc.

Deductive reasoning and devotion to detail helped Sherlock Holmes unravel some of the greatest mysteries of his day. This fictional detective would have felt at home at Rimkus Consulting Group, Inc. A consulting and engineering firm, Rimkus gathers and analyzes scientific evidence to solve problems perplexing insurance companies, law firms, corporations and other clients worldwide.

"We're called in when something bad happens — a fire, explosion or industrial incident, product or equipment failure, vehicle accident, natural disaster or hazardous emission," explains Frank Culberson, president and chief executive officer. Using sophisticated computer tools, Rimkus' technical teams re-create the event to determine what happened, why and who's responsible. They also can assess damages and establish remediation costs.

"Often, our clients are dealing with big-dollar insurance claims or lawsuits," Culberson says, "or they want to know what happened so they can prevent a recurrence."

From offices in nine cities, Rimkus tackles the most complex technical problems. Its 120-person staff includes representatives of all engineering disciplines as well as architects, environmental scientists, metallurgists, toxicologists, chemists and industrial hygienists.

"We're a one-stop shop," Culberson says. "That's important, because solving complex problems may require multiple disciplines."

Rimkus' experts can provide credible testimony, in laymen's terms, in depositions, at court and in hearings. In addition, the company's graphics division can produce photos, illustrations, models, videos and computer-generated 3-D animation to supplement oral and written reports.

Even Sherlock Holmes would be impressed. ■

236 ENERGY INDUSTRY

HOUSTON ★ People ★ Opportunity ★ Success

Ascension Capital Advisors, Inc.

Paul B. Thompson, President

"Wealth is created by concentration, but wealth is preserved by diversification."

At Ascension Capital Advisors, President Paul Thompson isn't a betting man, nor are his many clients. "When you're dealing with personal investments, you need to follow a disciplined, strategic approach that is based on understanding the long-term goals and financial objectives of the individual, family or trust involved," Thompson says.

"Wealth is created by concentration, but wealth is preserved by diversification." Many people have created wealth in this country by concentrating on one specific area. It may have been drilling an oil well, building a company or speculating in one specific field. That of course is the American dream! But once wealth is created, most people will preserve it by diversifying into other areas.

As a native Houstonian with more than 15 years of experience in the financial investment community, Thompson founded Ascension Capital in 1997 because he believed that there was a need for a more personalized approach to helping individuals and families manage their investments.

"Ascension's success comes from our core belief that there are proven methods to increase investment returns while minimizing risks," Thompson says. "We believe that no single style of investing dominates over the long term. Our disciplined investment process avoids reactions to short-term investment styles or market moves that cost clients real wealth."

In many respects, Ascension manages clients' portfolios much like a pension plan at a major company, using a multi-asset, multi-style, and multi-manager approach to enable clients to minimize risks and maximize returns. Ascension works strictly on a fee basis, which not only reduces transaction costs but also removes any bias or conflict of interest from the client relationship.

"Ascension replaces personal hunches and guesswork with solid investment management discipline that puts some of the world's best money managers to work for our clients," Thompson says. "In essence, we bring an institutional level of service to money management that most individuals would otherwise not be able to access."

For more information on Ascension Capital Advisors, please call 713-952-6900 or visit their website at ascensioncapital.com. *Securities offered through Dominion Investor Services, Inc. Member NASD, and SPIC.* ∎

BANKING & FINANCIAL 237

HOUSTON ★ People ★ Opportunity ★ Success

Sterling Bank

Sterling Bank, for over 25 years, taking care of Houston area owner-operated businesses.

Sterling Bankers understand our success depends on our customers' success. At Sterling Bank, it's all about people and always will be.

The more other banks become national, the more Houston-based Sterling Bank remains local. Founded as a neighborhood financial institution in one location, Sterling has emerged as a financial institution focused on owner-operated businesses with 22 locations. Dramatic growth also appears in assets, which have risen to nearly $2 billion.

What has fueled Sterling's careful, yet dramatic, growth? Sterling bankers remind themselves of the answer each day: "Our business is all about people and always will be."

Though commitment to personalized banking remains Sterling's broad centerpiece of operations, the organization also moves forward with specific goals and objectives. Under Chairman George Martinez and President Downey Bridgwater, Sterling focuses on those businesses that have borrowing needs up to $2 million.

"Most banks have the same products," Bridgwater said. "Most banks have the same technology. I believe personal service makes the difference. We concentrate on companies that are underserved by large national and out-of-state banks."

HOUSTON ★ People ★ Opportunity ★ Success

In addition to specializing in service to owner-operated businesses, Sterling tries to attract bankers who understand their important role in Greater Houston's financial world. Sterling also remains alert to the possibility of acquiring other community banks.

Bridgwater noted that wherever steady growth takes Sterling Bank, the operation will remain focused on the personal touch.

Sterling will beneficially modify banking customs if those changes result in better service. For example, banks traditionally have centralized many of their decision-making responsibilities. Sterling takes the opposite approach.

"We have empowered each of our bankers to be decision-makers and to take care of the customer immediately," Bridgwater said. "We don't believe in the flagship-bank concept."

Bridgwater emphasized that while some banks' policies obstruct fulfilling customer needs, Sterling "keeps customer needs in the forefront. For example, banks can get so absorbed in selling products that they don't focus on the customer. If you're focused on selling, you're not listening to and fulfilling the needs of the customer."

"As part of that focus, we also try to keep our internal customer—our employees—fulfilled. We spend an enormous amount of time on the growth and development of our employees. If we're not meeting their needs, how motivated will they be to fulfill our customers' needs?"

In a business where independent banks often become dinosaurs, Sterling has relied on the personal touch to turn itself into a tiger. ■

Sterling Bankers are empowered to make decisions and take care of their customers' needs immediately.

BANKING & FINANCIAL 239

HOUSTON ★ People ★ Opportunity ★ Success

AIM Funds

AIM's investment decisions are made by teams of managers who collectively contribute ideas and help ensure management continuity.

Houstonians wanting to invest with a successful money management firm don't need to call New York or other world financial centers. Instead, thousands of investors from Houston—as well as 6 million shareholders from across the United States and around the world—have turned to AIM Funds, one of the nation's 10 largest and most successful mutual fund companies.

Ted Bauer, Bob Graham and Gary Crum, all of whom remain active in the day-to-day management of the company, founded AIM on a dream and a vision. When AIM started out in 1976, the company had only a table, two chairs and a telephone. By mid-1999, the company had more than $121 billion in assets under management and more than 2,100 employees worldwide, most of whom are based in Greenway Plaza.

Over the years, such funds as AIM Weingarten Fund, AIM Constellation Fund and AIM Value Fund have become household words for millions of investors. AIM funds are sold through financial consultants as a reflection of the company's belief that investors can benefit significantly from having the advice and guidance of a professional who can create investment plans to meet clients' individual needs.

As a member of the $295 billion AMVESCAP group, AIM offers more than 50

240 BANKING & FINANCIAL

HOUSTON ★ People ★ Opportunity ★ Success

mutual funds, multiple investment management styles, a broadened product range and a variety of investment services. Managing global portfolios successfully requires insight into the intricacies of different markets, cultures and financial systems, and AIM has access to more than 80 experienced portfolio managers and more than 100 analysts worldwide.

"It took years of strategic planning and disciplined growth to get to where we are today," says Bauer, AIM's chairman. "And it couldn't have been done without our team of exemplary employees, whose collective commitment to excellence in everything from investment management to customer service brings value to our clients."

AIM also was built on innovative money-market and fixed-income products. In 1977, the company introduced the first underwritten high-yield bond fund. Three years later, AIM launched the first low-cost institutional money-market fund.

Today, The AIM Family of Funds® offers a full, diversified line of retail mutual funds and investment products for investors at all levels of risk tolerance. AIM also serves many of the largest banks in the United States through trusts, pension funds, profit-sharing plans, securities-lending programs and other custodial relationships.

AIM's equity funds follow three disciplined investment strategies designed for a variety of market conditions—growth, value and a blend of growth and value called growth at a reasonable price. The company's diverse array of fixed-income products range from conservative government securities to higher-yielding income funds.

"While we are proud of our past, our focus is on the future," Bauer says. "We continue to position AIM as the model investment-management firm of the 21st century—a company that can offer an unsurpassed array of quality products and services to investors worldwide."

For more information about AIM, please visit the company's web site at www.aimfunds.com. ∎

In the fast-paced mutual fund industry, customer service has become an increasingly valuable asset in developing and maintaining relationships with AIM's clients.

BANKING & FINANCIAL 241

HOUSTON ★ People ★ Opportunity ★ Success

MCG/Dulworth, Inc.

MCG

MCG/Dulworth, Inc. Board members include (left to right)

(seated)

Jim Phillips, Chairman

Jack Dulworth, Founder

(standing)

John Moore, Vice President

Dee Sullenger, Vice President

Lori Thomas, Vice President

Chuck Bracht, President

Management Compensation Group/Dulworth, Inc. helps businesses, families and individuals attain their long-term goals through informed planning. MCG offers both planning services and products in the areas of employee benefits, retirement planning, compensation consulting, executive benefits and individual planning.

The firm's many services reflect the diverse professional backgrounds of several principals.

Jack Dulworth founded the firm in 1952 as an independent insurance brokerage organization. Jack specialized in financial planning for high-net-worth individuals and small business owners, and this service continues in one of MCG's three marketing units.

Jim Phillips joined the organization in 1977, adding an employee benefits practice to the firm's capabilities. Now MCG's Chairman, Phillips oversees health & welfare and retirement benefits for mid-sized companies, typically with fewer than 3,000 employees.

President Chuck Bracht brought an executive benefits focus to the firm in 1983. The typical client company has 400 or more employees, and a desire to restore to top management benefits which have been limited by the tax code.

MCG has also established itself as a leader in compensation consulting for profit and non-profit organizations of any size.

Bracht commented upon MCG's advantages: "I believe that no other firm surpasses us in experience. Of our staff of 26 employees, only eight are involved in marketing. This reflects our client-oriented perspective; our focus is service."

MCG's future glows as brightly as its nearly 50-year history. For individuals and for companies of almost any size, MCG has the answers that will lead to successful planning. ■

HOUSTON ★ People ★ Opportunity ★ Success

Gull Industries

Since 1968, Gull Industries has provided the World with high quality metal finishing products. Pictured in front of one of their facilities is original owner Erma Mowry Knowlton (left center) is assisted by son, J. Kelly Mowry, President (pictured to her right) and by (from left to right) David L. Dennison, Vice President; Robert Garza, Maintenance Manager; Betty Spoon, Office Manager; Leonard Trinidad, Manager, Shop 1; Alberto Mani, Manager, Shop 2/Gull Industries-Lubbock; and Alex Chanthanark, Assistant Manager, Shop 2.

The new century marks more than one milestone at Gull Industries. The north Houston metal-finishing company enters its fourth decade of expanding operations to meet the needs of customers around the globe.

Gull continues to grow steadily in sales, productivity, employment and manufacturing space, yet it remains one of Greater Houston's better-kept industrial secrets.

"Everyone knows us, and still no one knows us," says J. Kelly Mowry, president of Gull Industries.

Gull Industries provides metal finishing, and the company's processes include precision dense chrome (Gullite), electroless nickel, nichrome (high-production nickel chrome), vapor honing and duplexed coatings.

"Though Houstonians know about Frito bags and the lunar lander, they probably don't know that we're involved in those products," says Mowry, whose late father founded Gull Industries. "For example, one of our metal-finishing processes assures the quality of bag-forming equipment for corn- and potato chip makers in the U.S., Europe, Australia and many other places. Without our finishing on the bag-forming equipment, it would wear out rapidly, and that bag of chips might cost $1.50 instead of 69 cents!"

Both an engineer and a pilot, Mowry explains that it's difficult for most people to get through a routine day without encountering Gull Industries' work. Even the bright, distinctive sprinkler heads in most Houston hotels result from Gull Industries' finishing.

Gull Industries takes pride in both exceptional service and maintaining one of the nation's most environmentally safe plants. The company dedicates itself to exceeding government requirements by implementing additional procedures, such as establishing air and water-quality systems when regulations do not even require one. Gull Industries' commitment to keeping its workplace safe for employees and neighbors earned the 1998, City of Houston Environmental Achievement Award. ■

MANUFACTURING/INDUSTRIAL

HOUSTON ★ People ★ Opportunity ★ Success

Stewart & Stevenson

Enron Field stands on the same downtown plot where Stewart & Stevenson planted its modest roots back in 1902. The Astros will begin playing baseball at the new park in 2000, but Stewart & Stevenson has been busy hitting industrial home runs for nearly a century.

Founded by blacksmith C. Jim Stewart and woodworker Joe R. Stevenson before the city had paved streets, the young company quickly grew into Houston's largest and most successful blacksmith shop. As "horseless carriages" began growing in popularity early in the 20th century, Stewart & Stevenson nimbly adapted its business from blacksmithing to auto and body repair.

"If a car's body was damaged, Houston had no infrastructure for fixing the damage," said C. Jim Stewart III, vice president and great-grandson of one of the two founders. "My great-grandfather and his associates successfully repaired the cars."

That smooth transition has typified almost a century of success and diversification for Stewart & Stevenson. The firm has been adept at identifying, entering and succeeding in new markets. From blacksmithing to more sophisticated endeavors, such as military truck manufacturing, energy industry equipment and aviation ground-support equipment, the still-Houston-based company has a shining record of local, regional and international achievement.

244 MANUFACTURING/INDUSTRIAL

HOUSTON ★ People ★ Opportunity ★ Success

Stewart & Stevenson serves global customers from locations throughout the world, including seven in South America. It operates 29 facilities in the U.S., including 15 in Greater Houston.

"Our diversification and loyal employees have been the cornerstone of our success," Stewart explained. "When one area of business is down, another is up." Certainly none has been more "up" than military transportation. At its Tactical Vehicle Systems' Sealy plant, Stewart & Stevenson has already manufactured 12,000 vehicles that were more than twice as old as some of the people driving them."

The Army vehicle represents only one milestone for this tradition-rich company. Its 1938 General Motors' distribution agreement for diesel engines was perhaps the most significant contract in company history. At one point during World War II, the company was turning out 30 diesels daily to power Sherman tanks.

More than 30 years ago, Stewart & Stevenson opened another important door when it formed the airline Products group. It manufactures ground support equipment that moves aircraft, delivers auxiliary power and transports luggage for commercial airliners.

In power generation, marine products, petroleum products and other transportation products, Stewart & Stevenson continues to develop new areas of manufacturing leadership.

Stewart & Stevenson values individual tradition even more than corporate tradition. Jim Stewart's sons represent fifth-generation employment. Many employees honored at the annual service awards banquet have served the company for more than 40 years.

"Dedication and loyalty of employees has been one of the two most important reasons for our success," Stewart said. "With 30 years of service to our company, I'm one of the new kids on the block. "The second reason for our success is the loyalty of customers in the markets we serve.

"Thanks to our employees and customers, we are proud to salute Houston in the new millennium as a company that has been part of our city's fabric for nearly 100 years." ■

MANUFACTURING/INDUSTRIAL 245

HOUSTON ★ People ★ Opportunity ★ Success

Cooper Cameron Corporation

The Established Market Leader in petroleum and industrial equipment and services.

Cameron products and services are helping the oil and gas industry meet the difficult challenges of ultra deepwater reservoirs.

Even from the company's first day in July 1995, Cooper Cameron Corporation was an established and recognized leader in petroleum and industrial equipment and services. Following its spin-off from Cooper Industries, the new Cooper Cameron Corporation was blessed with solid market positions and respected product brand names.

Proud, tradition-rich names like Cameron®, Cooper-Bessemer®, W-K-M®, Willis®, Turbo Air®, Demco®, Superior® and many more gave the enterprise something large to live up to. Given this leadership head start, management determined that "standing still" was not an option.

From the beginning, examples of market leader innovation have been easy to see: Cooper Turbocompressor's Turbo Air low-maintenance, oil-free air compressors. Cameron Control's new CAMTROL™ subsea drilling and production control systems. Cameron's award-winning LoadKing™ free-standing riser systems for deepwater wells. Ingenious VBR II™ ram packers for Cameron blowout preventers to form an "iris" around drill pipes of various sizes for safer drilling operations.

The company has pioneered a variety of innovative and cost-saving *service* options as well. For example, the Cooper Cameron Valves Double C Service program with its industry-leading 2-year valve warranty option. Cameron's comprehensive new CAMSERV™ aftermarket services to help reduce your Total Cost of Ownership. The Cooper Turbocompressor quick-turnaround Short Cycle Order Response product repair service. And Cooper Energy Services' remanufactured products program offering fully warranted engines *and* compressors for about 75% of the cost of a new product.

HOUSTON ★ People ★ Opportunity ★ Success

Many customers today are not looking as much for technical advancements and innovative services as they are for something that will get the job done at the lowest reasonable cost. For them, reliability and functionality are the primary buying factors.

Cameron has responded with its modular, pre-engineered MOSAIC™ subsea production systems. MOSAIC systems are so flexible, they can be economically adapted for virtually any subsea development concept. And nobody offers more dependable valve options than Cooper Cameron Valves: ball valves, gate valves, butterfly valves, Orbit® mechanical cam process valves, chokes, couplings, and a wide array of accessories to satisfy any flow control need.

Superior 2400 Series engines from Cooper Energy Services are designed to run 24,000 hours between top end and 48,000 hours before major overhauls. You get a lot more up-time and a lot less maintenance.

From reliable, no-nonsense equipment and comprehensive support service packages to technically advanced products and integrated systems, you'll find something to like about the new Cooper Cameron. You might even find it in cyberspace.

Our industry-leading web site now offers more than 10,000 pages of information. You'll find everything from product and personnel information to financial highlights and training seminar dates. TRANSACT, a restricted access section of the web site, offers electronic ordering of spare and replacement parts.

You will also find engineering drawings, technical bulletins, installation procedures and much more in TRANSACT. And it's available 24 hours a day, 7 days a week at the click of a mouse.

All this from a company that hasn't even celebrated its fifth birthday. You might say The Established Market Leader is getting more established every day. ∎

Cooper Energy Services and Cooper Cameron Valves provide dependable products for oil and gas transmission and storage.

MANUFACTURING/INDUSTRIAL 247

HOUSTON ★ People ★ Opportunity ★ Success

Suhm Spring Works, Inc.

Today, Suhm Spring Works, Inc. benefits from the leadership of three native Houstonians. (Left to right) Mark Scarborough, Vice President, Russell Morgan, President and Great Grandson of the Founder, Richard Vargas, Assistant Vice President.

Many manufacturers have come and gone over time, but Suhm Spring Works Inc. has been in business for 115 years.

German immigrant Carl J. Suhm founded the company in 1885 with one guiding principle—to produce a superior caliber product to meet his customers' needs. That principle hasn't changed, and will continue to serve Suhm Spring Works and its clients well into the 21st century and beyond.

The company is an industry leader in mechanical springs, wire forms and stampings, producing them in diameters from .005 to 2.875 inches in round, square or rectangular shapes. Much of the work is based on precision design and performed by true craftsmen—85 employees who work in popular and exotic materials, either building from a client's drawings or designing and developing the products required to solve a problem. Computer models provide precise stress and load analysis for each customer's specialized springs.

In order to provide customers with the most current and wide range of capabilities, the company continually invests in new technology and new equipment. Also, through an on-going education program, each technician is thoroughly trained to know the ins and outs of the spring fabrication process. From top to bottom, high quality craftsmanship begins with high quality design, a service clients always can count on with Suhm Spring Works.

HOUSTON ★ People ★ Opportunity ★ Success

Suhm Spring Works products can be found around the world, primarily serving the oil and gas, petrochemical, heavy equipment, commercial nuclear, aerospace and defense industries.

Principals Russell Morgan, Richard Vargas and Mark Scarborough ensure Suhm Spring Works adheres to ISO 9001 quality assurance guidelines. Their respect for quality is an attitude within the company that is as strong today as it was over a century ago.

In addition to being a long-standing member of the Houston community, Suhm Spring Works is an active member, participating in a number of civic and charitable organizations. Over the decades, Suhm employees have seen Houston grow and change into the dynamic international city that it is, and look forward to the next millennium and the promising future for Houston. ■

Suhm has been operating continuously with Houston as its base since 1885. (Third from left), Gene Suhm, Son of the Founder, (Fourth from left) Carl Suhm, Founder of Suhm Spring Works.

Headquartered in Houston, Texas since 1885

MANUFACTURING/INDUSTRIAL 249

HOUSTON ★ People ★ Opportunity ★ Success

PRIME Service, Inc.

PRIME's fundamental philosophy - know and satisfy your customer

Headquartered in Houston for 37 years, PRIME is one of the largest companies in the rental industry, providing safe, reliable, high-quality equipment to the construction, industrial and residential marketplace.

"Our industry is rapidly changing, but I still believe that the school of hard knocks has taught us many tricks of the trade that the new entrants into the industry have yet to learn," said Pete Post, President and COO of PRIME Service, Inc. "We should not lose focus on the basic products we deliver day in and day out to our customers, which are service and labor-reducing equipment of high quality at a competitive price."

Houston Proud

PRIME's 182 locations and 3,000-plus employees are concentrated across the Sunbelt, where construction continues year round. PRIME field offices also are located in Mexico, Canada and Puerto Rico, and in other parts of the United States. Houston's central location along the Sunbelt makes it an excellent hub for PRIME. "We're totally committed to Houston; we're here to stay," Post said.

PRIME can service anything from a complete plant turnaround to a homeowner's need for a pressure washer. About 50 percent of PRIME customers are commercial contractors; 45 percent are industrial; and 5 percent are homeowners. One reason PRIME has remained a leader in the rental equipment business is its on-going Preventive Maintenance Program. Because down time due to equipment malfunction means lost productivity and profits, PRIME provides maintenance and repair service seven days a week, 24 hours a day.

HOUSTON   ★   People   ★   Opportunity   ★   Success

Prime Performance

PRIME's strategy involves a heavy commitment to training and a process to measure internal performance and improvements. "Within our training programs at PRIME, we teach our trainees the human side, as well as the technical side of the business," Post said. "We tell them about the customer loyalties built up over many years due to consistent high levels of service and understanding the needs of each customer."

Quality training has contributed to a satisfied workforce, with a turnover rate of only 2 percent annually among employees who have been with the company five years or longer. PRIME's nine-person executive management team has more than 180 years' experience. "When you consider we are a service industry and prone to experience high turnover, we believe we are accomplishing our goal in retention of good people," Post said. "And, good people make things happen."

Customers agree. In PRIME's internal newsletter, customer comments are published regularly. "I just wanted to express my thanks for the timeliness and excellent quality of response that your people provided," wrote one Chevron Products Company customer. "I feel your performance is an excellent example of the performance one would hope to achieve from a closely working alliance relationship. We could not have returned to operation so quickly and efficiently without your excellent help."

For more information about PRIME Service, Inc., call 281-578-5600 or access their web site at www.prime-equip.com. ∎

HOUSTON ★ People ★ Opportunity ★ Success

Hitachi

Hitachi, the world's 10th largest manufacturer, maintains an important office in Houston, site of Hitachi Construction Machinery America.

Nearly 80 employees are Houston-based, though they conduct business throughout North America. They serve a company that has built a record filled with distinction.

Hitachi Construction Machinery manufactures more models of excavators than any other company. Hitachi accounts for about 40 percent of the world's hydraulic mining shovel market and 20 percent of the world's excavator market.

Now the company introduces an array of new products, including three mini-excavators, five cranes and two construction-size excavators. Industry-leading technology sets these and existing Hitachi products apart from the competition. For example, a new boom crane (load capacity 77 to 220 tons) features unusually precise independent main and auxiliary hoist drums. They provide the ultimate in lifting control. Hitachi has again designed the ergonomically adjustable seat and seat lever for the operator's immediate comfort.

In addition to its large Houston office, Hitachi operates North American manufacturing facilities in North Carolina, Mexico and British Columbia.

Under President William Horaney, the company enters the new millennium poised to build upon its reputation as a leading global manufacturer. Hitachi's goal is to be viewed as the very best excavator supported by the most customer-committed organization in the world. ■

HOUSTON ★ People ★ Opportunity ★ Success

Madden Bolt

A strong foundation building to the future

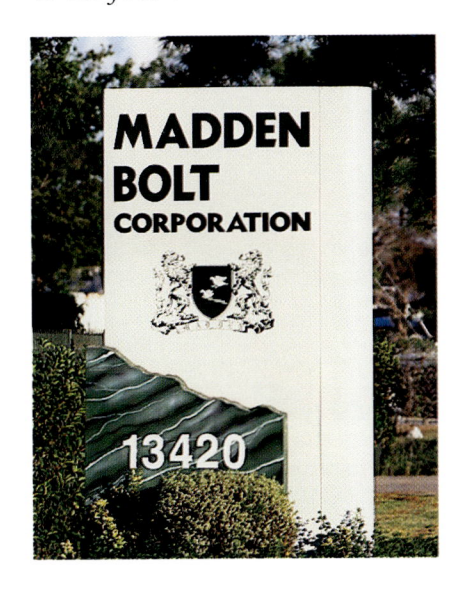

Madden Bolt:
Past-Present-Future

When David Madden founded Madden Bolt in 1988, the company had just six employees and operated from a leased steel fabrication building with broken glass windows, dirt floors and only six bolt fabrication machines.

Today, the company annually sells more than $5 million quarter-inch to four-inch diameter custom bolts, holding together everything from a Hawaiian chemical plant to parts of Enron Field.

Madden Bolt owns a new facility on six acres of land along Hempstead Highway with all the comforts of home. The property even hosts a catfish pond with resident ducks, turtles and wild birds. Four of the original six employees are still with the company, contributing to a 55-member work force that today also includes two of Madden's sons: Brian and Kevin.

"Houston has been one of the biggest factors in our success," Madden says. The area's petrochemical industry uses the company's bolts daily in upgrades, expansions and for maintenance, and the Port of Houston ships tons of Madden bolts all over the world.

The company struggled its first few years, having begun during the depths of Houston's oil-related recession. But Madden attributes his success to three key principles:

1. Old fashioned service to the customer every time
2. Teamwork, dedication and the attitude of all the employees
3. The great location and dynamics of Houston

This family based business still features the bolt sleeve that David and brother Richard invented in 1983. More importantly, David says, the company that features his family's name is a successful tribute to his parents, especially the strong foundation he built while working in his father's own bolt manufacturing business decades ago.

For more information, visit www.maddenbolt.com or call 713-939-9999. ■

MANUFACTURING/INDUSTRIAL

HOUSTON ★ People ★ Opportunity ★ Success

Houston Foam Plastics

Custom foam design and fabrication for engineered cushion packaging and insulation

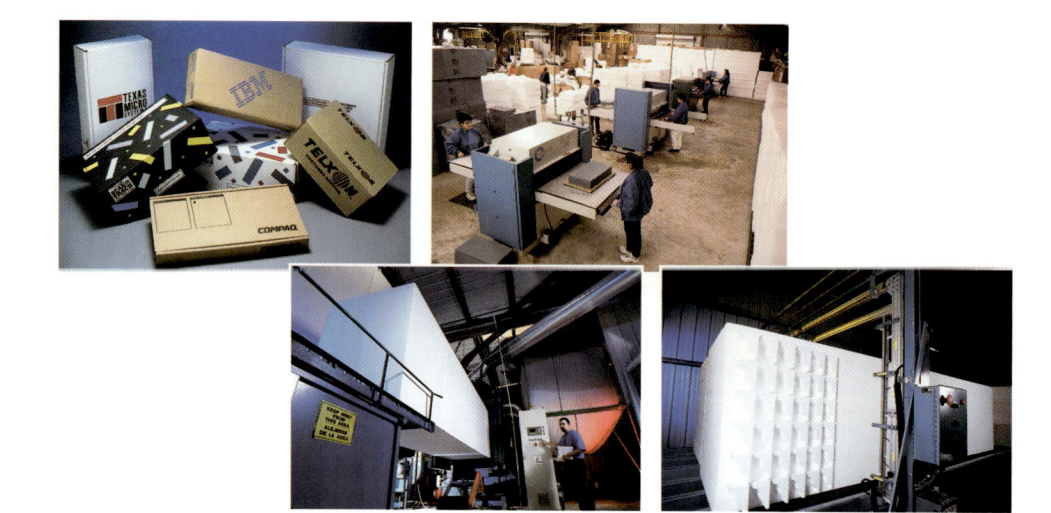

In 1970, Gene Kurtz had a young family, a home mortgage, and high aspirations. Like many Americans, he dreamed of starting his own business.

Unlike most, Kurtz pursued his dream, borrowing capital to start Houston Foam Plastics (HFP), an entrepreneurial venture that has grown over the past 30 years into one of the nation's largest producers of custom foam packaging, construction, and insulation materials.

Kurtz, along with Vice Presidents Scott Jones, Bob Kurtz, and Treasurer Patti Bisceglia, oversee an operation that boasts some 170 full-time employees. The company's original manufacturing site has expanded into facilities that now comprise five full city blocks near downtown Houston. The HFP group has also built a network of affiliated companies that provide similar services throughout the United States, Malaysia, China, Ireland, Brazil, and Mexico.

Among the company's first, and still loyal, packaging customers were Houston's emerging computer and electronics manufacturers. These companies needed a supplier that could provide customized, reliable, full-service packaging support. Houston Foam Plastics filled that need.

In partnership with its high-tech clientele, HFP has developed a time-proven approach to customer service. After assisting the customer with material selection, HFP then designs, tests, and produces the most cost-effective, protective packaging available.

Extensive warehouse and transportation facilities allow HFP to provide "just in time" service to both packaging and construction customers. With its own fleet of trucks, the company delivers material to customer's manufacturing or construction sites as needed, saving customers the cost and inconvenience of maintaining high-volume inventories.

Houston Foam Plastics strives to maintain the same quality relationship with its neighbors that it has with its customers. HFP believes in hiring technical, administrative, and manufacturing personnel that reside in the immediate area. Its employees participate in neighborhood clean-up efforts, providing both manpower and equipment. Also, the company recently donated a full city block to a neighborhood church for use as an outdoor recreation center.

Over the years, HFP has witnessed increased public concerns regarding the recyclability of plastics. They have responded to these concerns by maintaining a recycling collection facility in the heart of Houston, located within blocks of their manufacturing facility. As an environmentally responsible company, HFP transforms discarded packaging along with its own post-industrial waste into renewed packaging and quality insulation products. ■

HOUSTON ★ People ★ Opportunity ★ Success

Hydralift, Inc.

The new concept 'Hydralift Rig' Package was delivered in late 1998 to the 'Stena Tay' Semisubmersible. This state-of-the-art vessel is now drilling for Shell on a long term contract.

Hydralift designed and manufactured twelve 70-metric-tonne Knuckle-Boom Cranes for the 3 state-of-the-art class Enterprise drillships, which are part of the fleet operated by Houston-based Transocean Offshore Inc., an international offshore drilling company.

Hydralift Inc. follows in the footsteps of parent company Hydralift ASA in Norway, setting industry standards as a global supplier of offshore and drilling equipment packages and cranes. The Houston-based company is revered for its comprehensive range of products and systems for offshore oil and gas exploration and production, as well as for shipping and land-based industry.

Hydralift Inc. serves clients by developing and designing specialized solutions based upon their standard product range to meet customers' particular needs. Its success in satisfying these needs is reflected in significant revenue and staff growth over the years, and in its recent move to a new 51,000-square-foot office near Bush Intercontinental Airport.

Internationally, Hydralift has delivered more than 5,000 electro-hydraulic cranes to ships, drilling rigs, platforms and specialized support vessels since first established in 1965. Recent deliveries include the new concept "Hydralift Rig," complete derricks and drilling equipment, riser and guideline tensioning systems, mooring equipment, cranes and sub-sea handling systems. By implementing the latest technology into its work, the company can easily modify designs to fit specific applications. ■

MANUFACTURING/INDUSTRIAL

HOUSTON ★ People ★ Opportunity ★ Success

Port of Houston

Known as "the port that built a city," the Port of Houston has had a defining impact on Houston's economy throughout the 20th century and, based on the Port's long-term strategic plan, is likely to play a pivotal role in Houston's economy throughout the 21st century.

Since its founding in 1836, Houston had always aspired to be a major international trading center. Fueled by the growth of the cotton and timber industries and aided by numerous railroad lines, Houston made great progress as a trade center throughout the 19th century. But Houston's full potential as a trade center expanded significantly in 1914 when the Houston Ship Channel was completed, establishing Houston as a deep water port for world trade.

In the 1920s and 1930s, the construction of oil refineries and petrochemical plants along the Houston Ship Channel—combined with Houston's emergence as the energy capital of the world—further enhanced the Port of Houston's position as the most important port in the Gulf of Mexico. Today, the Houston Ship Channel is home to a $15 billion petrochemical complex, the largest in the nation and second largest worldwide.

Throughout the 20th century, Houston continued to invest in the Port of Houston. The Port is the largest U.S. port for foreign cargo (107.8 million tons) as well as the second largest U.S. port and the eighth largest port in the world in total tonnage (170 million tons). More than 100 steamship lines offer service between Houston and 200 ports around the world. More than 7,000 ships call on the Port annually and over 100,000 barges navigate the Houston Ship Channel.

In addition to attracting trade for the area, the Port of Houston is a major contributor to Houston's overall economy, generating $7.7 billion dollars in business revenues annually and supporting more than 200,000 direct and related jobs statewide.

One of the most successful investments in the Port of Houston has been the Fentress Bracewell Barbours Cut Container Terminal, which handles more than half of the container cargo in the Gulf of Mexico. Growing by more than 17 percent annually, the 230-acre facility now handles nearly 1 million containers and more than 8 million tons of products. Further development at Barbours Cut Terminal is not possible due to the lack of expansion space. The Port's productive growth in container traffic has prompted the Port Commission to plan for the development of a new container terminal in southeast Harris County. By developing Bayport, the Port can keep pace with the anticipated and expanding growth patterns in the container industry.

In planning for the future, the Port of Houston has begun work on deepening the channel from 40 to 45 feet and widening it from 400 to 530 feet. When completed, the project will enhance Houston's competitiveness by allowing ships to utilize their capacity more fully, thus lowering unit transportation costs. The improvements also will reduce the potential for collision and oil spill risks in the channel and will improve navigational aids.

As it prepares for the 21st century, the Port of Houston is also entering new markets. One of the most successful and promising has been the development of the cruiseline business, with Norwegian Cruise Line offering seven-day cruises to the western Caribbean. The "Texaribbean Cruises" offer tourists from the U.S. west and midwest the opportunity to sail from Houston rather than taking a lengthy and costly flight to board a ship in Florida. And in May 2000, Premier Cruise Line will begin offering exclusive cruises to Vera Cruz in the western Caribbean, along with stops in Cozumel and Playa del Carmen, on the newly refurbished IslandBreeze cruise ship.

For more information about the Port of Houston, please visit our web site at www.portofhouston.com. ∎

HOUSTON ★ People ★ Opportunity ★ Success

Palletized Trucking Inc.

(L to R) Marillyn King, Rex King, with daughter Sally King, and son Michael Rex King, all officers of the company. The King family is looking forward to serving Houston in the new millennium.

After 30 years, Palletized Trucking Inc. is still providing one basic service: It safely moves freight to where it's needed - and when it's needed.

Palletized Trucking is a leader in the Houston market, providing a diversified range of services - van freight, heavy hauling utilizing flatbeds and multi-axle low boys, import/export containers by the hundreds, warehouse and food products shipments.

Rex and Marillyn King founded the company in 1969. Rex had been a Continental Can executive, transferring from Kansas to Houston to take charge of shipping and packaging. They found Houston to be a growing, dynamic city with great opportunities - and a need for better service in trucking.

They used their savings and the proceeds from their Kansas farm and bought a minority interest in a small trucking company. But after six years, the deal turned sour, and Rex was out of a job.

Disappointed and broke, he went back to Continental Can (in Florida) for about six months. As fate would have it, the first call Rex received on his first day back in Houston was from a man needing several loads moved from a warehouse to the city docks. Without explaining that he was no longer in the trucking business, Rex rented a tractor, borrowed two trailers and did the job himself. More opportunities for trucking arose, so he borrowed on his insurance policy and a bank loaned enough to buy three used trucks.

HOUSTON ★ People ★ Opportunity ★ Success

For two years, the Kings' home was the headquarters for Palletized Trucking, with Rex dispatching, driving and repairing trucks on an empty lot on weekends. Then a lot with a vacant filling station was purchased and converted into a small terminal.

The business continued to grow, and in 1980, they moved into a beautiful new terminal located on 10-plus acres at 2001 Collingsworth.

Palletized Trucking was one of the first carriers hauling containers in and out of the Port of Houston. The company has diversified over the years to keep up with the many changes in the area economy and markets. Palletized Trucking trucks now are seen delivering to all 48 contiguous states.

The Kings' children, Mike, Sally and Ron, have accumulated almost 60 years with the company, and are well positioned for succession in the new millennium.

"It's a good family management team," said Mike. "Dad has always encouraged us to work, and his attention to detail, hard work and energy are the reasons for the company's success."

Sally said, "It's also Mom's high level of integrity and wanting the best for the employees and their families, such as our profit-sharing program."

Safety is of utmost importance at Palletized Trucking. Safe Drivers (both company drivers and lease contractors) are recognized at annual safety award banquets. The company also has won state and national safety awards.

The Kings are civic minded, and many worthy organizations have benefited by their generosity. Marillyn and Rex were named Texas Motor Transportation Association's "Leaders of the Year" in 1990, and have received many other honors of recognition.

The Kings are truly grateful for their faith in God, for Houston, and for the opportunity to start over and fulfill the American dream. ■

Marillyn and Rex King, founders of Palletized Trucking Inc. in 1969, celebrated 30 years in business at their trucking terminal.

The beautiful skyline of Houston shows off the oldest truck in our fleet, a completely restored 1948 Mack. This "show" truck was restored by V-P Michael King.

INTERNATIONAL/TRANSPORTATION 259

HOUSTON ★ People ★ Opportunity ★ Success

Houston Airport System

The tails of foreign and domestic airliners line the Mickey Leland International Airlines Building at Bush Intercontinental Airport. The Houston Airport System is currently in the midst of a $1.7 billion construction and development program, which includes the expansion of this terminal.

In a century defined in part by the invention of the airplane and its impact on transportation and trade, Houston's investments in planning and building a comprehensive airport system have continued to pay big rewards for the city, the companies that do business throughout the region and the traveling public.

Houston's first investment in air transportation was the purchase in 1937 of a private airfield where William P. Hobby Airport is now located. At the time, the airport was served by Braniff and Eastern airlines. It wasn't until the 1940s that the airport's first field lighting system and concrete paved runways and taxiways were completed. In 1950, Houston became an international airport with Pan American Airway's new flight to Mexico City. Seven years later, KLM Royal Dutch Airlines began European service out of Houston with flights to Amsterdam.

By the early 1960s, the introduction of jet-powered commercial aircraft was creating an obvious need for additional air transportation capacity and Houston began construction of a new airport located 22 miles north of downtown. When it opened in 1969 as Houston Intercontinental Airport (IAH), the facility served more than 4.5 million passengers in its first year and was described as Houston's greatest transportation achievement since the Houston Ship Channel.

Today, the Houston Airport System is the fourth largest system in the United States and the sixth largest in the world. In fact, the Houston Airport System has set records for air passenger volumes in 39 of the past 40 years, topping 40 million air passengers in 1998 alone. Led by Continental Airlines at IAH and Southwest Airlines at Hobby, Houston is now served by 25 domestic and international scheduled passenger airlines providing nonstop or direct flights to more than 150 destinations worldwide.

A big part of the growth the Houston Airport System has been international traffic. In fact, during the past two decades international air traffic has grown at a faster pace than domestic passenger volumes. Intercontinental Airport (which was renamed in 1997 in honor of former U.S. President George Bush) was the eighth largest international gateway in the United States in 1998, handling 4.5 million passengers traveling between Houston and 40 countries around the world.

HOUSTON ★ People ★ Opportunity ★ Success

Air cargo through Houston has also continued to soar, topping 700 million pounds in 1998. Houston is now served by 13 all-cargo airlines and more than 500 freight forwarders that transport everything from large oilfield equipment to delicate perishables such as flowers and fresh seafood.

More than 115 million pounds of air cargo was processed by United Parcel Service at the Houston Airport System's Ellington Field. Located near NASA's Johnson Space Center, the airport serves more than 100,000 Continental Express passengers. It is also the home of the Texas Air National Guard and the Texas Army National Guard as well as air cargo operations, private and corporate aircraft, and other aerospace-related businesses.

The outlook for air transportation in Houston is one characterized by strong growth during the new century. Passenger enplanements are expected to double by 2017, representing an average annual increase of almost 4 percent. Similar growth is projected for air cargo activity, increasing to 1.6 billion pounds in 2017. To meet the growth, the Houston Airport System has developed a long-term airport master plan and has already embarked on a $1.7 billion airport development program that includes construction of a new runway, expansion of terminal facilities and new state-of-the-art air cargo facilities.

For more information on the Houston Airport System, please visit its web site at www.ci.houston.tx.us/has. ■

William P. Hobby Airport is an important, medium-sized, domestic, passenger traffic center and serves as Southwest Airlines' second largest hub. This airport provides Houstonians with a second air transportation gateway, an amenity not available in most other cities.

INTERNATIONAL/TRANSPORTATION 261

HOUSTON ★ People ★ Opportunity ★ Success

Circle International

General Manager Chris Cahill proudly exemplifies the hard-working dedication and resulting success of Circle International.

Chris Cahill (left), General Manager, and Sammy Martinez (right), Warehouse Manager, check inventory in the yard of Circle International's brand new 100,000 sq. ft. facility.

For the past century, Circle International has solved transportation and logistics problems in almost every spot on the globe.

Founded in 1898 as a customs broker, the company today provides a broad array of services. Its principal product lines are air and ocean freight forwarding, customs brokerage and compliance consulting, and logistics services including trucking, warehousing, distribution, inventory control and related materials management activities such as pick-and-pack, sub-assembly, product integration and order fulfillment. Through its Circle Trade Services unit, the company also provides product procurement, inventory financing and trade facilitation programs.

HOUSTON ★ People ★ Opportunity ★ Success

Circle Houston opened its doors in 1972. At the beginning, the focus was customs brokerage, according to General Manager Christopher Cahill. In 1991, the activity grew into air/ocean forwarding operations, then later to full-scale services supporting engineering and construction projects, oil and gas industry and high-tech products. Circle clients now enjoy a complete array of service options only available from a "true" Third Party Logistics provider.

Circle International is a leader in the logistics industry in Houston. Its revenues have quadrupled since 1995 and profits have risen 600 percent. Its growth is partly evidenced by the company's move last summer to a new 107,000-square-foot facility, with a 6.5-acre marshalling yard, near Bush Intercontinental Airport.

"The Houston area's strong economy helped us grow in the mid-90s, and our new services and pursuit of new markets help us continue to be successful. We take an aggressive approach in providing customized logistics solutions for our clients that yield win-win results," says Cahill.

The logistics solutions Circle International devises are based on clients' specific needs. Circle logistics professionals work closely with clients to analyze material and information flows in order to streamline the overall process. At both the strategic and daily detail levels, cost-effective procedures and quality measures are developed and monitored, with the focus on continuous improvement in cycle times, order accuracy and flexibility.

The company's large international presence is an advantage to its clients. "One World, One Team" is more than a slogan—Circle International has 367 offices in 97 countries, all working together to ensure the seamless flow of cargo and information from purchase order creation to final delivery. ■

The management team of Circle International's Houston Branch demonstrates strong leadership for the 73 employees.

INTERNATIONAL/TRANSPORTATION 263

HOUSTON ★ People ★ Opportunity ★ Success

PageSoutherlandPage

As the state's oldest architecture and engineering firm, PageSoutherlandPage has been creating - and re-creating - great architecture in Texas and Houston throughout this century. In fact, the company's work over the past 101 years is a physical collection of the major trends and styles in architecture of the past century.

But, while architectural styles have changed over the past century, some things—like the importance of the functionality of a building or office—never change, says John Cryer, principal and head of the Houston office of PageSoutherlandPage.

The diversity of the projects designed by PageSoutherlandPage in Houston—such as the restoration of downtown Houston's Rice Hotel and the construction of the Center for Comparative Medicine at Baylor College of Medicine—reflects the firm's ability to both capture the past and design for the future.

"The challenge for today's architectural and engineering firm is not just in mastering the technical aspects of designing a building, although obviously that is very important," Cryer says. "The most critical part of any project is designing a space that is functional today but also flexible enough to remain functional even as new technology and new ways of doing business create different demands on the space. Change is constant and buildings must be designed with change in mind."

In Houston, PageSoutherlandPage has played an important role in the rejuvenation of downtown Houston and other areas. In addition to the restoration of the Rice Hotel and its conversion to loft apartments, PageSoutherlandPage has designed The Gotham, The Metropolis, St. Germain on Main, Keystone Lofts and Commerce Tower.

In the educational area, PageSoutherlandPage has designed and renovated schools to meet a variety of student needs from K-12 to the college level. "We have developed new ways to create environments that enhance student success, that maximize facilities' values for taxpayers, and that effectively integrate multimedia and communication technologies with classroom instruction," says Cryer. "What's the payoff of our education design? It's more than just safe, flexible, and economical learning places—it's providing engaging, nurturing learning environments for the students who use them."

In addition to the new center for Baylor College of Medicine, PageSoutherlandPage has an extensive practice in designing buildings for the healthcare industry. "Architects and engineers must constantly search for innovative ways to help hospitals and health networks excel in this competitive, evolving environment," says Cryer. "That's why PageSoutherlandPage developed a consensus-building approach to healthcare facility design—one that evaluates input from patients, physicians, staff, and administrators to assess current facility requirements and predict future needs. Technological advances and new financial strategies mean that any renovation or new construction must be done with an eye on tomorrow."

With more than 250 professionals and offices in Austin, Dallas, Houston, and Washington D.C., PageSoutherlandPage design services include site selection, feasibility analysis, strategic planning, master planning, programming, energy analysis, interior design, architecture, and engineering.

As a result of its work, PageSoutherlandPage is consistently ranked among the upper third of the top 500 national design firms by *Engineering News-Record*, and among the top 10 percent of all national healthcare design firms by *Modern Healthcare* magazine.

For more information on PageSoutherlandPage, please visit its web site at www.psp.com. ■

HOUSTON ★ People ★ Opportunity ★ Success

Greater Houston Partnership

Local elected officials and their staffs work with the Partnership to bring business to Houston.

The Greater Houston Partnership is the primary advocate of Houston's business community, and is dedicated to building economic prosperity in the region. The Partnership is accredited by the Chamber of Commerce of the United States.

On January 28, 1840, Mirabeau B. Lamar, president of the Republic of Texas, signed the charter creating the Houston Chamber of Commerce. This set in motion what was to become, 149 years later, the Houston region's leading business organization. In 1989, the Houston Chamber of Commerce joined forces with the 62-year-old Houston World Trade Association and the fledgling Houston Economic Development Council, giving birth to the Greater Houston Partnership. This unique umbrella organization was united under one leadership and focused on one goal—building economic prosperity in the region.

As Houston's leading business organization, the Partnership has been at the forefront of every major development in Houston during the 20th century. The Houston Ship Channel, Texas Medical Center, NASA's Johnson Space Center, George Bush Intercontinental Airport, the Houston Livestock Show & Rodeo, the Greater Houston Convention & Visitors Bureau and many other regional assets and community organizations are a direct result of the leadership, vision and commitment of the Partnership and Houston's business community.

HOUSTON ★ People ★ Opportunity ★ Success

Greater Houston Partnership Facts:
- A private, non-profit organization
- 2,200 member businesses, employing one out of every three area workers
- 70 staff members
- 50 committees and task forces
- 3,200 active volunteers
- 81 percent of annual revenue from member dues, publication sales and events

The Partnership's Chamber of Commerce Division is dedicated to improving the business climate and quality of life in the Houston region through programs that address aviation, education, environment, transportation, regional planning and emerging business issues. It lobbies actively at the local, state, and national levels.

The Partnership's Economic Development Division creates jobs in the region by working to retain Houston companies and attract corporate expansions and relocations. In 1998, the Partnership assisted 35 companies with relocation, expansion, or retention projects with an annual economic impact of $1.3 billion.

The Partnership's Member Services Division nurtures existing Houston-area businesses through CEO Roundtables, Sales Lead Roundtables, business development and networking programs.

The Partnership's World Trade Division works to enhance Houston's role as a center of international business and helps Houston firms promote their products and services in the international marketplace. During 1998, it hosted 89 inbound and outbound trade missions involving countries around the globe. It also sponsors seminars and workshops to teach import/export skills.

For more information on the Greater Houston Partnership, please visit our Web site at www.houston.org. ∎

Local, state and national media carry the Partnership's message and position on issues. The Partnership is home to the International Press Center-Houston, designed to help domestic and foreign journalists research and develop stories on news in the greater Houston area.

PROFESSIONAL SERVICES 267

Jim Olive Photography/Stockyard Photos

From aerial photos of offshore oil and gas platforms around the world to photographs of Houston's dramatic skyline, Jim Olive Photography has helped hundreds of Houston's companies visually tell their story and market their products and services.

For Jim Olive, Houston is a photographer's dream, providing a rich selection of images, lighting and settings that he can draw from to create award-winning photos that visually tell a compelling story.

A native Houstonian, Olive has been photographing Houston for more than 30 years. His photos have captured the heart-pounding excitement of the U.S. space program during the Apollo flights and documented the life-saving heart procedures of Houston's pioneering cardiac surgeons. His photos of Houston and Houstonians have been published in Time, Life and numerous other national and international publications.

Olive revels in the diversity of photo assignments that Houston offers. "Houston is a fascinating city for a photographer who enjoys new challenges," Olive says. "You might spend one day shooting drill bits or a manufacturing plant and the next day you could be photographing a biotechnology company or capturing some of the breath-taking architecture that has made Houston famous."

Olive's photo assignments have enabled him to cover the extraordinary tapestry of people, companies and organizations that have been the strength of Houston's growth and diversity. Reflecting Houston's international focus, for example, Olive has traveled on assignment to more than 62 countries to photograph Houston companies, their people and their products.

An avid fisherman and conservationist, Jim has also used his photography to capture the natural beauty of the Houston region, from the sealife and birds in Galveston Bay to the forests and fauna north of Houston and to the bluebonnet-covered rolling hills west of Houston.

As a result of his years of photographing Houston, Olive has a treasure trove of images of Houston that are often used by publications around the world. For a sampling of Olive's photography, visit his web site at www.stockyard.com. ∎

HOUSTON ★ People ★ Opportunity ★ Success

Andrews & Kurth

Since 1902, Andrews & Kurth L.L.P. has been applying its founding principles to the practice of business law, principles which continue to apply today as Andrews & Kurth reaches greater heights in the 21st Century.

From our earliest days counseling the railroads that fueled America's growth, to our present work, helping emerging companies reach new technological frontiers, clients have trusted Andrews & Kurth to handle their most important legal interests.

"The aims and ideals of the firm and of the individuals composing the firm are to practice law as a profession, not as an occupation, the chief aim…to so serve in the profession that the firm would have always the full confidence of clients and the trust of all people," said founder Frank Andrews in 1934.

The language is a bit old-fashioned, but the message still rings true. "Our commitment to quality, service and integrity, our focus on client needs and objectives, and our emphasis on problem-solving will continue as the touchstone for our performance as we enter the next century," said Howard T. Ayers, Andrews & Kurth managing partner.

Today, a firm of more than 250 dynamic and forward-thinking attorneys, Andrews & Kurth handles the vital interests of established companies and emerging businesses around the globe. In addition to its founding office in Houston, Andrews & Kurth serves clients from offices in The Woodlands, Dallas, Washington D.C., Los Angeles, New York and London.

Andrews & Kurth. Providing innovative solutions to complex problems since 1902. Visit our web site at www.andrews-kurth.com or telephone 713-220-4200. ■

PROFESSIONAL SERVICES

HOUSTON ★ People ★ Opportunity ★ Success

Fredricks Commercial Brokerage

Robert Spiegel and Brent Fredricks are on top of the Houston real estate market.

> "Fredricks Commercial Brokerage has provided excellent service to our Company in site assemblage work and surplus property sales."
>
> James R. Spitzer
> Real Estate Manager
> Houston Division
> ALBERTSON'S, INC.

Fredricks Commercial Brokerage is becoming the forerunner in providing the highest quality personalized service for companies requiring tenant representation services or site acquisition and disposition services. With over 18 years of experience in buying, selling, leasing and managing commercial properties in the city, owner Brent Fredricks and his associate Robert Spiegel represent domestic and international corporations, institutions and individuals in single and multi-tenant retail properties, office buildings and industrial properties. The firm also operates Estate Property Services, L.L.C., offering commercial and residential sales and management services on behalf of estates and estate administrators.

Houston developers as well as national and publicly traded companies prefer Fredricks Commercial Brokerage because the firm is big enough to be effective, yet small enough to be responsive. Fredricks, a second-generation Houstonian, prides himself on building one-on-one relationships with customers and strives to respond quickly to service each client's special needs.

For more information or current references on Fredricks Commercial Brokerage contact 713-572-3500. ■

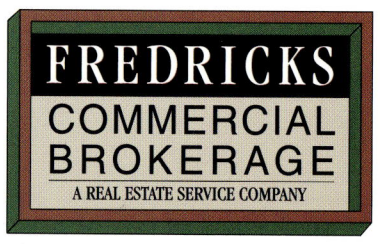

FREDRICKS COMMERCIAL BROKERAGE
A REAL ESTATE SERVICE COMPANY

HOUSTON ★ People ★ Opportunity ★ Success

Tindall & Foster, P.C.

*Immigration
& Family Law*

Front Row:
Karen Feldman, Harry Tindall,
Charles Foster, Kay Linh Pham

Back Row:
Alice Gruber, Angela Pence,
Robert Loughran, Richard
Sindelar, Robert Nadalin,
Heather Hughes, Matt
Thompson, Lisa Reed

Since its founding in 1973, Tindall & Foster, P.C. has grown to become one of Houston's leading boutique law firms specializing in employment-related immigration law and family law.

Founding partners Harry L. Tindall, who heads the family law group with 3 attorneys, and Charles C. Foster, who heads the immigration law group with 10 attorneys, say the firm's growth reflects both local and national trends.

"The legal issues involved in both the immigration and family law fields have grown increasingly complex over the past quarter century," says Tindall. "To successfully represent clients in complex cases today requires a law firm with a greater degree of specialization and experience in their respective fields."

Foster points out that Houston has become a truly global city, driven by the energy industry, foreign trade through the Port of Houston, the Texas Medical Center and Houston's cultural arts community. Working with companies throughout the United States, Europe, Latin America, Japan, China and the Middle East, the firm's business-related immigration law section is ranked as one of the largest in the nation in terms of size and clients.

To compete in global markets, Foster says, Houston companies are actively recruiting and transferring foreign nationals with specialized skills and experience.

"Tindall & Foster represents key employees who are seeking appropriate nonimmigrant or temporary working visa status in the United States. Some of the greatest needs are from companies whose futures depend on recruiting individuals with very specialized backgrounds in new technology," Foster says. "This includes like Compaq Computer and BMC Software as well as the energy industry and the institutions of the Texas Medical Center."

Both Tindall and Foster are recognized leaders in their respective professional fields. Foster is a past national President of the American Immigration Lawyers Association and Chairman of the American Bar Association's Coordinating Committee on Immigration, while Tindall is past Chairman of the Texas State Bar's Family Law Section.

For more information about Tindall & Foster, P.C., please visit the firm's website at www.tindallfoster.com. ∎

PROFESSIONAL SERVICES 271

HOUSTON ★ People ★ Opportunity ★ Success

Chicago Title

Leading the Industry

Chicago Title is a leader in the title insurance industry. With a history dating back to the very inception of the title business, Chicago Title also plays a significant role in Houston's booming real estate sector.

The Chicago Title and Trust Company was the very first trust company authorized by a new state law which emerged from the ashes of Chicago's 1871 great fire. Chicago Title was among a select group of firms who saved their real estate records and established what evolved into the title insurance industry.

The company's Houston heritage dates back to the late 1800's, and today this independent, publicly traded company has the history and strength to focus on the operating efficiencies and strategic initiatives that will be required into the 21st century.

With more than 30 branch offices throughout the Greater Houston area, including Brazoria Ft. Bend, Harris, Montgomery and Galveston counties, Chicago Title has a commitment to putting their customers' needs first. As part of the fabric of Greater Houston, Chicago Title is poised to continue as a strong partner in Houston's booming real estate community.

"We're your neighbor," says Bob Goodside, Vice President and Area Manager. "Our employees and agents have helped us meet and anticipate the needs of our customers as we have grown to become a nationally recognized leader in real estate and financial services. That strength will serve us well into the next millennium." ∎

272 PROFESSIONAL SERVICES

HOUSTON ★ People ★ Opportunity ★ Success

PricewaterhouseCoopers

PricewaterhouseCoopers

PricewaterhouseCoopers refers to the U.S. firm of PricewaterhouseCoopers LLP and other members of the worldwide PricewaterhouseCoopers organization.

This whirlpool symbolizes the dynamic energy that PricewaterhouseCoopers brings to the new millennium —in our community, with our clients, and with our employees.

PricewaterhouseCoopers has a strong tradition of supporting organizations that create tangible results in the community. Our professionals build homes through Habitat for Humanity, tutor and mentor students with Junior Achievement, raise funds for the United Way, and participate in races that support many local charities (such as the American Heart Association and American Diabetes Association). PricewaterhouseCoopers invests heavily—with both "people" and financial resources—in organizations that build infrastructure for today's youth and tomorrow's leaders.

In the arts community, PricewaterhouseCoopers continues its pledge to strengthen cultural and arts organizations that bring beauty and creativity to Houston. We are strong supporters of the Houston Grand Opera, Alley Theatre, TUTS, the Museum of Fine Arts, and the Museum of Natural Science.

PricewaterhouseCoopers has been created to help our clients meet the challenges posed by the globalizing economy. We are one of the largest knowledge businesses in the world, a leader in every market in which we operate. We bring an enviable breadth and depth of resources worldwide. Drawing on the knowledge and skills of 155,000 people in 150 countries, we help our clients solve complex business problems and measurably enhance their ability to build value, manage risk, and improve performance.

All of our services involve a careful balance—between our global expertise and local experience. We strike this balance by taking the most relevant and innovative ideas from wherever they arise, and apply them as workable, practical solutions in a local context. We follow this approach in every one of the 150 countries where we work. This attitude fosters the rich cultural diversity within PricewaterhouseCoopers.

For more information about PricewaterhouseCoopers, visit our web sites at www.pwcglobal.com or www.e-business.pwcglobal.com. ■

PROFESSIONAL SERVICES

BDO Seidman, LLP

Growing companies need an accounting firm that offers the services—and attention— they need to grow.

BDO Seidman, LLP
Accountants and Consultants

In today's global economy, more and more businesses want to make their mark on foreign soil. BDO Seidman, LLP, is helping them lay that foundation for success.

BDO Seidman serves growing businesses through more than 40 offices located across the United States. The Houston office opened in 1961 and has been serving a wide variety of clients over the years whose needs range from local to national to international. BDO's Managing Director for Houston, Charles Dewhurst, states, "Houston is a gateway for U.S. companies interested in expanding internationally and Latin American companies intent upon doing business here. We're well-suited to serve clients on both sides of the border."

Houston partners Carlos Ancira, Jr., and Daniel Dominguez focus in particular on Latin American opportunities. "We're experienced in helping U.S. clients go abroad and foreign businesses come into this country," says Ancira. "We understand where they're coming from and what it takes for them to enter a foreign market."

Dominguez adds, "In the last 20 years, we've seen many foreign companies that are interested in Houston because they're energy-related. Basically, Houston is a gateway for all of the operations located south of us."

As the U.S. member firm of BDO International, BDO Seidman leverages a global network of resources to serve clients abroad through more than 500 member firm offices in over 85 countries. Given these resources, Dewhurst says, "BDO Seidman can tap financial and commercial markets all over the world." ∎

HOUSTON ★ People ★ Opportunity ★ Success

Apollo Paper Company

Rocketing into the 21st century

The dedicated professionals of Apollo Paper Company at their northwest Houston location.

DAVID DIETRICH PHOTOGRAPHY

Thirty years ago, Apollo 11 landed the first men on the moon. "Apollo" was the epitome of the future: leading edge, vision driven. That spirit resulted in the formation of Apollo Paper Company.

As the millennium rockets toward us, Apollo Paper Company still embodies those visionary values. The company has been in business in Houston and Dallas for 30 years, and recently joined forces with a 10-year-old company in Bryan/College Station. The resulting firm now has more than 160 employees, 22 trucks and annual sales of more than $50 million.

Apollo Paper Company is a leader in the business, supplying paper, packaging sanitary maintenance/janitorial and printing materials. They stock padded mailing bags, bubble packaging, mailing tubes, corrugated rolls and Kraft paper. From sisal twine and tissue paper to freezer paper, utility mailing bags, air freight containers or rolls of corrugated, Apollo stands ready to supply its customers' needs.

Dedication to customer satisfaction is Apollo Paper Company's fuel. In addition to upgrading their facilities in Houston and Dallas, the company is constantly taking advantage of the strength of the latest technology to enhance and facilitate business with their growing customer base. They are adding bar coding, EDI, electronic commerce and an on-line version of their catalog.

"Apollo plans to chart the future course of the shipping, packaging and maintenance industry," says M.E. "Nick" Nicholson, president and CEO. ■

PROFESSIONAL SERVICES

HOUSTON ★ People ★ Opportunity ★ Success

American Bureau of Professional Translators

Today's shrinking electronic world requires translations that are timely and right the first time. ABPT's experienced staff can cut your time in translation without cutting any corners.

Doing business in multiple languages has become a critical factor for success in Houston.

After Chernobyl, scientists from the former Soviet Union and other countries came to Houston to discuss the health effects of low-dose radiation. The American Bureau of Professional Translators handled their interpretation needs.

At the 1990 Economic Summit in Houston, leaders of seven countries convened to consider diverse international economic and political issues. ABPT provided interpretation services for the German and French delegations.

When a corporation needs complex, technical manuals to be translated for use overseas, they also call on ABPT for assistance.

Since 1986, clients have counted on ABPT to help them communicate effectively in a multinational business environment. Through offices in Houston, Dallas and Mexico City and a network of over 1,000 translators and interpreters worldwide, ABPT provides translation and consecutive and simultaneous interpretation services, on or off-site, in every commercial language. It also offers specialized services, such as translating web sites and localizing software to countries' specific requirements.

"We employ well-educated professionals with experience in such industries as energy, medical or legal," Director Richard Rosenthal says. "We don't just translate or interpret word for word. We choose language that's understandable and culturally sensitive and that conveys the intended meaning. We will work around the clock, if necessary, alongside clients' technical staff as partners to complete jobs accurately, on time and on budget.

"The biggest barrier to international success isn't geographical, it's cultural and linguistic," Rosenthal concludes. "If you don't overcome that barrier, you'll lose to competitors who will." Contact us at (713) 789-2500 or email: info@abpt.com. ∎

PROFESSIONAL SERVICES

HOUSTON ★ People ★ Opportunity ★ Success

Moss Landscaping, Inc.

As a college student at the University of Texas headed for what he thought would be a career in the oil business, Gary Moss began cutting grass for several Austin condominium associations. As demand grew, Moss employed fraternity brothers to assist with his lawn maintenance business.

Those modest business roots sprouted. Now more than 20 years later, Moss Landscaping, is known in Greater Houston's most distinguished neighborhoods as an institution in custom design, construction, drainage, pest control management and overall maintenance.

Moss never dreamed that his successful college enterprise would grow beyond an endeavor that paid his college expenses. In those days, he focused primarily on pursuing his business degree at the University of Texas, studying geology and petroleum management in hopes of entering the energy business. Then, in the early 80s, declines in domestic petroleum production, Moss considered a different career. He decided to pursue his interest in landscaping on a professional basis and spent his summers driving back and forth to Texas A&M, studying agronomy and horticulture.

After graduation from Texas, the second-generation Houstonian continued to build his landscaping business in Austin. He added business accounts, including IBM and Texaco, and he married fellow Houstonian Louise Andrews.

As his firm's reputation spread, the young graduate opened a Moss Landscaping office in Houston in 1989. The Austin business was sold in 1995 to allow Moss to focus on the Houston market.

Today, careful hands-on growth and ongoing contact with customers have helped the Moss organization forge one of the most successful companies in Houston's residential market.

"Teamwork is very important within our company," Moss said. "We're very proud of our people and their accomplishments. We have created a strong incentive program that enables us to send happy, motivated workers to our projects." ■

PROFESSIONAL SERVICES 277

HOUSTON ★ People ★ Opportunity ★ Success

Robert Huff Landscape Illumination

Design is the most important aspect of achieving a spectacular effect in landscape illumination. For this reason, Robert Huff or one of his design associates personally supervises the individual placement of each fixture on your grounds.

What makes Robert Huff Landscape Illumination distinctive? Founder Robert Huff believes the ability to provide the best possible combination of design and installation of custom-made equipment will create optimum value. These philosophies have established his organization as **"the premier landscape lighting company not only in Greater Houston, but throughout Texas."**

Huff, who founded the firm 14 years ago, has invested 27 years in landscape lighting design. He still believes that careful planning and personal supervision assure that each project concludes precisely as the client wishes.

To assure satisfaction, Huff or one of his associates visits every current project at the end of each day.

Huff's approach works, as thousands of highly satisfied clients will attest to. Most clients come on referral, thanks in part to many Greater Houston business leaders, civic leaders, sports celebrities and other public figures whose homes he has illuminated. They have spread the word which has created great success and growth for the company.

"Many companies in our business do several things, and outdoor lighting happens to be of them," Huff says. "We do one thing—landscape and security lighting. We continually work on developing an even stronger professional organization so we can keep improving what we do for our clients."

It's difficult to improve an organization that uses outdoor lighting as an artist uses a brush. The Huff organization—which has grown from one person to nine—will carefully enhance the beauty of a home with just the right touch of light and shadows. Huff describes the approach as blending "art with science."

Although the main thrust of the company's business has always been the upscale residential market, Huff also has several hotels, country clubs, restaurants and corporate headquarters in his resume' of satisfied clients.

Huff has observed a major change in client demand. He explains, "When we started, about 80 percent of our customers wanted landscape illumination for aesthetics and about 20 percent for security reasons. Now it's about 80-20 the other way, though our clients always demand and receive the best in aesthetics for their personal homes."

For a free consultation, please phone Robert Huff at 713-861-2000. ■

HOUSTON ★ People ★ Opportunity ★ Success

Furniture Marketing Group of Houston, Inc.

Sophistication of Wood, Architectural Distinction— A Million and One Options. "A favorite with the Fortune 500® crowd."

Anticipates Technology, Grows with Your Organization, Fully Stackable—Even to the Ceiling. "The industry's most successful new system."

Driven by a single-minded commitment to provide its customers with the very best solutions to their office furniture and service needs, Furniture Marketing Group is making its mark in Houston as a company that delivers its promises. FMG-Houston began in 1996 with the purchase of a small Haworth furniture dealership that was built around a few large Houston client companies including Administaff Inc. and American General Corporation.

In just three short years, FMG-Houston has tripled sales, grown to a company of 35 employees and added Enron, Nextel, BindView Development Corporation, AquaSource and Computer Sciences Corporation to its local client list.

FMG-Houston has both national and global capabilities with affiliate divisions located in Dallas, Austin, London and Sydney. In the past two years, FMG's divisions have designed, delivered and installed projects in 24 countries worldwide. FMG is also the largest volume dealer of Haworth products in the world. With annual sales of $1.7 billion, Haworth is recognized as perhaps the premier office furniture company in the industry.

"FMG's overall size, which in terms of annual sales was $120 million last year, has allowed the Houston division to rapidly demonstrate the ability to attract new business and to retain these companies as long-term clients," said Joe Farrell, president of FMG-Houston.

"As a smaller local division we are very approachable and proactive to quickly address the needs of our clients. We have a 'can do' culture where the collective efforts of our employees are totally focused on exceeding customer expectations," asserted Farrell.

"Another major asset is our partnership with Haworth. With Haworth's worldwide reputation for building innovative, cost effective and high quality products, we have a complete package at FMG-Houston that provides our customers with a positive, turnkey office furniture experience," said Farrell. ■

PROFESSIONAL SERVICES

HOUSTON ★ People ★ Opportunity ★ Success

City Central Courier

City Central Courier is poised for the new millennium with Internet capabilities which are virtually unprecedented in the delivery service industry. City Central is a Houston based messenger and delivery company established in 1982. They have grown from a staff of seven to over a hundred.

"What sets us apart from our competition is our flexibility, said City Central Courier's President Steven Willard. "Whatever our customers want, we can do it. We can mold ourselves around our clients to fit their needs, not the other way around. This has been very successful for the company. Now we are counting on new technology of the Internet to take us to the future."

By visiting City Central Courier's web site at www.citycentralcourier.com and inputting delivery data, a state-of-the-art system will simultaneously dispatch a messenger to your site and track their estimated time of arrival to the delivery point. Also, download daily delivery reports and information that might be useful for the client operations.

Now the client can place an order with a click from their desktop. "Our goal is to make ordering a delivery easier than ever before," states Willard. "Can you imagine monitoring an image of your delivery ticket on our Web site, even printing that ticket for your records or billing that charge to your client all at once?"

City Central Courier is a time-sensitive delivery company with coverage only limited by their client's delivery point. As you can see, City Central Courier will be a presence well into the new millennium. For more information about City Central by phone, call 713-623-0303 or visit their web site at www.citycentralcourier.com. ■

HOUSTON ★ People ★ Opportunity ★ Success

The University of Texas Medical Branch

UTMB is dedicated to educating health science professionals and researchers, caring for patients and solving biomedical puzzles through scientific inquiry

The University of Texas Medical Branch Hyperbaric Facility in Galveston, Texas.

Since its founding in 1891, the University of Texas Medical Branch at Galveston has been a leader in health science education, research and patient care. Now a major academic health science center, UTMB is poised to expand its tradition of service, diversity, education, innovation and community well into the future.

UTMB educates tomorrow's healers and tomorrow's scientists through its schools of Medicine, Nursing, Allied Health Sciences and Graduate Biomedical Sciences. Its diverse student body and hands-on approach to learning help ensure that graduates will be ready to meet any challenge the health-care field can pose. The Institute for the Medical Humanities and the Marine Biomedical Institute offer opportunities for specialized study in those fields.

As an international research center, UTMB contributes to the body of knowledge in many important fields. Areas of research strength include infectious disease, gastrointestinal health, environmental health, aging, cancer, structural biology, molecular sciences and molecular cardiology. The university's scientists work in an interdisciplinary environment that seeks to bring together a variety of perspectives and expertise to solve some of the world's most puzzling biomedical mysteries.

UTMB's educational and research endeavors ultimately have the same goal: to improve the health of society. The university also contributes to this ideal through its extensive network of hospitals and clinics. From primary care to the specialized care available only at the nation's largest academic medical centers, patients benefit from UTMB's experience and expertise. Clinical areas of excellence include senior health; cardiology; behavioral health; trauma care; care of special populations such as the indigent, women and children, and prison inmates; telemedicine; hyperbaric medicine; and aerospace medicine. ■

HOUSTON ★ People ★ Opportunity ★ Success

Baylor College of Medicine

1900 ★ 2000
BAYLOR COLLEGE OF MEDICINE
Education • Research • Patient Care
100 YEARS OF SERVICE

Baylor College of Medicine celebrates its 100th anniversary this year, and as a result of its foundation for excellence and vision for the future, is positioned as a "Leader in medicine for the next millennium."

The key to Baylor's success has been its ability to meet the needs of a changing health care environment and pursue innovative endeavors in line with its long-standing mission of education, patient care and research.

"As one of the premier health science centers in the country, Baylor is uniquely poised to reach a new level of medical and scientific leadership," said Dr. Ralph D. Feigin, Baylor president and CEO.

To provide the best academic medical environment, Baylor continually pursues the latest student training programs and recruits top faculty, who in turn attract top students. It has strengthened joint efforts with affiliates and created strategic new alliances with corporations. This environment provides not only the best results for patients, but also an ideal learning environment.

The College has redoubled its commitment to research that results in scientific breakthroughs. The promise of new gene therapies has dramatically changed the science of medicine, especially the treatment and prevention of diseases. Strategic collaborations already propelling the College to the forefront include the new International Center for Cell and Gene Therapy, an effort with The Methodist Hospital and Texas Children's Hospital, and the Breast Center at Baylor.

Today, Baylor continues to build a future among the nation's most celebrated medical institutions as it sets it sights on even greater levels of achievement. ■

HOUSTON ★ People ★ Opportunity ★ Success

E-Eldercare

In consultation with J.C. Sharma, M.D., medical advisor, Tom Pointer, president, and Barbara Lewis, care coordinator, reviewing a client's assessment and care needs.

Tom Pointer, president, discusses the benefits of Eldercare Employee Assistance Program with Larry Corley, president of Energy Project Services.

Margaret Chandler, care manager, assists the elderly with their health care needs.

A Greater Houston company, E-Eldercare, is pioneering the way in providing eldercare services to the aging population by arranging placement in appropriate living facilities, health care needs, and financial management nationwide.

Eldercare in the workplace costs U.S. businesses an estimated $29 billion a year. Now E-Eldercare's EEAP (Eldercare Employee Assistance Program) enables employees to assure good care for older family members without having to take time from work. Eldercare is an increasing demand on employees' time.

Founded by Tom Pointer, CPA, Internet-based E-Eldercare seems destined to become an essential workplace employee benefit program. Several companies, including Energy Project Services, have already discovered that E-Eldercare works.

"I was concerned about my employees and the eldercare issues that most of us will face," said Larry Corley, president of Energy Project Services. "This program will be a great asset for our employees, and for me, too.

"My elderly parents live in Dallas, and both have faced health issues. I know that any problems that arise while we have E-Eldercare will be handled promptly and efficiently. This program is a win-win situation for companies, employees and elderly parents."

E-Eldercare's flexibility extends proper care both to the ailing senior or to one in good health who is dealing with physical or cognitive decline. E-Eldercare is a single source for an individuals parents. E-Eldercare saved the day for Tony Arfele by helping his parents find a better assisted living facility.

As a CPA, Certified Financial Planner, and Certified Senior Advisor, Mr. Pointer is also able to provide financial consulting, estate management and other financial services related to long-term care planning for the senior. For more information on E-Eldercare, please call 281-397-9997 or access our website at www.e-eldercare.com. ■

MEDICAL